THE WORLD AND GOD

THE WORLD AND GOD

A Study of Prayer, Providence and
Miracle in Christian Experience

BY

H. H. FARMER

D.D.

PROFESSOR OF SYSTEMATIC THEOLOGY
WESTMINSTER COLLEGE, CAMBRIDGE

London
NISBET & CO. LTD.
22 BERNERS STREET, W.1

First published . . . December 1935
Revised and reprinted . September 1936
Reprinted . . . . May 1939
Reprinted . . . . January 1942
Reprinted . . . . December 1943

PRINTED IN GREAT BRITAIN

TO
JOHN OMAN

GENERAL INTRODUCTION

THE Editors of this series are convinced that the Christian Church as a whole is confronted with a great though largely silent crisis, and also with an unparalleled opportunity. They have a common mind concerning the way in which this crisis and opportunity should be met. The time has gone by when " apologetics " could be of any great value. Something more is needed than a defence of propositions already accepted on authority, for the present spiritual crisis is essentially a questioning of authority if not a revolt against it. It may be predicted that the number of people who are content simply to rest their religion on the authority of the Bible or the Church is steadily diminishing, and with the growing effectiveness of popular education will continue to diminish. We shall not therefore meet the need, if we have rightly diagnosed it, by dissertations, however learned, on the interpretation of the Bible or the history of Christian doctrine. Nothing less is required than a candid, courageous and well-informed effort to think out anew, in the light of modern knowledge, the foundation affirmations of our common Christianity. This is the aim of every writer in this series.

A further agreement is, we hope, characteristic of the books which will be published in the series. The authors have a common mind not only with regard to the problem but also with regard to the starting-point of reconstruction. They desire to lay stress upon the value and validity of religious experience and to develop their theology on the basis of the religious consciousness. In so doing they claim to be in harmony with modern thought. The massive achievements of the nineteenth and twentieth centuries have been built up on the method of observation and experiment, on experience, not on abstract *a priori* reasoning. Our contention is that the moral and spiritual experience of mankind has the right to be considered, and demands to be understood.

Many distinguished thinkers might be quoted in support of the assertion that philosophers are now prepared in a greater measure than formerly to consider religious experience as among the most significant of their data. One of the greatest has said, " There is nothing more real than what comes in religion. To compare facts such as these with what is given to us in outward existence would be to trifle with the subject. The man who demands a reality more solid than that of the religious consciousness, seeks he does not know what."[1] Nor does this estimate of religious experience come only from idealist thinkers. A philosopher who writes from the standpoint of mathematics and natural science has expressed the same thought in even more forcible language. " The fact of religious vision, and its history of persistent expansion, is our one ground for optimism. Apart from it, human life is a flash of occasional enjoyments lighting up a

[1] F. H. Bradley, *Appearance and Reality*, p. 449.

mass of pain and misery, a bagatelle of transient experience."[1]

The conviction that religious experience is to be taken as the starting-point of theological reconstruction does not, of course, imply that we are absolved from the labour of thought. On the contrary, it should serve as the stimulus to thought. No experience can be taken at its face value ; it must be criticised and interpreted. Just as natural science could not exist without experience and the thought concerning experience, so theology cannot exist without the religious consciousness and reflection upon it. Nor do we mean by " experience " anything less than the whole experience of the human race, so far as it has shared in the Christian consciousness. As Mazzini finely said, " Tradition and conscience are the two wings given to the human soul to reach the truth."

It has been the aim of the writers and the Editors of the series to produce studies of the main aspects of Christianity which will be intelligible and interesting to the general reader and at the same time may be worthy of the attention of the specialist. After all, in religion we are dealing with a subject-matter which is open to all and the plan of the works does not require that they shall delve very deeply into questions of minute scholarship. We have had the ambition to produce volumes which might find a useful place on the shelves of the clergyman and minister, and no less on those of the intelligent layman. Perhaps we may have done something to bridge the gulf which too often separates the pulpit from the pew.

[1] A. N. Whitehead, *Science and the Modern World*, p. 275.

Naturally the plan of our series has led us to give the utmost freedom to the authors of the books to work out their own lines of thought, and our part has been strictly confined to the invitation to contribute, and to suggestions concerning the mode of presentation. We hope that the series will contribute something useful to the great debate on religion which is proceeding in secret in the mind of our age, and we humbly pray that their endeavours and ours may be blessed by the Spirit of Truth for the building up of Christ's Universal Church.

PREFACE TO THE SECOND EDITION

IN this edition I have corrected a number of minor errors and made one or two alterations in terminology; otherwise the text remains the same.

Perhaps it may be added that since the book was first published, an English translation of Karl Heim's *Glaube und Denken*, to which reference is made more than once in the text, has been issued by Messrs. Nisbet, under the title of *God Transcendent*.

H. H. F.

CAMBRIDGE,
    August, 1936.

PREFACE TO THE FIRST EDITION

SECTIONS of this book formed part of the Russell Lectures delivered at Auburn Theological Seminary, New York, in April, 1934. It is a pleasure to acknowledge once again the great kindness which the Faculty of that institution showed me during the delivery of the lectures. Other sections formed part of the Carew Lectures delivered at Hartford Theological Seminary, Conn., as long ago as October, 1930. To the Faculty of that institution also I tender my sincere thanks, not only for their kindness on the occasion of the lectures, but also, and even more, for their friendship during four years of happy fellowship with them as a colleague.

My indebtedness to other authors, so far as I have remained aware of it, will be apparent enough from the references. I wish, however, to make special acknowledgment of the inspiring and shaping influence on my thought, such as it is, of my revered teacher, Dr. John Oman, though this also will be apparent enough to any who are acquainted with his writings.

To the following also I tender my sincere thanks: the Editors of the Library of Constructive Theology, the Rev. Dr. W. Douglas Mackenzie, President Emeritus of the Hartford Seminary Foundation, and Dr. A. Wood, all of whom read the manuscript, wholly or in part, and made many valuable comments and suggestions; the Rev. Dr. C. A. Anderson Scott, and the Rev. Prof. R. H. Strachan for reading the proofs; Mr. and Mrs. V. A. Burrows for preparing the index.

The Princeton University Press and Mr. Paul Elmer More kindly gave permission for an extended quotation from the latter's book *The Sceptical Approach to Religion*. The Student Christian Movement Press also kindly gave me permission to quote certain passages from my book *Experience of God*.

H. H. F.

WESTMINSTER COLLEGE,
    CAMBRIDGE,
        November, 1935.

CONTENTS

INTRODUCTORY

Belief in personal God central in Christian thought and experience, 1. Modern monism as inhibiting such belief, 3. The loss of the sense of the supernatural, 6. Modern illustrations, 7. The purpose of the book, 9.

PART I

GENERAL PRINCIPLES AND CATEGORIES

CHAPTER I

Experience of God as personal approached through human personal relationships, 13. The distinctiveness and immediacy of such relationships, 14. Relationship of trust analysed, 19. Two indispensable elements in awareness of persons : (a) value-resistance, 21 ; (b) value-co-operation, 22. This appears in awareness of God as (a) absolute demand, 23 ; (b) final succour, 25. Yet awareness of God not merely anthropomorphic, 26.

So analysed, awareness of God as personal seen to be characteristic of all living religion, 27.

CHAPTER II

Two ways of apprehending the world : (a) analysis, 33 ; (b) synthesising intuition, 34. (b) related more immediately to interest, 35. In awareness of God mind functions primarily by (b), 38 ; the interest concerned being the organism's urge towards its own fulfilment or norm, 39. Can we speak of the latter as interest ? 40.

In religion the mind intuits the universe as congenial to the fulfilment of the personal life, or, less abstractly, God as final succour, 42. Yet personal life cannot be fulfilled without sense of God as absolute demand, 44. Thus awareness of God as personal as analysed in Chapter I seen to be deeply implicated in inner necessities of personality, 48.

Contents

INTRODUCTORY

THE conviction that God is personal, and deals personally with men and women, lies at the heart of Christian experience and thought.

Sufficient proof of this, if proof be needed, is afforded by the New Testament. Every category, phrase, doctrine, movement of thought, presupposes and implies the possibility for all, and the actuality for the writers, of a personal relationship to a personal God. " God is love ; and he that abideth in love abideth in God and God abideth in him." " If God so loved us, we ought also to love one another." These statements can have no straightforward meaning if God be not thought of as in some sense personal, constituting with men an ultimate order of personal relations. " The God and Father of our Lord Jesus Christ." " He that hath seen me hath seen the Father." Thus to use the term " father " in respect of God, thus to derive its meaning and content from Jesus, involves that whatever else may be true of God, this at least is true, that He is personal and personally related to men. To see Jesus is to see a personal life entering into personal relations with, and seeking personal ends for, men and women.

The experience of the forgiveness of sins and reconciliation with God, which is so central in the New Testament, obviously lies within the same sphere of personal relations with God. Doubtless it is possible, starting from an impersonal conception of God, to excogitate possible meanings for such words as sin, forgiveness, reconciliation, but these would not be the New Testament meanings, nor would they be the meanings with which anybody, out of the midst of a

B

living experience of divine forgiveness, would spontaneously
invest the terms. Sin, for the New Testament writers, is
something which involves an estrangement from, even an
enmity to, God of a personal kind. And forgiveness, being
the overcoming of that estrangement and enmity, is necessarily of the same order. Only because the forgiveness of
God is a transaction between persons is it able to be—as
Jesus said it should be—the inspiration of a man's forgiveness of his fellows. So also the term faith, in the New
Testament, appears to signify fundamentally trust in, self-
commitment to, a divine Person, the God and Father of our
Lord Jesus Christ. Trust is in some ways the most distinctive of all relations between persons, and on it, as
Herrmann has shown, all achievement of a genuinely
ethical, and therefore truly personal, life depends.[1]

This being so, it would seem that we here confront one
of the main difficulties in commending the Christian faith
to this age, and in maintaining it as a living power amongst
those who profess it. For the modern man, seemingly, has
a certain inhibition in his spirit from experiencing, and
thinking of, God as personal. This is doubtless the result
of many co-operative causes working over several generations, such as, for example, the increasing depersonalisation
of industrial relationships since the beginning of the machine
age ; the desocialised life which vast numbers live in the
great cities ; the unification of human life into a world-wide
economic system which few seem to understand and none
can control, though all are subject to it as to an impersonal
Fate ; the shaping of the modern mind by the abstract
methods and categories of science. Perhaps the most
inclusive description of the situation would be to say that
the modern man has become profoundly naturalistic, or
monistic, in his way of looking at his world. He has lost
the sense of there being anything beyond, or above, or

[1] *Ethik*, 5 Aufl., p. 38.

outlasting, the ongoing natural process of which he is a part ;
he tends all the time to look backwards and forwards
horizontally along the ever-changing time-series, but never,
or seldom, upwards, vertically to anything, or anyone,
apprehended as being above the time-series and giving it
whatsoever meaning or direction it may have.

Monistic notions of the world process have, of course,
always had a great attraction for thinkers all down the ages
from the Pythagoreans onwards. Sometimes, as Ménégoz
says, this type of thought is " enveloped in the frigidity of
pure rationalism ; sometimes it expresses itself under the
form of an austere moralism ; sometimes, again, it is
suffused with the warmth of a passionate mysticism . . .
but at bottom it remains invariably the same."[1] In the
century since Hegel such ideas, without the precision given
them by the philosophers, have become very widespread,
partly through the influence of Hegelian schools of thought,
but more because of the fact that they have become fused
with the doctrines of evolution and of the supposed immutable laws of nature, as these have been popularised by
science ; so that increasingly the conception of the universe
as a monistic system has become almost unconsciously part
of the mental furniture of the modern man. In so far as
such ideas receive articulate expression, it is usually in
some form of vague " life-force " philosophy. The order of
the world, as manifested in the sequence of its ascending
stages from the mechanistic levels of matter up to the
emergence of the spirit of man, is regarded as the result of
an immanent creative force which is somehow working
throughout the whole system towards the increase of what
is vaguely called " value." If a place is found for human
endeavour in this scheme, it is only as a sort of localised
manifestation of the general creativeness, a manifestation

---

[1] *Le Problème de la Prière*, p. 19. Cf. Siebeck, *Uber Freiheit, Entwick-
lung und Vorsehung*, p. 33.

which, according to its quality, is either caught up into the
general movement as a contributory factor, or is, in time,
inexorably annulled and cast on one side as a useless
aberration.[1]

How much this has been the prevailing, and often unconscious, temper of modern thought is shown by the way
in which it has soaked into the minds of those professing to
be earnest participants in the Christian tradition and
experience, though with these the fact is often concealed,
both from others and from themselves, by the continued
use of a traditional Christian phraseology which presupposes what is in reality an entirely different thought
of the ultimate nature of things.   Thus there can be
observed again and again a certain reluctance to speak
of God as personal.   The word providence may be
used, and a genuinely religious act of self-commitment
may accompany the use, yet the underlying thought is
not of providence in the character of the God and Father
of our Lord Jesus Christ, but in the character of an all-
inclusive, ongoing process which somehow, through the
operation of natural laws, is creating and conserving " higher
values."   The same tendency appears in the loss of any
poignant sense of sin ; in a reluctance to think of Christ as
any other than a remarkable concretion within the evolutionary process of general principles of truth and goodness ;
in the complete elimination of anything even remotely akin
to what used to be called miracle ; even, at times, in a
hesitancy to affirm a life beyond death, the individual being
regarded merely as a vehicle of process destined, when it
has served its purpose, to disappear.   It is perhaps in regard

---

[1] The affinity between Hegelianism and some of our modern " life-
force " philosophies is obvious ; in both everything, including man, is
reduced to the position of phases in, or vehicles of, an all-embracing
process.   Bergson, Lloyd Morgan, Dewey are all Hegelians in modern
dress, and, as Ménégoz hints in the passage just quoted, "*plus ça change,
plus c'est le même chose.*"   Cf. Oman, *The Natural and the Supernatural*,
p. 284 : " Prof. Lloyd Morgan is merely Spinoza turned biologist."

to prayer that this way of thought makes itself most apparent. Prayer of petition is frowned upon, and the act of prayer tends to become merely the cultivation of a state of mind in which the individual's place in the universe, and his duty to be so far as may be a vehicle of its creative energy, are realised and accepted. To be sure, the deeper religious instinct to engage in petitionary prayer continually breaks through this monistic scheme of ideas, even if it be only in the form of praying that one may be enabled to accept whatever the process may bring forth. But such petitionary prayer is regarded on the whole as a lower stage in the spiritual life, to be increasingly discarded as the latter matures. A variety of reasons are offered in justification, but the real reason is the deep-seated prior conviction that petitionary prayer is futile and useless in a universe which, in its separate events, is governed by immutable laws, and, as a totality, is already a settled harmony with which the soul must seek to realise its unity and be at peace.[1]

We may put the point in another way by saying that the

[1] The last chapter of Ritschl's *Justification and Reconciliation* affords an example of the way in which a mind, which otherwise shows a profound grasp of the Christian experience and message, when it comes to the question of petitionary prayer, suddenly reveals itself to be dominated by ideas of providence and of the reign of law such as are criticised above. The chapter contains more than one statement which suggests a virtual identity between the rule of providence and the all-embracing, unalterable dominion of natural law, and the suggestion is confirmed when, in the later sections, prayer is reduced almost completely to a thankful submission to the divine will. Lordship over the world, therefore, which, according to Ritschl, it is the whole purpose of religion to bestow upon man, is, even in its highest Christian form, only submission to it.

Re-reading some of F. W. Robertson's sermons lately, one was startled to discover how even his powerful Christian spirit, when it came to deal with prayer, revealed at once the influence of the same ideas. The elimination of petition is set forth as the mark of maturity in prayer, and one of the reasons given is the necessity of having that humility which " looks on ourselves as atoms, links in a mysterious chain, and shrinks from the dangerous wish to break the chain " (*Sermons*, People's Edition, 4th Series, p. 33). This is monism again. Yet elsewhere nothing is more eloquently insisted on than the personal quality of God. The wish " to break the chain " is surely the desire to preserve precisely that personal quality.

modern man has lost the sense of the personal in God
because in his naturalistic and monistic thinking he has lost
the sense of the supernatural. To many people the word
supernatural immediately suggests the contranatural, in the
sense of happenings which involve the direct overriding of
what is called the natural order ; but that is to miss entirely
its deepest significance. For religion the supernatural
means, in the last resort, the personal. To be a person means
to be a being who is not a mere item in process, not a mere
function of environment, not a mere product of forces which
grind on in mechanical necessity to their predetermined
end, but rather one which, while rooted in the process,
stands in a measure above it and is able to rule it to freely
chosen ends. Hence it is that in so far as religion has at its
heart the sense of God as personal, and of man as called to
achieve his own personality through fellowship with God
as personal, it inevitably begins to speak of the supernatural.
The personal is the true supernatural, as the natural, with
its blind concatenation of physical and psychical cause-
effect relationships, is the true impersonal. The religious
instinct to cling to the concept of miracle is at bottom not
the result of a craving for portents to gape at, or for accom-
modations on the part of the universe to merely selfish
desires, but for personality in God, and so for the possibility
of a genuine achievement of personality in man ; it is a
protest against an all-inclusive monism which leaves the
soul choking for want of air.

These things, it is hoped, will be made clearer in the
following chapters. Meanwhile we may illustrate, from two
other aspects of our present era, how intimately related to
one another are the belief in the supernatural—in someone
above the process with whom man may have relationships
—and the sense of man's own significance as a person.

The first is the profound devaluation of the individual
which is characteristic of such phenomena as Communism,

Fascism, Nazi-ism.[1] The state is all, the individual nothing save as he is an item in the state's total life. Doubtless there are here at work forces of a more temporary and transient kind, but it is impossible not to see also the outworking of something more deep-seated, without which the temporary and transient influences could never have produced the result in question. The devaluation is, in part, the inevitable outcome of a monistic philosophy of process ; and the inevitability derives not so much from the necessities of logic as from the deeper necessities of the human spirit. A monistic naturalism may conceivably, in theory, find room for an exalted notion of man, but practically and psychologically the two views cannot long abide together. If I do not derive my being from God, and the significance of my being from His supernatural (=personal) purpose resting upon me, then I derive them merely from the natural forces—psychological, biological, sociological— which constitute race, and race may annul me when any tyrant, who can persuade himself and others that the process is for the moment supremely embodied in himself, may so decree.

The second is a certain vague sense of the meaninglessness and emptiness of existence which underlies and subtly tones so much of contemporary life. There is not lacking evidence that the so-called " modern temper " has been, since the war, an increasingly depressed and puzzled one. There is to be observed everywhere, in greater or less degree— sometimes coming to the surface in articulate speech, more often persisting as an underlying ground-tone—a baffled and frustrated sense of the futility of human life. As

---

[1] In the original teaching of Karl Marx there is not lacking a sense of the significance and value of the individual personality. Russian Communism, however, at least in its present form (whatever may be its ultimate outcome), is indistinguishable from Fascism in its ruthless subordination of the individual to the State. (Cf. *The Times*, August 7, 1935.)

Lippmann puts it : " The modern man finds it hard to believe that doing any one thing is better than doing any other thing, or, in fact, that it is better than doing nothing at all."[1] This also is the result of a monistic philosophy of process. For, without the sense of being related to the supernatural personal, man sooner or later becomes conscious of being merely carried along in a flux of events, of whose ultimate outcome he can form no conception in terms of his own interests and deeds. The rise of dictatorships is related to this attitude of mind. As we shall maintain later, the Eternal as the supernatural personal reveals itself to the heart of man through an unconditional demand, and only through his response to this unconditional demand can man be released from the process and given a truly personal life. If this is lacking, there is nothing in the end but an intolerable emptiness and hunger for his heart ; with the result that, seeking escape, he is ready to seize on the figure of a national leader or a political dictator and make *him* the supernatural personal, to whose demands unconditional obedience must be given, for whom, if need be, there must be readiness to die. The rise of modern exaggerated nationalism, sometimes finding expression through mythological symbols and quasi-religious devotion, and the rise of modern monistic naturalism, are related to one another. The one is an escape from the sense of emptiness and futility which sooner or later overtakes the other. It is substitute religion, and the dictator is a substitute deity.

If there be any truth in these remarks, it follows that to expound the thought of God as personal, and to help to restore it to a more living and central place in the experience and witness of Christian men and women, is one of the major tasks of the theologian to-day. The unconscious tendency to accommodate oneself to the age and to present an attenuated gospel, in which all personal categories used in

[1] *Preface to Morals*, p. 4.

relation to God are toned down, or explained away so soon as question is raised, must be steadfastly resisted. This may invite the charge from certain quarters of being out-of-date ; but we can afford to wait and, unless we are greatly mistaken, signs are not lacking that we shall not have to wait long. Monistic naturalism is under judgement to-day, certainly in events, and increasingly in some of the best thinking of the time.

To the fulfilment of this task this book is offered as a contribution.

In an exposition of the Christian awareness of God as personal it is possible to pursue three lines of thought. First, we may seek to indicate what appears to be central and indispensable in such awareness, under what conditions it is given, the manner of its development in reach and content, the way in which it enters into and determines the whole personal life. Second, we may make suggestions how what is thus given in the life of personal fellowship with God may be reflectively related to what appears to be given in other departments of experience and knowledge. Third, we may consider the theoretical difficulties which inhere, or are alleged to inhere, in the concept of personality as applied to God. In this work it is not proposed to pursue the third of these lines of thought, partly for reasons of space, partly because such questions have been extensively argued by other writers,[1] but chiefly because incomparably more important than meeting abstract philosophical difficulties is the endeavour to open men's mind to that personal approach of God to the soul which, if there be any truth in our position at all, is already going on in the concrete actualities of their daily experience. The real difficulty with most people is not the conundrums which the philosophers ask (such as, for example, whether personality can

---

[1] As, for example, in another volume of this series—Matthews, *God in Christian Thought and Experience.*

be attributed to a Being who, by definition, would seem to have no not-self, no environment), but their own inability to interpret the thought of God as personal in terms of the world as they know it, or seem to know it, in their personal dealing with it. For this reason we have deemed it necessary, while eschewing the more abstract theoretical questions, to say something about the relation of the awareness of God as personal to the so-called " reign of law " described by science.

The three topics indicated in the sub-title, namely Prayer, Miracle, and Providence, are thus singled out, because in them are focused the fundamental factors of the Christian's life of personal fellowship with God. To discuss them is to discuss the living awareness of God as personal ; to discuss the living awareness of God as personal is to discuss them. In particular, as already hinted and as will be more fully expounded later, it is of the highest importance to approach the concept of miracle from within the sphere of personal relations with God ; only thus can it be rescued from the gross misunderstanding and ill-repute into which it has fallen, and be restored in thought to that position which, despite all the admitted difficulties and confusions, it has never entirely lost in living and spontaneous Christian experience. It is significant that, whilst attempts have often been made to retain a place for prayer and for a species of trust in Providence along with a fundamentally impersonal conception of God, the attempt is never made to retain a place for miracle under the same conditions, save in a form that evacuates it of all distinctive meaning. This would suggest that the issue between personal and impersonal conceptions of God reaches sharpest definition in relation to the concept of miracle. That this is so, the sequel will perhaps make clear.

PART I

GENERAL PRINCIPLES AND CATEGORIES

CHAPTER I

BASIC ELEMENTS OF PERSONAL RELATIONSHIP

WE begin with the question : What is essentially involved in the living awareness of God as personal ? By " living awareness " we mean an awareness quite other than the merely theoretical ascription of personal quality to the ultimate on philosophical grounds : it is an awareness which includes feeling and will as well as ideas, and so determines in a measure the whole character and direction of the personal life. By " what is essentially involved " we mean those basic elements without which, so far as can be judged, such awareness of God would not arise.

In order to answer this question, we propose to begin with something which is perhaps more familiar and more easily susceptible of analysis, namely our awareness of one another as personal beings. This method is the more justified because, as the whole course of our thought will show, the experience of our fellows and the experience of God as personal are intimately bound up with one another, God, the neighbour, and the self constituting an ultimate and continuous order of personal relationship.

Nothing is clearer in our everyday life than the distinction between dealing with a person and dealing with a thing. The fact that in the animal world we have to deal with creatures who are neither the one nor the other merely emphasises the more the clarity, certainty, and uniqueness of our awareness of personality when it confronts us, and enters into relationship with us. One way of reflectively realising the absolute nature of this distinction, which is so

13

fundamental and familiar in the ordinary way that we take it for granted and never think about it all, is imaginatively to put oneself in the place of Pygmalion when the statue began to *speak*. The point is not that one would be exceedingly startled that a dead object should suddenly become alive ; rather it is that, whether startled or not, there is in the awareness of having now in the room a personal being in addition to oneself a profound reorientation of the whole mind. There is, as it were, a shift in the foundation, a change of key, with the result that the whole pattern and tone of awareness becomes different. Everything is now in a different perspective or dimension. The statue's addressing of itself to *you* in speech is like the sudden moving of the lever of a kaleidoscope ; the bits of glass fall into such an entirely new pattern that it is difficult to believe that they have not themselves been transformed into entirely different things.

It is indeed in the peculiarly direct and living relationship of speech that the sense of the distinction between persons and things reaches its maximum. As I talk to my neighbour, hear his views, suggest things which he repudiates, repudiate things which he suggests, watch the play of his features, gaze into the eyes wherein so much of personal quality seems to be concentrated, sense feelings of accord or tension passing back and forth, it is totally impossible for me to react to him in the same way that I would react to the dog, and still more impossible to entertain the idea that he might after all be only a mechanical talking doll. There is something intrinsically coercive and self-evident in the apprehension that I am in that quite distinctive sort of relationship to that quite distinctive sort of entity which I call personal. The whole thing is *sui generis*. Martin Buber has suggested[1] that the peculiar distinctiveness of this relationship comes to expression in the use of the second person pronoun singular—" you " or " thou ". At the

[1] *Ich und Du, passim.*

point where an entity is grasped in a living immediacy of
direct personal relationship the word " thou " is inevitably
sooner or later used, and only at that point is it used.
Probably everybody has experienced, sometimes with
surprise, the difference between thinking about, and passing
judgement upon, a person whom he has never met, and then
encountering and speaking with him face to face. Up
to the moment of encounter he has been merely a " he ",
almost, so far as our attitude is concerned, an " it ", a mere
symbol for the convergence of certain relationships ; doubtless a personal meaning is attached to the symbol, but only
in an abstract, theoretical way, much as a certain value
might be attached to x in an algebraic equation. But now
when we meet him and speak with him, and our purposes
meet and interact in the direct *rapport* of speech, he becomes
a " thou " to us, and instantly the relationship is different,
so different that all our previous theoretical ideas about
" him " may be swept on one side.

There is then, we affirm, in certain circumstances a direct
awareness of personal entities other than ourselves, with
whom we stand in an order, or dimension, of personal
relationships. It has, however, been questioned by some
whether such awareness is as immediate as it appears to be,
and, as the question is of some importance in relation to
later developments of our thought, some consideration
must be given to it.

There can be no question that the awareness has in actual
experience what Tennant calls " psychical immediacy ",
that is to say, it is not at the moment of its occurrence the
result of a process of mental construction or inference ;
rather it has an intuitive and intrinsic certainty which
neither requires, nor admits of, any attestation other than
its own self-evidence. It is maintained, however, that
though psychically immediate, it is not psychologically so.
All that is immediately given is the sense-impressions which

the bodies of others make upon us. These from our earliest years we have learnt to interpret as the bodies of beings with an inner life like our own ; we have analogically projected our own inner life into their bodies as presented to us through the senses, and this has been so abundantly justified in practice that it has become an " inevitable and self-evident belief." The analogical projection, or inference, or construction, has become so fused in experience with the immediate sense-impressions which human organisms make upon us, that it seems to share in their immediacy.

It is open to question whether this is really adequate to the facts. It is difficult to see how the individual, if he is initially shut up within the circle of his own private sense-impressions, could ever transcend it ; and to posit an innate power of analogical projection operative in the earliest stages of experience, in order to explain the mystery, savours a little of " faculty " psychology. We have no experience elsewhere of analogical inference producing that type of full assurance, evoking the profoundest responses of the mind, which we have of one another's existence as personal beings, and into which the very young child apparently very swiftly enters in advance of any prolonged experimental verification. That analogical projection may play a part need not be denied, but without a prior awareness, however dim, of some sort of personal, or at least living, other presented in and through sensations, there would seem to be nothing to call it into activity. Even the savage's projection of spirits into natural objects presupposes the awareness of living beings other than himself, and it may have derived much of its liveliness as belief from an immediate intuition, true so far as it went and awaiting further experience to be more fully understood, of " something far more deeply interfused " presenting itself through the physical environment. Animism, in short, as Stout has suggested,[1] may be fundamentally a valid insight, and, so

[1] *Mind and Matter*, p. 33.

far from being the result, may be rather the presupposition of the savage's analogical projection of himself into things, and of the admittedly useful part such projection can, and does, play in a developing understanding of the world.

Three misconceptions seem to lie behind the reluctance to grant that there is anywhere in our relations with others as personal a real, and not merely an apparent, immediacy of apprehension.

First, there is a tendency to confuse immediacy with independence. It is supposed that, if an awareness is to be properly regarded as immediate, it should be capable of taking place independently of any other sort of awareness. Hence, inasmuch as we can have no awareness of others save in and through the sensations which their bodies evoke in us, it is inferred that the latter alone are the immediate data in the experience, anything else being only derivative interpretation or acquired meaning. But this does not follow. The argument seems to rest on the absolute separation of mind and body which since Descartes has lain like a blight on reflection upon these matters. If our fellow-beings in this world are inseparable organic unities of body and self, then it is to be expected that we should become aware of them as such—as self active in and through its unity with a body, as body acting in and through its unity with a self, neither being prior to the other, but both being given together. When a man who is angry with me glares at me with clenched fist, his personal attitude, as a conscious being, to myself is not inferred from the physical manifestations, but is apprehended as being dynamically contained in, and continuous with, them ; he presents himself as a single personal totality containing, as it were, the two mutually involved and quite inseparable dimensions of mind and body.[1]

Second, there is a tendency to suppose that, if we have an

[1] Cf. Köhler, *Gestalt Psychology* (Eng. Trans.), p. 201.

c

immediate awareness of others as personal beings, it ought never to happen that we imagine ourselves to have that awareness, when in fact we are mistaken ; yet, in fact, that does sometimes happen. The schoolboy in the orchard mistakes the scarecrow for the farmer and flees. Here is plainly a false interpretation of visual impressions ; must not then all awareness of others be fundamentally interpretations of the same kind, except that in most cases subsequent experience attests their truth ? But this also does not follow. Given a prior experience of embodied personalities the laws of association will account for false apprehensions like that of the schoolboy ; and the question of the nature of that prior awareness, and whether there is something immediate in it, is not affected one way or the other by the occurrence of such mistakes. Moreover, we are not concerned to affirm that the immediate awareness of personality in another is necessarily given through any and every impression his body may make upon us ; it is only when those impressions are part of a certain direct, responsive relationship, a certain *mutuum commercium*, between two individualities *within a common situation* in which the wills of both are involved, that through them the dimension of the personal is immediately perceived in the way indicated.

Third, there is a tendency to suppose that if an awareness is immediate it cannot be subject to development and have a history. We may fully admit, however, that to the full and indubitable awareness of others as personal many factors contribute of which the psychologist can give an account—imaginative interpretation, analogical projection, experimental verification, and so on. All that we are concerned to maintain is that whatever else may be involved, there runs throughout all our awareness of being set in a system of relationships with other personal beings—from the vague awareness of the infant up to that most vivid and irresistible awareness which is given in the co-operation of friendship and trust—a core of immediate apprehension, or of remembered immediate apprehension. Such apprehension could not arise apart from sense-impressions, but is never merely a construct from them.[1]

This immediacy in the awareness of the " other " as personal does not preclude us, however, from giving some description of certain elements which appear to be central and indispensable in it. In order to do this we may take a look at the relationship of friendship and trust, in which, as we have just suggested, such awareness reaches a maximum. Trust is a grasping of, a responding to, a communicating with, certain entities as personal, or it is nothing. We do indeed sometimes speak of trusting ourselves to natural laws and physical objects, but we do not mean the same thing as when we speak of trusting a friend ; if there is anything of the same feeling present, it is because in a dim way we are responding religiously to the world and discerning something quasi-personal within it.

Two things at least seem to be central in genuine trust in a person.

First, there is an awareness of the other's will as standing over against our own in a certain polarity or tension. It is precisely the mark of trust to respect and rejoice in this, and not in any way to seek to circumvent or overcome it. The other's will presents itself as an inaccessible source of activity, continuously creating, as it were, an invisible frontier between his being and ours, a frontier where there is always at least potential resistance, and over which there is no passing save in so far as he invites us so to do. Here indeed is the paradox of trust, and that which shows that we are in an entirely different order of relationships from

[1] For a fuller discussion of these matters the reader may refer to Tennant, *Philosophical Theology*, Vol. I ; Webb, *Divine Personality and Human Life ;* Stout, *Mind and Matter.*

those in which we stand to the physical world. In the latter the basis of our confidence about future events is that they are the necessary resultant of quasi-mechanical forces operative within a given sphere ; in the relationship of trust the basis of our confidence is precisely that events are not so determined. If we thought that the other man's will were so determined we should have no trust in him whatsoever, for at any moment he might come under the influence of forces of a stronger kind than those which now determine his conduct, and his whole behaviour might be deflected in a totally new direction, as iron filings are re-arranged into a new pattern so soon as a magnet is brought near. We put the point in another way if we say that directly we begin to try to force the will of our friend into conformity with ours, to appeal to powerful instincts and passions, such as fear or cupidity, to manœuvre him into situations where he has little option save to do what we want, we demonstrate that we do not and cannot trust him. For if we can thus manipulate him through his passions and instincts, so may someone else in our absence ; no basis of confidence remains.

Essential, then, in trust is the acceptance of the inaccessibility of the other man's will to ours, its unalterable polarity and tension with ours. How, then, do we ever come to commit ourselves to what is thus entirely inaccessible to our control ? Here the second thing enters in qualifying the first. We are ready to commit ourselves to it in so far as we are able to believe that both his will and ours, though not subject to one another, are subject to the same standards of *unconditional* worth or value. By being subject to the same standards of unconditional value, both wills are lifted above the merely mechanical determination of conduct by powerful environmental stimuli, and, despite incidental divergences, can rest on one another in that quite peculiar and satisfying way which is trust. Trust, then, in the fullest sense, is only possible between beings who are

implicitly, if not explicitly, aware of one another as personalities, or moral subjects, that is to say, as conscious beings
who are enabled to stand above the flux of process because
both are inwardly under the rule of the same world of final
value. It involves an awareness of the completest independence of purpose in the midst of the profoundest
community of ultimate values, of the profoundest community of ultimate values in the midst of the completest
independence of purpose. And, we repeat, in this relationship of trust the most distinctive and living awareness of
the other as personal is achieved. This might be said to
be what personality supremely is, namely that type of
conscious being who is capable of entering into such a
mutual relationship of trust.[1]

Now what is thus given at a maximum in the relationship
of trust would appear to be present, in greater or less
degree of vividness, in all awareness of others as personal.

First, there is always some awareness of purpose or will
or self-activity, however it may be called, coming forth
from the other man and meeting ours, within a common
situation, in a certain peculiar and irreducible tension or
resistance. This does not mean that we have to be at
cross-purposes with a man before we apprehend him as a
person. As we have seen, the sort of tension or resistance of
which we are thinking is the basis of the friendliest co-
operation and trust. The other's will stands as a limit to
ours. Physical objects also limit our purposes, but the
limitation is of an entirely different kind, as our response
to it clearly shows. The resistance of physical objects can
only be overcome, if it is overcome at all, by direct manip-
ulative control. The resistance of a will can never be overcome save by what we call agreement or reconciliation.
For in the degree that it is otherwise overcome it ceases to
be a personal will any longer, and so cannot, *qua* will, be

[1] See Herrmann, *op. cit.*, p. 39f.

said to be overcome at all. Popular sentiment shows this. Most sensitive people feel that the attempt to manipulate the activity of an individual apart from his own genuine insight into, and acceptance of, the ends in view is what they call " an abuse of personality ", and what is meant by that phrase is well understood by most, even though it is difficult to express it precisely in terms. On the other hand a man who is unduly submissive to another's purposes is said to have no personality, to be a non-entity, a " rubber stamp ". Always personality becomes most vividly an entity to us by offering what we may call purpose- or value-resistance.

And yet, also, second, there is always some awareness of the other's will as operating in the same world of rationally apprehended facts and values as one's own, as offering, therefore, potentially at least, what may be called value-co-operation as well as value-resistance. There is awareness of community with the other man even when one is at cross-purpose with him. Indeed it is only because the situation is a common situation, having in a measure a common significance and relevance to both as specifically human beings, so that each can in a measure grasp what the other values and intends, that the peculiar tension just referred to can arise. The other man's peculiar power to resist and frustrate me—so very different from the inert resistance of things or the blind resistance of animals—lies in his power to understand what I am doing and to adjust himself accordingly ; but that implies also his power to co-operate and help. He can do the one because he can do the other, and the other because he can do the one. My vivid awareness of his resistance is surrounded, as it were, by a pervasive sense of his community with me as a personal being who could as well be a friend as a foe.

The awareness, then, of the other as potentially co-operative in his resistance, or as potentially resistant in his co-operation, lies at the heart of our awareness of personality in one another. It reaches its maximum, as we have said, in the most distinctive of all personal relationships, which is trust. We may note, in view of what will be considered later, that the same awareness comes to expression in the distinctively personal relationship of prayer. We ask, request, pray persons to do things, in a way that we do not animals or things. Prayer is an act which is conscious of another will as being beyond the control of our purpose and yet at the same time potentially co-operative with it ; it is conscious, that is to say, of its object as personal, or it is not prayer.

In the light of this, let us now return to the question of what is central in the living awareness of God as personal. If there is continuity between the personal world in which we live with our fellows and that in which we live with God —and Christianity, alike in its doctrine and in its ethics, emphatically affirms that there is—then we should expect that what is central in the one sphere would be central in the other. Man could hardly react in one way in apprehending his fellows as personal, and in an entirely different way in apprehending God as personal, however great the difference in the total content of the two experiences, corresponding to the profound difference in the realities which evoke them, must necessarily be. The facts show this to be so.

First, central in the living awareness of God as personal is something which happens, and must continue to happen, in the sphere of the *will*. The religious man is aware of a certain peculiar type of resistance being set up within the sphere of his values and preferences : the resistance, namely, of absolute, sacred, unconditional values—values which are apprehended as calling for obedience literally at any cost. Such values are felt as asking in principle even the sacrifice of life itself, thus setting up a resistance to the most basic and powerful of all instincts, the instinct to remain alive.

It is in their accent of unconditionality that their quite peculiar resistant quality is felt. The strength of their claim to obedience does not wax or wane with the strength or weakness of a man's desires for them, or the weakness or strength of his desires in other directions ; they are not felt as being, fundamentally, a function of desire at all, but as, potentially at least, a check, limit, or resistance to any desire whatsoever. Further, it is in and through the accent of unconditionality that the awareness of meeting another's will in and through such values is given. For, as Heim has said, man cannot lay an unconditional on his own will by his own will. Whatever he imposes on himself he can lift from himself at a pinch ; but that which can be lifted, even if it be only at a pinch, is not an unconditional.

Whose will is it, then, that is met in such unconditional value-resistance ? To the religious mind it is the will of God, the will, that is, of the ultimate purpose which lies at the heart of all being. Whoso says God, says, for the religious mind, the ultimate WILL haunting the soul with the pressure of an unconditional value, with the demand for an unconditional obedience ; and whoso says the pressure of an unconditional value, the demand for an unconditional obedience, says, for the religious mind, the ultimate WILL of God. And " will " means " person " ; in and through the resistance of values the dimension of the personal is immediately known. The religious mind does not first feel the impact of unconditional values and then argue from them to the hypothesis of an ultimate holy purpose as the best explanation he can offer of so strange an experience ; to suppose that would be to confuse religion with philosophy, and to leave entirely inexplicable the tremendous power of religion in the experience of man. No, the awareness of God as personal will is given immediately in the impact of unconditional value itself, so that the religious man says, not that God is a necessary postulate in order to make sense

of such absolute resistance to his will, but that He is a
" consuming fire ", or that " He is living and powerful and
sharper than a two-edged sword."[1]

But this does not exhaust the religious man's living
awareness of God as personal. For, second, there is always
at the heart of it the awareness of God, not merely as
unconditional demand, but also as what may be called
ultimate or final succour. And these two awarenesses are
not, in the living religious experience, separable from one
another ; they are given in and through one another. The
unconditional demands, the values of God, are apprehended
as pointing the way to the highest self-realisation, the final
security of man. The divine will resists and sets a limit to
our personal desires and preferences of a peculiarly absolute
kind ; none the less it can be trustfully obeyed, for it is in
the same world of values with ourselves, or rather it is the
ultimate foundation of it. In its very resistance, therefore,
it is, in a unique and ultimate way, co-operative. In the
highest reaches of Christian experience this dual awareness
has often found striking expression, as, for example, in the
phrases " Whose service is perfect freedom ", " In His will
is our peace ", and clearest of all in Jesus' words, " He that
loseth his life for my sake shall find it." But it is an awareness which runs through all religion of this type, and in its
original unanalysed unity it is the living awareness of the
Eternal as personal. This unconditional value-resistance
which also points the way of man's final succour is immediately known as the approach of the personal ultimate, or
the ultimate personal, to the soul, calling for the personal
response of obedience and trust. For a personal reality, as
we have said, is supremely and essentially known both
through its value-resistance and through its intuited community of values with those of the percipient's own personal

---

[1] I have given a fuller exposition of this coercive impact of God upon
the soul through absolute values and demands in *Experience of God* (S.C.M.,
1929), to which the reader is referred.

life. Both factors are essential. To know God livingly and fully as personal He must be apprehended at one and the same time as "consuming fire" and as "refuge and strength." It is an idle question to ask why this should be the manner of God's self-disclosure to the soul of man. The necessity lies in the character of God Himself, and in that order of personal relations, of relations between personal wills, which springs from Him. It is given in the original unity of the universe, inherent in which is the primordial *rapport* between man and God, and God and man.

It is perhaps not unnecessary to insist that we have been merely trying to set forth the central awarenesses in and through which the *personal* quality of God is apprehended and without which, so far as can be judged, it would not be apprehended at all. We do not suggest that what has been said exhausts the religious experience of God ; rather it indicates merely a sort of focal point around which there is a vast penumbra of awareness of the infinite, mysterious, divine reality, from the depths of whose transcendent and unimaginable being there comes forth this revealing resistancy, and succouring promise, of personal purpose. It is *God* who is apprehended as personal and not merely another creature like ourselves. In and through the central impact of absolute values there is perceived what may be called in a clumsy phrase " ontal depth " or " the dimension of the eternal ". It is like a promontory jutting out into the sea from some vast, misty, dimly sensed *hinterland* of mountains, or like the dimension of depth which by means of the tiny, flat surface of the retina is seen stretching away into the infinite blue.[1]

[1] The supposed crude anthropomorphism of the primitive in worshipping his idol is surely often grossly misunderstood. It is never *mere* anthropomorphism. There is always a penumbra, an atmosphere, an overtone, of meaning which goes beyond the mere image, and makes the whole response of the mind specifically religious in content and feeling, specifically a response to *God*, and not to something which is in the least danger of being confused with man.

Moreover, there always accompanies this awareness a reverberation of feeling concerning which we can only say that it is that peculiar feeling-tone which accompanies the awareness of God. Doubtless it may be subsumed under the generic name " awe ", but generic names for feelings tell us very little ; even feelings which have a family likeness differ greatly according to the situation to which they refer. A situation in which God is livingly apprehended is like no other, and the feeling which attends it is like no other ; it may lie nearer, say, to the awe felt in the presence of the forces of nature than to some other feelings, as red might be said to lie nearer to orange than to some other colours ; but it is not that awe, any more than red is orange. It is itself—the peculiar reverberation of the soul of man to ultimate being apprehended as meeting him in holy demand and final succour.[1]

In this analysis of the essential elements in the living awareness of God as personal, we have based ourselves of necessity on the Christian experience, which is the only one we know at first hand and which is, as has been said above,[2] through and through personalistic in its experience and thought of God. It is a further step, warranted, we believe, by the facts, but taking us beyond what is immediately given in our own religious awareness into what is more theoretical, when we seek to apply our conclusions to all religious awareness whatsoever. We propose the thesis that to uncover what is central in the awareness of God as personal is to uncover what is the essence of living religion

---

[1] The affinity between what we have called " holy demand and succour " and Otto's familiar " *mysterium tremendum et fascinans* " will be noted. Otto's net, however, was of far too wide mesh to catch and isolate the essential religious fact. Not all awareness of " *mysterium tremendum et fascinans* " is religious ; it is religious when the " *mysterium tremendum* " takes on the quality of unconditional value-resistance, and the " *fascinans* " takes on the quality of uniting man, in and through that resistance, to a final security and well-being.

[2] See the introductory chapter.

all down the ages. *The essence of religion in all its forms is a response to the ultimate as personal.* To one who believes that God is in fact personal such a conclusion is, indeed, unavoidable. For if God be indeed personal, and if the religious experience of mankind be a response to Him, then it is to be expected that at no point will the peculiar differentiæ of personal relationship fail to appear, even though it be in a disguised, attenuated, corrupt, or merely germinal form. And the facts, so far as they can be known, appear to verify this expectancy.

We suggest that always at the heart of man's religious response to his world there can be discerned (*a*) an awareness of unconditional demand ; (*b*) an awareness of man's well-being as somehow bound up in his obedience to that demand ; (*c*) an awareness of the final reality of his world meeting him in such absolute demand and proferred succour ; (*d*) a certain reverberation in feeling of the nature of worship or awe. The unconditional demand may be from our point of view very superstitious, unethical, even repulsive, in its content, as in the irrational taboos or the blood-sacrifices of primitive religion, but the important thing is not its content so much as its form as unconditional. The succour may be conceived in crudely materialistic or hedonistic terms—protection from enemies, abundance of herds and flocks, etc.—but it is always in terms of what is felt to be supremely valuable, filling for the moment at least the whole horizon of desire.[1] The god worshipped may be one of many, but within the sphere allotted to him, and in relation to the practical situation in the midst of which the religious awareness arises, he is apprehended as the final reality, the one supernatural ultimate with which man has to deal and from which there is no further appeal to anything beyond. Every religious response at the moment of its occurrence is monotheistic, or rather henotheistic. The reverberation

[1] See further below, p. 139.

in feeling may be mixed with other feelings and impulses—
fear, sex, egotistic power-feelings—but it always has something of the distinctive quality which comes, and can only
come, from the specifically religious awareness and response.

Doubtless the question whether there has ever been, or
ever could be, a religion without any awareness of the
ultimate as personal is in part a matter of definition. If
anyone choose so to define religion that it does not essentially
include such awareness in any shape or form, and to abide
by the definition, there is nothing more to be said. Yet a
definition cannot be a matter of arbitrary choice, or prejudice. It must be related, on the one hand, to all that
prima facie, according to the general sense of mankind, is
indicated by the term, and, on the other hand, to what
appears to be given as its essential import in one's own
experience. It should include without strain both the
outwardly presented historical facts so far as known, and
the inwardly felt personal experience, doing full justice to
both and setting them in orderly perspective with one
another.[1] It is certainly arguable that those who so conceive
the essence of religion that it does not necessarily include
any awareness of the ultimate as personal do not fulfil
either of these conditions ; they do justice *neither* to religion
as a historical phenomenon *nor* even to such experience of
their own as they are disposed to regard as religious.

Thus, concerning the former point, it is often asserted that
history presents us with cases of religion without the
thought of God as personal. The instances cited are
Buddhism and Hinduism, whose fundamental conception
of the ultimate reality, with which man has to deal, in many

---

[1] Bradley's curt statement : " The doctrine that there cannot be a
religion without a personal God is to my mind certainly false " (*Essays on
Truth and Reality*, p. 432), carries little weight as stated, for it is not
supported by a carefully wrought-out theory of religion, based on an
examination of the religious consciousness and of the facts of the history
of religion.

ways gives the impression of being impersonal through and through. Yet surely we have to distinguish between the conceptual thought of metaphysical reflection and the religious response as such, for which such reflection seeks to provide a more or less adequate intellectual expression. It cannot be without significance that in so far as Buddhism and Hinduism have become religions of the masses, the impersonalistic metaphysic has receded into the background and the object of religious devotion has become pronouncedly personal. The impersonal Absolute had to be conceived as presenting itself in personal form before it could decisively and formatively lay hold on the religious impulse. The Buddha has been deified, the Bodhisattvas and the Amida Buddha are personal beings. In Hinduism the neutral, all-embracing Brahma is believed to have manifested itself in the Trimurti, that is, the three divine personalities of Brahma, Vishnu, and Siva, and these have become, along with other deities, the real objects of a religious devotion which in the Bhakti cults is of a warmly personal kind. This might be regarded as merely a declension to a lower level ; yet it is equally reasonable to regard it as the genuine religious response of the soul breaking through, doubtless in a form not uninfluenced by the pressure of that against which it asserts itself, a metaphysic which has failed to do it justice.[1]

And concerning the second point we may venture to doubt whether, for example, some of our contemporary naturalistic monists, who expressly refuse to ascribe personality to God whilst seeking to retain something which they call religion, really succeed in uniting such an impersonalistic philosophy with the religious response itself.

[1] Cf. an interesting passage in Ménégoz, *op. cit.*, p. 467, where he seeks to show that Oriental impersonalistic monism has evolved in certain thinkers into theism, as though not only the necessities of religion, but also those of reason require the thought of God as personal. Cf. also Wobbermin, *The Nature of Religion* (Eng. Trans.), p. 195 f.

What happens appears to be that, on the one hand, an impersonalist theory of the universe is wrought out on rational grounds, and, on the other hand, certain religious moods are experienced wherein, altogether apart from the theory so wrought out, there is a blissful sense of union with the All, or the Wholeness of things, or the Life-force, however it may be expressed. At first sight these two seem to be readily harmonisable with one another. But the question is whether they can be harmonised with one another *at the moment of the religious feelings*. It is doubtful whether they can, whether it is possible in the midst of such feelings to affirm with clear conviction the strictly impersonal nature of the ultimate without the feelings radically changing their quality, if not completely vanishing away. In other words, what happens is that at the moment of religious response there is an implicit awareness of the personal quality of ultimate reality, union with which is so blissfully felt. One might say, borrowing some phrases of Ménégoz, that such devotees are caught, fortunately, in a religious atavism which breaks through the artificial barriers of logical thought. From this point of view the type of religion under discussion would be regarded as rudimentary religion partly inhibited from its proper development by a false metaphysic, rather than as religion functioning at its maturest level, as so many seem to regard it.[1]

---

[1] The same thing can be illustrated from acosmic pantheism or mysticism. Here union with God is sought by escape from the world. As Heiler points out (*Das Gebet*, p. 249), historically a purely impersonalistic mysticism has seldom been achieved ; always it has tended to take on a personal colouring. Where it has been thoroughly wrought out it has been through an artificial method of spiritual discipline designed to suspend the power of thought altogether, and to reduce the mind to a bare unity without content. Here least of all can an impersonalistic philosophy be said to be united with religious feeling, for at the summit of supposedly religious awareness the mind is out of commission, and incapable of entertaining a philosophy at all.

CHAPTER II

INNER ROOTS OF PERSONAL RELIGION

THE truth of the analysis just given of the basic elements in the awareness of God as personal is further evidenced when these elements are set in relation to the nature and ends of distinctively personal life in man. They are then seen to be indissolubly bound up together. The sphere of religion is the sphere of the personal, and to penetrate deeply into the one is always to penetrate deeply into the other.

We must first take note of a distinction which in these days is almost a commonplace, that, namely, between the two main ways in which the mind apprehends its world.

There is, first, the way of analysis. In analysis we endeavour to break down that which in the business of practical living is first given as a totality, or as a unique and unrepeatable situation in our personal experience, into constituent, and as far as possible similar, parts ; we then seek to discover generalisations conceived as governing the relations between these parts in all situations whatsoever. We distinguish, sort, catalogue, pigeon-hole, diagrammatise. The process is essentially one of abstraction ; that is to say, it is a process of isolating in thought aspects of the situation which in fact are not met in that isolated form at all. The rich particularity and variety of the immediately given, its appeal to feeling and its challenge to will, the atmosphere of meaning by which it is surrounded and permeated, as a sponge is surrounded and permeated by the water in which it floats, are all left on one side and in its

place is substituted a thought-pattern, or chart, of generalised symbols conceived as standing in some sort of universal
and necessary relationship to one another. The sick man
ceases to be a living personality in whom the awful drama
of death's challenge to ambition and love is being wrought
out, and becomes a case of Bright's disease, one like tens of
thousands of similar cases before. The water which to
David spoke of the loyalty and sacrifice of his men and of
his own unworthiness, so that he could not drink it, thirsty
as he was ; which to St. Francis was dear Sister Water ;
which, according to Jesus, being given to the needy, might
take a man into eternal life—is, for scientific purposes,
just H_2O, a formula which would stand with equal accuracy
for a puddle in a pit for snakes.

The most specialised and advanced type of this analytic
activity is physics, which endeavours to analyse the phenomena of the physical universe into elements and functions
of the most abstract mathematical kind. But even those
sciences which are largely descriptive and classificatory are,
in their degree, abstract. Even to call a familiar garden-
flower by its official class-name is in a measure to evacuate
it of its romance and beauty, and to transport the mind
into a grey, attenuated world. None but the scientist, and
he only for scientific purposes, would wish to call a hedgerow
flower "*lonicera periclymenum*", when he might call it
" sweet honeysuckle ". The fact is, all generalisations, even
the simplest ones of daily life, are abstract. " All men are
two-legged." Yet in the business of living we only perceive
this two-legged man and that two-legged man, and each
perception has been part of a total situation occurring at a
particular point in time and space and never really occurring
again. Never in any concrete, historical situation do we
confront an entity " all men " or an entity " two-legged-
ness ". If we experience these in any sense at all, it is only
in the world of thought. It is beyond our purpose to discuss

D

the age-long question of the precise status of such "uni-versals" in the real world and in our knowledge of it ; it is enough to note, as it has some importance in relation to what will be said later, that there is this quality of abstract-ness in all generalised statements.

In contrast with this analytic approach there is, second, the way of approach which dominates us in practical affairs. Here the mind works in a predominantly synthetic way, not breaking impressions up, but rather fusing them together into significant totalities. This synthesising activity of the mind is, however, different from the analysing activity not merely in being synthesising. It is also different in that it cannot be made a matter of volition in anything like the same degree, if indeed at all. There is, doubtless, a certain inborn impulse to analyse situations into likenesses and unlikenesses—it is amongst the child's favourite activ-ities to play with boxes, or to sort or tidy up—and such an impulse is essential to the practical life itself. But, beyond a certain point, unless the mind deliberately analyses impressions, they will not be analysed at all. They will not analyse themselves. But to synthesise impressions by a deliberate act of will into total significant situations, appre-hended as such, is impossible. The impressions must fuse themselves, or rather the mind must fuse them in a sort of intuitional flash which is as a rule quite beyond volitional control. Thus in reading a poem the mind either intuits it as an artistic unity in and through the serial impressions, or it does not ; if it does not, no amount of wishing or straining will avail. Yet anybody can understand the grammatical rules of the structure of the poem, if he apply his mind to it. The same thing appears in the way in which a number of lines on a sheet of paper will suddenly present themselves as a significant pattern or shape to someone staring at them. Many, however, will stare in vain, though all can count and measure the lines.

The reason why these synthesising intuitions are not under volitional control is that they are part of what is essentially a feeling response to the world, the word " feeling " being used to cover any awareness, not necessarily a fully self-conscious and explicit awareness, of the significance of a situation for the individual's own life. They have all to do at some point or other with the relationship of whatever is going on to our own interests and values. This might appear dubious in respect of the simplest patterns which the mind intuits in the impressions which it receives, such as those of spatial configuration ; but even these, we may surmise, have had genetically a connexion with some biological interest or need, though it may now be impossible to trace it. Much of the simpler patterning with which our minds immediately invest reality may be of the nature of survivals of more primitive " interest-situations ". Indeed, it is possible, as Bergson has suggested, that the whole range of our awareness of reality has been determined in the past, and still is in a measure determined, by the biological task which has been set the organism by its intrinsic needs and capacities. Certainly it is difficult to understand why, seeing so many of the colours of the spectrum, we cannot see more, or why our thinking, for all the strenuous efforts we make, cannot altogether escape what Coleridge called " the despotism of the eye ". From this point of view our physical world, as it is apprehended in everyday life, is a shape or pattern, with vague fringes, strained out of the infinite number of possible experiences which an infinite universe offers to sentient beings ; and the sense of the unity of our world, never wholly absent, is, in part at any rate, the organism's awareness of its own persistence as an organic unity, as it grasps that in its environment which is relevant to its own deepest interest, which is to realise its own life.

It must not be supposed, however, that the synthesising activity of the mind is merely a function of the past biological history of the organism as this is written in its present disposition and structure, though this probably provides a sort of framework for all awareness of this kind. There are synthetic unities of awareness of a higher order, such as the perception of the beauty of a poem or a sonata, which transcend what would usually be regarded as the merely biological utilities, whether of the past or the present. From the merely biological point of view it is a little difficult to see what purpose, or interest, is served by admiring the beauty of the sunset. Yet, here as elsewhere, the connexion between synthesising intuition and interest may be supposed to hold, provided we interpret man's essential "*bios*" widely enough, and do not restrict it to its merely physical basis. The whole realm of beauty, as of other higher values, opens up to man because his nature is so constituted that he needs that realm in order to grow to what he has it in him to be and the deepest thing in him is seeking to be. It is the peculiarity of the human organism that its interests lie as much in the relatively unexplored world of truth and beauty and goodness as in the much more completely explored world of "bread and butter." "A *man's* life consisteth not in the abundance of the things that he possesseth." It is written, "*Man* shall not live by bread alone," and it is so written in Scripture, because it was first written in the essential constitution of man's being.

The synthesising attitude is, therefore, essentially the practical attitude, the word practical being used in the broadest sense to cover every form of awareness of a situation as related to the interests of the personal life. The analytic activity, which abstracts this or that aspect of the total situation and considers it, therefore, apart from its significance for the individual percipient—for only in and through the total situation has it any significance for *him*—comes into operation as a sort of temporary withdrawal from the real business of living. Yet the motive of the withdrawal, as Macmurray has insisted,[1] is fundamentally practical. It takes place primarily because of some difficulty in practical adjustment to a situation whose relation to the values of the personal life is one of partial frustration and hindrance ; it is a method of grasping *general* cause-effect relationships in order to use factors in the situation as *your* means to the effects *you* desire in it. It follows that the two ways of approach must not be too rigidly separated from one another. The results of abstract reflection are taken back into the practical situation, often enriching its content and giving the mind a deeper grasp of, and a truer response to, its total significance. Thus a knowledge of psychology can be a real equipment for dealing with men, though without a species of intuitive tact and insight, which such knowledge cannot bestow, it is valueless ; the merely academic mind which is fumbling and helpless in practical situations, which, having learning, lacks wisdom, is here as elsewhere rightly an object of scorn.

It is perhaps not unnecessary to insist that in thus relating the synthetic intuitions of the mind to its own interests we do not impugn the veracity of these intuitions as a report of the real world. Such intuitions may be true or false, but they are not false merely because on the subjective side they are a function of interest. Into the epistemological question of what constitutes knowledge, and how the so-called " subjective " and " objective " factors are related in the process of knowing, it is not necessary to enter. It is enough to guard against the error, into which many fall, of thinking that where interest and valuation enter, genuine knowledge of necessity departs. There is no reason why certain aspects of the world should not increasingly disclose themselves to the right sort of interest even as other aspects disclose themselves to the right sort of impersonal, abstract ratiocination.

[1] *Interpreting the Universe*, p. 36.

It is the relation of situations to interest that produces the essential privateness and uniqueness of events as they enter into the living experience, the personal history, of men and women. Each man's situation, and the things which happen to him in it, are peculiarly his own, because they are in their totality a function, not only of outward causes, but also of the individual interest which he brings to them. Two men are left a legacy, and we say that the same thing has happened to them both. But the same thing has not happened to them both. For the whole event is the receiving of the legacy plus the individual's inner response to it, the manner in which it enters into his personal history and is synthesised by, and with, his values, interests, plans, and insights. From this point of view it was quite untrue to say : " All things come alike to all ; there is one event to the righteous and to the wicked." Science, we have said, for its own purposes abstracts from this inwardness of events, thus depersonalising them. But for the understanding of living religion, and particularly of the awareness of God as personal, this is precisely what must not be done.[1]

Turning now to consider, on the basis of these remarks, the main question of this chapter, it is clear that in the awareness of God the mind is functioning in a synthetic and intuitive way. Religion has always found its natural allies in art, poetry, music, and it is generally recognised that it is in great danger of losing its soul when it attempts to be analytically and abstractly precise in theological science. Not that theology is valueless, for, as has already been remarked, abstract thought and synthetic insight must not be rigidly separated from one another. The results of theological reflexion can be taken up into the living religious response of the soul, clarifying its vision (or obscuring it, if it is improperly done) and deepening its grasp. None the

[1] This will be of importance in the later discussion of providence and miracle; see particularly pp. 114, 233 f.

less the suspicion of theological discussion which deep religious natures have sometimes felt, even if it has been frequently ill-founded, bears witness to the type of response which religion must be taken fundamentally to be.

Granting then that in the awareness of God the mind is responding synthetically and intuitively to its environment, the question we have first to consider is what is the fundamental interest of the personality to which such awareness is related. The answer is that it is rooted in the deepest interest of the human organism, the interest which it has in fulfilling itself, in becoming that which by the primordial constitution of its being it is intended to be.

What right have we to speak of such an interest of the human organism ?

It is the mark of living organisms as distinct from other types of organised totalities, such as crystals or machines, that they have the power to grow to, and maintain themselves in, a certain normal or specific condition amidst all the changes and challenges of their environment. They appear to be governed by an immanent teleology which adjusts the reactions of the parts to external events and to one another in the interest of the whole, the peculiar class-type of whole to which the organism belongs. The hen's egg grows into a hen and not into an adder, and no known change in environmental conditions can so deflect this inner norm that the creature shifts from the one line of development to the other. In relation to growth this immanent teleology produces the paradoxical situation that the organism is in a sense already that which none the less it is not yet. It is what it will be ; the oak in some baffling way is in the acorn, yet the acorn is not the oak. Whatever may be the obscurity surrounding the border line between the organic and the inorganic, it is this quality of responding as a totality, of " aliveness to " the relation of environmental impacts to its *telos*, its maturity or wholeness, that generally distinguishes things which are alive from those which are not.

We are aware of the vexed question how this quality of living organisms is to be regarded on the one hand from the standpoint of biological science, and on the other hand from the standpoint of the philosophy of the organism. The danger of thinking of the immanent teleology of the organism as though it were a conscious purpose, or as though it were a mysterious entity added to the parts of the organism and compelling them *ab extra* to a co-operation otherwise repugnant to them, has often enough been pointed out. The general statement that the organism has an interest in fulfilling and maintaining itself might therefore be open to objection. Yet when we consider the higher ranges of life, and particularly man, with whom in this discussion we are alone concerned, no other term than interest seems adequate to the part which the immanent teleology plays in the conscious life. For, in the first place, in a highly sensitive and close-knit unity such as man the immanent teleology of the organism must enter into all the more fully conscious interests and activities, providing an underlying and pervasive feeling-tone, and determining, in a measure, their quality and direction as specifically human functions. And that broadly is what interest is, a response to environment taking an organically relevant direction through feeling. The feeling of zest and well-being which pervades the personality and its activities when body and mind are in harmonious and healthy balance illustrates the way in which the functional and teleological unity of the organism enters as a determinant into consciousness. And, in the second place, in the consciousness of man the urge of the organism towards its proper maturity becomes, in the pursuit of the ideal life, an interest of the fully self-conscious, purposive kind. The response of average men to presentations of an ideal of personal life, even when it has but the vaguest content, shows that such presentations are moving in the realm, not of merely abstract ideas, but of ideas which, being rooted in, and appealing to, the deep springs of man's being, have an intrinsic psychological force.

We are prepared then to speak without further apology of the interest of the human personality in achieving and maintaining its own proper maturity, albeit it is an interest which strictly speaking is not one amongst others, but one which in a sense underlies them all. It is, in fact, the deepest and most pervasive and most formative thing in embodied personalities, manifesting itself on the lower levels in the unconscious processes which the physiologist studies, and on the highest levels in the ideals and aspirations and feelings of guilt and remorse of the moral and religious life. And in this interest, we affirm, is rooted the synthetic, intuitive response to the world which is involved in the awareness of God.

It is some confirmation of the rightness of thus relating the awareness of God on its subjective side to the immanent teleology which constitutes man specifically man, that religion is in some ways the most distinctive of human functions ; there is nothing even dimly suggestive of it in animal life. Moreover, it is, so far as can be judged, universal in man in one form or another. It appears in the dimmest beginnings of the race and persists right up into its highest developments, keeping pace with, often inspiring, always able to absorb and nourish itself on, all man's cultural achievements. It is further confirmation that religion, perhaps more than any other interest, inevitably grows feeble and corrupt if it be isolated from the other interests of life, instead of informing and giving meaning and direction to them all. And it is still further confirmation that it has been possible for different thinkers, each with a show of truth, to discover the essence of religion in one or other of the three fundamental aspects of consciousness. Some, like

Hegel, have sought to centre religious need and truth in reason ; others, like Kant, in the will ; others, like Schleiermacher, in feeling. Each is right, and yet each is in a measure wrong. For religion is in some way a response of the whole personality, thinking, willing, feeling. It is the personality grasping, intuiting something through its own profound interest in its own fullest realisation.

What, then, does it thus grasp ? What is the content of the religious intuition ?

In religion the personality of man synthetically grasps its environment as a totality ; it grasps the " ultimate " of its world, that which holds together its apparent discord and confusion in a final and unalterable unity of meaning. As Whitehead says : " Religion consists in a certain widespread, direct apprehension of a character exemplified in the actual universe."[1] And the character which the religious spirit intuits is a character which, despite every incidental appearance to the contrary, is in harmony with, and can succour and support, the deep-seated interest of which we have been speaking, the interest of human personality in achieving its own highest and completest life. We might put it more humanly and pictorially by saying that in religion the spirit of man discerns itself to be at home in the universe.[2]

That this is so is hardly capable of demonstration. If it is true, the religious mind will instantly sense that it is, so far as it goes, a true report of one of its deepest springs. It is confirmation, however, to note how large a proportion of the definitions of religion given by various writers, as for example they are summarised by Runze,[3] approach more or less closely to the thought that in religion the soul of man

---

[1] *Religion in the Making*, p. 86.

[2] Elsewhere I have suggested that the whole evolution of life has depended on a fundamental optimism, or faith, in living creatures that they are adequate to their world. See *Experience of God*, p. 23.

[3] *Psychologie der Religion*, p. 127.

achieves, or maintains, or affirms, its essential selfhood in and through an awareness of its essential unity with the ultimate ground and meaning of the world. It is further confirmation, too, that in the highest moments of religious awareness, as, for example, in genuine conversion, there is usually a thrilling and blissful sense on the one hand of a newly achieved harmony of the self, and on the other hand of a newly achieved harmony with the world. As Hocking has shown, " unity and integration in the self are concomitant with unity and integration in the world known by that self."[1] Only by discerning the unity of its world can the inner conflicts of the personality be resolved, and only as the inner conflicts of the personality are being resolved can the unity of the world be discerned. It is a single unitary response in which the objective unity meets the need for inward wholeness in an emancipating awareness of God.[2] Moreover, such awareness is always of God as in some sense personal, for only an ultimate which is personal could give the universe a character congenial to the personality's highest life. Thus from another angle we see why living religion always tends to personalise God.

Now it is to be observed that we have thus reached only that aspect of the awareness of God as personal which in the last chapter we designated the awareness of Him as ultimate and final succour. What then of the other central aspect of the awareness of God as personal, the awareness, that is, of Him as absolute sacred demand, demanding if need be the surrender of life itself ? The two things, we said, are not to be separated from one another, the sense of God as

---

[1] *Meaning of God in Human Experience,* p. 533. The words quoted are from Bennett's *Dilemma of Religious Knowledge,* p. 107.

[2] Conversion in this sense, so far from being an unusual phenomenon, is the type of all maximal religious awareness. It is because the unifying of the self is impossible without awareness of the unity of the world with the self, that psycho-therapists working without religion, without a doctrine of reconciliation, are foredoomed to failure, or only partial success.

consuming fire and as refuge and strength being given in a single response of the soul to His approach to it. It is clear that our thought is incomplete until we relate the awareness of sacred value, the unconditional demand, also to the immanent teleology of the organism ; and we must so relate it that its necessary unity with the awareness of final succour is again, from this new angle, made clear.[1]

If we would understand the relation of the impact of absolute values to the immanent teleology of the organism, we must begin by realising that personal life must be self-achieved or it is not truly personal. Man is constituted a personal being by the fact that his *telos* is such that it is not to be achieved by smooth, effortless growth, but only through the co-operation of his own self-conscious insights and decisions. His destiny as personal implies that he should himself in some sense and in some degree be in charge of it. This requires two things. First, it requires that man should become aware, however dimly and partially at first, of the direction of the immanent norm of his own nature and co-operate with it, putting his own self-conscious causality into it. Second, it requires that man should cease to be a mere function of his world. Only when he becomes capable of at least temporarily suspending, or arresting, the flux of the instinctive life, through which, so to say, the environment merely soaks into the organism through

---

[1] In the various descriptions and definitions of religion reviewed by Runze in the passage already quoted, there are a number which, unlike those referred to above, place the main emphasis on the aspect of obedience, abasement, dependence, submission to moral duty, etc. Runze himself draws attention to the distinction between those views which regard the religious object as a limit to man and those which regard it as man's emancipation. Our endeavour is to bring both aspects into organic relationship to one another. It is important to do so, for to set all the emphasis, as so many writers do, on the function of religion as sustaining and succouring human personality is to play right into the hands of those psychologists who would explain religion as merely a device to help ourselves along. Yet the element of absolute demand, requiring the surrender of life altogether if need be, is equally central.

stimulus and out again through reaction, can anything in the nature of self-determination, genuine will, i.e. truly personal life, begin.

Both these requirements are fulfilled at once by the impact of unconditional values on the soul of man.

Thus, first, we may suggest, in the awareness of such unconditional values the norm of his whole organism, its deep urge towards its own self-realisation, breaks into the self-consciousness of man. On the lower physical and subconscious levels it sustains the organism in its growth to, and maintenance in, specific humanness, but on the higher level of self-consciousness it could hardly remain operative without being explicitly apprehended in some form or other. And it is difficult to see how it could be so apprehended save through some imperative of value, some awareness of what is not, but ought to be. If, *per impossibile*, the acorn suddenly became self-conscious, it would become aware of the fact that it is not yet what in a deeper sense it already is, namely the oak, in a species of moral apprehension, in a compulsive sense of what it ought to be and by its own self-direction ought to seek. What is impossible in the acorn is, however, normal in man. Just because it is part of the specific maturity of personality that it can only be achieved through self-direction, the norm, in its own interests—if we may so put it—must cease to exercise automatic control and present itself as a summons, a most imperative summons since it has the whole nisus of the organism behind it, but still only a summons. The conscious self of its own initiative must give the word and obey ; if it does so, then the deeper urge of the organism, in pause, as it were, during the crisis of decision, is released and can move through new challenges to new stages of growth.

That the personality should thus apparently be split into two fundamental factors—on the one hand the deeper urge of the whole organism towards self-realisation, and on the other hand an ego or centre of free activity on whose co-operation such self-realisation depends—is doubtless very baffling to the mind. In the fact of the self and its freedom amidst limiting conditions, both internal and external, we are down on one of the ultimates and must expect puzzles. But, however baffling, the facts force us to some such mental picture. It finds justification in the fact that men should so spontaneously feel, after moral failure, that they have gone contrary to what they call their true self, fallen beneath the level of their proper manhood, corrupted somehow the deeper springs of their being. The stings of remorse and the sense of guilt are in part the registering in feeling of the disorder of the whole personality, when the summons of its immanent norm has been disobeyed. Moreover, remorse smothered and sin persisted in do seem to lead to a progressive degradation and disintegration of the whole personality on all its levels, running out into debased and unnatural physical appetites as luridly pictured in the first chapter of the Epistle to the Romans. On the other hand, it is a fairly common experience that in some decisive act of moral obedience, when at last we can bring ourselves to do it, especially if it involve self-commitment in faith to God, the whole inner life seems to gain release and to move forward to a new level of peace and insight and power.[1] It accords, too, with the view presented that it is in adolescence, when the whole organism is on the threshold of maturity, that the call of absolute values is apt to present itself most vividly to the mind. The youth often feels a profound urge to surrender absolutely to a high vocation and enterprise, such as probably never is experienced with quite the same compulsive vividness at any other time. Adolescence is the best time to give the life to Christ.

But, second, the impact of unconditional values not only provides for that co-operation of the self with the immanent

---

[1] Cf. Brunner, *Das Gebot und die Ordnungen*, p. 145.

norm of the organism which is essential to personal life, but also for that independence of the environment and of the flux of the merely instinctive life which is equally essential. Only as man realises that there are values into the balance with which no personal preference whatsoever must be put, that there are ends in the service of which he is called upon to say " No " even to that most powerful of all his desires, the desire to remain alive, does he begin to stand on his feet as specifically man. Then, and only then, does he have frontiers between himself and his world within which he can begin to rule himself. The point has been so powerfully put by Oman, that it would be idle to try to say it in other words : " The recognition of anything as sacred, as of an absolute value above desire and even above life, was the well-spring of all endeavour after emancipation from a material world merely appealing to his appetites, because this alone in his life was not measured by them. Manifestly, therefore, he was finding a higher power which made this victory possible, and this he made plain by revering it above all might of visible things and obeying its requirements at all costs of loss or hazard. This valuation as sacred, therefore, we ought to esteem as the spring of all self-mastery and all mastery over the world, as the sublime attainment by which man became truly man. Man with a taboo, which he would not break for any earthly gain or even to save his life, was no longer a mere animal whose only inhibition was the threat of suffering or the fear of death. He might still fear what could only kill the body and his judgement of sacredness might still relate itself to that fear, but if there was something in his experience more sacred than life, the fear of death as the final ill was conquered in principle ; and this victory is the condition of all progress, for there is no real spiritual good possible at lower cost than the hazard of our material life, nor any impossible at that price."[1] Elsewhere

[1] *Science, Religion and Reality*, p. 292.

Oman has shown the qualities which distinguish man from the brutes—reason, tool-using, laughter—are rooted in the same awareness of sacred values.[1] " The moment he said, ' this is sacred, this is not the realm of ordinary values,' even granting that it was said of what seems to us is the insanest of taboos, he had said to his world as well as to himself, ' Thou shalt not '. Forthwith he began to be master of himself, and, thereby, master in his world. Then, in some true sense of the word he began to be free. Thus by the judgement of the sacred, man was set free from the leading-strings of nature, the nurse which, with the immediate values of the visible world, had hitherto nurtured all living creatures."[2]

The impact of unconditional values is, therefore, deeply involved in the immanent teleology of the human organism and its interest in achieving its true end. How then is it related to the discernment of the world as ultimately congenial to the achievement of that end, which, as we have seen, is rooted in the same interest ? The answer appears when it is realised that if the soul of man were presented with bare unconditional values, without any awareness of the universe as ultimately congenial to its highest life, it would be plunged at every critical stage in its development into a grave dilemma. On the one hand there would be the demand to surrender life itself, if need be, to the sacred end or value, and this, as we have seen, in the interest of achieving a genuine personal life ; yet on the other hand, to surrender life would appear on the surface to mean the extinction of the self altogether. To fashion a true self as distinct from a merely animal instinctiveness, it is necessary to be prepared to perish ; yet that would seem to

---

[1] *The Natural and the Supernatural*, p. 82 f.
[2] *Ibid.*, p. 85. Herrmann also has much to say throughout the first section of his *Ethik* on the indispensability of the unconditional imperative to man's release from his world and the achievement of personal life.

be to destroy the self once and for all. The impact of unconditional values, in other words, supplies the inner condition of the soul's self-realisation in the very act of proposing a failure in adjustment to outward conditions, a failure of the basis of all growth and progress, which is that one should continue to exist. Now the philosopher might seek to resolve this dilemma in a variety of ways, but we are concerned only with the way in which it is resolved in living religious experience. The fact is that in the moment of religious awareness men are hardly conscious of the dilemma at all. Why ? Because it is being solved all the time by the religious intuition of the actual character of the universe, by the intuition of God. The call to seek absolute values even at the cost of life is apprehended as the breaking into human awareness of a higher and more ultimate reality of succouring divine purpose. In surrendering even life itself, therefore, the personality is aware that it is not suffering a final and destructive rupture with its world, but rather is making an ultimate and blessed adjustment to it. The personality gains itself by losing itself, because behind all things there is a divine purpose which guarantees the personal life in the very act of asking its complete surrender even unto death.[1]

It is perhaps not unnecessary to add, that in relating the awareness of God to the inner processes and needs of the human organism, we do not in any sense commit ourselves to the view that religion is merely one way of being conscious of ourselves, without any objective divine reality being involved at all ; any more than to set forth the processes of digestion is to question the reality of food. As has been said, it is a crude and shallow epistemology which assumes that where interest enters in, genuine commerce with the real

---

[1] Here, possibly, we confront the deepest source of the belief, never very far from the central places of religion in all its forms, in some sort of survival after death. We return to this point below in the chapter on eschatology, p. 211.

E

world departs. To the ordinary religious person the analysis given in this chapter would probably not be very intelligible ; certainly he would not immediately recognise it as a description of what goes on in his mind during his moments of religious insight and feeling. Just as the eye is not aware of itself, nor of its history, nor of its biological indispensability to the organism, but only of the object seen, so the religious mind is for the most part merely aware of the divine reality with which it is in relationship. We take our stand on the veracity of that immediate awareness, and nothing that we have said can logically be taken as the foundation of a contrary position, or of the view that the sense of God is merely a useful biological or sociological illusion.[1] For us, as for the religious mind generally, the supreme reality which calls into being the religious awareness is God Himself. Whatever may be the deep inward processes involved, they are made active only by God's own approach to the soul ; without that approach they would remain quiescent, if indeed they could be said to have any reality at all. They are what they are only because God intends to enter into relation with them ; nay, He is already in relation with them, for He has made the soul, and in Him, in some ultimate and unanalysable way, it lives and moves, and has its being. It is God who has written the norm in the constitution of man's being and God who through the interplay of it with the environmental world makes Himself known. "Thou hast formed us for thyself, and our hearts are restless until they find rest in thee."[2]

To a discussion of the part that environmental factors play in the awareness of God as personal we now turn.

---

[1] Such views have been faithfully dealt with by a number of writers. For an excellent refutation of them in short compass the reader may refer to Bennett's *The Dilemma of Religious Knowledge*.

[2] Augustine, *Confessions*, Book I, Chap. I.

CHAPTER III

ENVIRONMENTAL FACTORS IN THE RELIGIOUS CONSCIOUSNESS

THE environment into which man is born presents itself to him under two aspects. There is, first, the social environment, and, second, the environment of what is loosely termed nature. The latter word is for exact thought very ambiguous, but we are not for the moment concerned to be exact ; the usages of popular speech are sufficient for our purpose, precisely because the broad distinction indicated is one which everybody in the practical conduct of his life is forced to make. The social environment is the environment of persons like ourselves with whom we constitute a social organism ; the natural environment is the environment of things which are not personal and not capable of being incorporated in the social organism or dealt with through its functions and forms. In modern times the distinction has been so emphasised and wrought out into scientific theory and method that the boundaries between the two are very sharply drawn even for the least educated. In most cultured people there is some awareness of the prime problem of modern philosophy which is now reflectively to bring the two so obviously different, yet so closely interrelated, spheres of history and nature, morals and mechanism, into a unity with one another. Yet even to the primitive mind, which had none of our modern conceptions of natural law and necessary causal relationships, and was ready in certain contingencies to see in any natural object a personal or quasi-personal activity, the broad

distinction must have been obvious enough, even though
at certain points the dividing line grew somewhat vague
There were his tribe and the set of reactions appropriate to
it, and there were the world of nature, of rivers and streams
and woods and stars, and the set of reactions appropriate
to that. The one was *his* society and the other was not.

Considered, however, as factors in the practical business
of living and in the shaping of men's minds, the two environments, though clearly distinguishable, are not separate the
one from the other. They are two aspects of one world, and
each merges into the other in the total situation with which
at any juncture man has to deal. When social necessities
and adjustments are in the focus of attention the realm of
nature is still there as a determining context and framework
if, *per impossibile*, it were not there, or were other than it is
the " feel " of the situation and the response to it would be
different. When natural necessities and adjustments are
in the focus of attention, as, for example, in tilling the soil
or escaping the storm, a social context or framework is
present in the same way. This is true even of the modern
man in whose mind there is apt to be, as we have said, a
sharp theoretical distinction, and, owing to excessive urban-
isation, a sharp practical distinction also, between society
and nature. Even the modern city-dweller has but to lift
his eyes to see the clouds and the sun, and a tornado in
some distant land may at any moment wreck his business :
if, on the other hand, wearying of the city, he says he will get
away from man and commune with nature alone in the fields,
he cannot do it, for he cannot get away from a self which has
been shaped by, and is indissolubly bound to, other men
and women. In more primitive peoples, this interpenetration
of the two environments in one situation and one response
is closer and more obvious. The primitive, we may suppose,
makes a more unitary response to a social-natural situation
which presents itself in a more unitary way ; none the less,

the factors in that response which are evoked by the social, and those which are evoked by the natural, elements in the situation are different, even though they merge in a psychical unity which the primitive man certainly could not himself analyse, and which the modern man has in a great measure lost.

In the light of this we may consider the question of the relation of the living awareness of God to environmental events.

We have seen that the religious intuition essentially concerns itself with the world as a whole ; whence it follows that the awareness of God, more than any other sort of awareness, is given neither through the social environment alone nor through the natural environment alone, but through both together as forming a single world. Only as He is apprehended, however dimly, as speaking through the total environment, is He apprehended as, so to say, distinctively God. It is possible, however, to discern in the unitary religious awareness those elements which derive more especially from the social environment, and those which derive more especially from the natural, even though we must continue to insist that to think of the one apart from the other is in some measure a false abstraction.

We said that the awareness of God as personal in and through the sense of absolute demand and final succour is, as it were, a focal point around which there is a penumbra of awareness of God as the infinite and eternal " Other ". In other words, because the lineaments of personality are discerned, it does not cease to be an awareness of *God* and all that that implies of in-finite, mysterious being, of ontal depth and ultimacy, of transcendence and lordship of all creation. If then we distinguish between (taking care not to divide) the awareness of God as meeting the soul in a personal relationship and the awareness of Him as infinite and transcendent, we may say that the former is especially related to the social environment, and the latter to the natural. It is especially in the sphere of personal relations that God is livingly known as personal, and especially in the sphere of natural phenomena that He is livingly known as infinite and transcendent. Yet, we hasten to add, neither sphere, and neither awareness, is apart from the other. We might put it thus : when the religious consciousness is functioning more within the realm of social relationships and responsibilities, then the awareness of God as near and personal is apt to be at its maximum, and the awareness of Him as infinite and transcendent falls more into the background, though it never disappears. When, on the other hand, the religious consciousness is function ing more in relation to natural phenomena, then the awareness of God as infinite and transcendent is apt to be at its maximum, and the awareness of Him as near and personal falls into the background, though, again, it never disappears. And the intense sense of the divine as personal on the vaguer background of the divine as infinite in the social world, as also the intense sense of the divine as infinite on the vaguer background of the divine as personal in the natural world, would not be possible were it not that the social environment and the natural environment are really one. Each is more or less clearly apprehended as the background of, and continuous with, the other by a mind which is shaped by both, and which in religion is responding to both as constituting its total world.

Let us now look at these points more closely. First, *the social environment.*

Here, we said, the awareness of God as near and personal, or, in terms of the analysis given, as absolute demand and final succour, is at its maximum, and the awareness of Him as infinite and transcendent, though never absent, falls more into the background.

Now, it is obvious that there is an affinity and parallelism between such awarenesses· and the relation in which the individual stands to his society. Indeed, this affinity and parallelism are so impressive that some writers have made them the basis of the theory that God is only another name for society. Durkheim, for example, lists a number of points wherein the qualities which the religious mind attributes to God as related to himself resemble those which can be discerned in society as related to the individual, and from this draws the conclusion indicated.[1] The position might be expressed thus : Man, it is said, is a cell in the social organism before he is anything else, and this fact, wrought up into the permanent structure of his being, underlies and determines all that may later develop in the way of self-conscious and intelligent life. Now a cell in an organism, it may be supposed, if it could be suddenly endowed with self-consciousness would, as we suggested earlier in another connexion, become aware of the immanent teleology or norm of the organism in the form of an absolute demand upon it ; furthermore, as its life depends on the life of the whole organism and on its fulfilling its own proper function within it, it would become aware that in obedience to that demand lies its final security ; finally, its dim awareness of the larger organism by which it is carried would convey the sense of being in relation to something infinitely and mysteriously transcending itself. So it is with man's relationship to society ; he is a cell, in the larger social organism, which has become self-conscious and intelligent, and his sense of God as absolute demand and final security and yet also as a mysterious and infinite transcendent, is merely the sense of the fashioning and determining pressure of the social organism as it passes up through the deep, unconscious structure of the soul into the little area of full and illumined awareness at the top.

If we reject the conclusion, as we do, that does not mean

[1] *Elementary Forms of the Religious Life* (Eng. Trans.), p. 206 f.

that we reject altogether the premisses on which it is based. The sociological theories of religion fail to cover all the facts of man's spiritual history, as has often been pointed out by critics of it, but they rightly emphasise and expound the social setting, the milieu of personal relationships, in the midst of which the experience of God arises, and by which it is sustained and conditioned all the time ; or, as we would prefer to say, through which God more and more makes Himself known as personal to the soul of man. If the personal infinite is to present itself to man through media, and not as a naked, unmediated divine reality—as we shall maintain later it is essential to a personal relationship that it should be presented through media[1]—then it is not surprising that it should be through a social environment whose pressures upon, and sustainings of, the individual have a certain correspondence with the more ultimate reality which they are designed to mediate and without which they would have no existence at all ; the more so if the divine end is, as Christianity believes, some sort of social end, a divine society or kingdom of love. It is therefore not for us in the least disturbing that human society should bear some of the lineaments of God. We gladly grant that the absolute demands and proffered securities of religion arise in the midst of, and draw their content from, and, indeed, are often bewilderingly confused with, the requirements and safeguards of a social environment which begins to school the individual with its authority so soon as he is born into it. We grant also that through society the individual has his first introduction to a mysterious and transcendent reality encompassing and surpassing the limits of his own existence. Only we insist that something other than society is involved, and that without it the specifically religious awareness would never arise. Somehow God seizes upon the pressures and utilities of man's social situation, which

[1] See below, p. 70 f.

adumbrate, and indeed are intended to be caught up into and become part of what He has to say—and speaks. The accents of God are heard within them, the dimension of the infinite and eternal personal is discerned through them. And when this happens the moral and social life of man is set in the way of developments which are not otherwise open to it, and which are inexplicable on any theory which takes account of merely sociological factors. Thus morality becomes more inward and searching, for God, unlike society, is apprehended as judging the internal motions of the heart and not merely the external conformities of the deed. Conscience takes on an authority which can, on occasion, defy all the behests of society, for man must now obey God rather than his fellows. The individual begins to be invested with an intrinsic worth and significance altogether apart from his social situation, for in him speaks none other than the voice and purpose of God. Yet, as may be clearly seen in Christianity, the social basis and reference remains ; the right inward motive which God requires is love to the brethren ; the conscience which defies society does so in the conviction that thus society's highest life is best served ; the individual has worth and significance in himself because of what he is intended to be in the realised divine kingdom of love.

God, then, is not another name for society, but in and through society's relationship to its members, that is to say, in and through the order of personal relations in which He has placed man, His touch falls upon the human spirit and awakens it to an awareness of a Beyond, an Infinite, which is itself personal, and meets the will as a higher Will to be obeyed and trusted. It is because the infinite as personal is most vividly known, if it is livingly known at all, in the sphere of immediate relations with finite persons, that sociological theories of religion have such plausibility. Yet the truth is almost the exact reverse of such theories.

God is not a symbol for society, but rather society is a symbol for God, an intrinsic symbol, one, that is to say, which is continuous with, and sustained by, the reality which it mediates.[1]

Second, *the natural environment.*

Here the reverse of what has been said of the social environment holds, the awareness of God as infinite and transcendent being at its maximum, and the awareness of Him as near and personal being relatively dim.

That the natural environment is peculiarly suited to mediate God as infinite and transcendent hardly needs arguing. The sublimity of nature is a quality which is almost lacking in the social environment save in so far as it may be copied in architecture. By its sublimity we mean its power to impress man with its transcendent greatness in comparison with himself. Two forms of it may, following Kant, be mentioned. One is the impression of transcendent vastness, the other is the impression of transcendent power, though these are probably never found apart from one another. Entering into them both is the sense of mystery, which also is not present in the same way in the social environment. In his fellows man sees his counterpart, but in nature he confronts something inscrutable which he cannot quite evaluate in terms of his own life. That doubtless is why obscurity, mistiness, shadowiness always tends to increase the impression of sublimity, and indeed can sometimes invest with sublimity what would otherwise seem insignificant.

Yet merely to be abased before the vast dimensions of the mountains or the stars or the seas, or to cringe before the irresistible might of the winds and storms, or to shiver a little at the uncanny quietness of some dim vista in the woods, is not yet to be religious, to discern God. Such experience only becomes religious when there is apprehended

[1] See below, p. 74 f.

through it that which is *super*natural, when through the
vastness of the overarching sky and the hills, the irresistible
forces of nature, another reality of a different order is given ;
one which, vast as the sky, is not the sky, eternal as the hills
is not the hills, mysterious as the woods is not the woods,
irresistible as the winds is not the winds, but that from
which these take their being. When this happens the
experience is of an entirely different kind ; it is not evoked
by a merely quantitative " stepping-up " of the sublime,
but by the discernment in and through it of another
dimension of being in which nature lies and by which it
is sustained.[1]

But to discern the supernatural within and above nature
is, we have seen,[2] to discern, however dimly, the personal
within and above it. The supernatural and the personal are
for the religious consciousness in the last analysis one and
the same thing. We have to ask, then, how there enters
into the overwhelming impression of the sublime in nature
that which makes it a revelation of the infinite as personal,
that is to say, of the true supernatural. Supremely this
comes about, as we shall maintain, through the fusion with
it of that more vivid awareness of God as personal which is
given through the social medium ; but, leaving this for the
moment on one side, we can discern the point where more
purely natural events in their relation to man begin almost
of necessity to take on at least a dim personal quality,
waiting as it were the reinforcement which comes from the
social side.

That point is where events detach themselves from the
general impression of mystery and vastness and power, which
nature makes upon the soul, by entering into the individual's
own personal situation as relevant factors of injury or

---

[1] Cf. Bruhn, Art. " Erhabenheit," *Religion in Geschichte und Gegenwart*,
Vol. II, p. 233.

[2] See above, p. 6.

blessing, that is to say, as factors of precisely that *value-resistance and value-co-operation* which we said earlier lies somewhere at the heart of all discernment of another as personal. A diffused, contemplative awareness of the world in general could never *per se* mediate a personal reality ; It is necessary first that the general should particularise itself by entering into relation with the individual's personal situation, personal destiny, personal *will*. Bergson has a passage in his *Les deux Sources de la Morale et de la Religion*[1] which puts the point in a vivid way. Criticising Lévy-Bruhl's theory that the primitive by a "*participation mystique*" discerns behind all events an occult cause, Bergson points out that all the examples given are events which concern man himself, more particularly accidents which happen to him, especially illness and death. The general action of inanimate objects on one another in a way that is either irrelevant to, or may be assumed in, the pursuit of his own purposes—the wind bending the trees, the clouds floating across the sky, the stream carrying his canoe—is in practice not regarded by the primitive differently from the modern man who has a theory of impersonal, mechanical cause-effect relationships between events. But when events, so to say, break from their routine and become significant for man, especially for a particular man in a particular situation, when there is unexpected resistance to, or assistance of *my* personal purpose, as, for example, when a rock falls and hurts me rather than my neighbour, or my enemy rather than me, then the sense of something intended, of will on the other side, begins to stir in the soul. Bergson shows, however, that this response is not confined to primitives. It is present in the mind of the highly civilised and cultured—a spontaneous, more or less subconscious attitude persisting beneath the mechanistic philosophies of the mind, subtly influencing language, and on overwhelming

[1] p. 150 f.

occasions ready to possess the whole soul. A man will say
" just my luck ", or speak of the " sheer cussedness of
things " ; he will talk to a recalcitrant piece of wood in
imperatives and adjurations and curses as though it had a
will thwarting his own. Doubtless his mind, on reflection,
will repudiate the idea that there is a will there ; but that
he ever speaks as though there were one present, and finds
some obscure satisfaction in it, indicates that there is active,
albeit in an attenuated form, a primordial, ineradicable
response of the soul of man to his world as it enters into
relation with his own will. Bergson shows that even in the
use of the word " chance " the same sort of response, again
in an attenuated form, finds expression. A tile blows from
the house-top and kills a passer-by. " We say, it is chance.
Should we say the same, if the tile were merely smashed
to pieces on the ground ? Perhaps, but that is because we
think vaguely of a man who might have been there, or
because, for one reason or another, this special place in the
road interests us particularly, in such a way that it
seems as though the tile chose to fall just there. In both
cases there is chance only because human interest is involved
and because things have happened as though man had been
taken into consideration, whether to render him service or
still more to do him an injury. Think only of the wind tearing
off the tile, the tile falling on the road, the impact of
the tile on the earth, and you see only mechanism—chance
disappears. For chance to intervene, it is necessary for the
effect to have a human significance ; such significance then
overflows on to the cause and colours it, so to say, with
humanity. Chance, then, is mechanism acting as though it
had intention. It might be said, that it is precisely by using
the word chance when events happen as if they intended
something, that we show that we do not suppose them really
to intend anything, but rather that everything can be
explained mechanically. That would be so, if nothing were

involved but reflective and fully conscious thought. But beneath the latter is a spontaneous and half-conscious thought which imposes on the mechanical chain of causes and effects something quite different, not indeed in order to explain the fall of the tile, but to explain why the fall should have coincided with the passing of a particular man, why it should have chosen this particular instant of time. . . . If there is no such thought of an element of intention in the matter, one would only speak of mechanism and not of chance."[1]

Many would wish to dismiss this sort of response of the human spirit as merely a primitive way of thinking which survives in modern people only because of the tenacity of ancestral habits. Obviously primitive expressions of it, as in the endowment of any and every object with a soul, or in the child's kicking the table over which he stumbles, should be, and are for the most part, left behind. But it is another matter to dismiss it altogether. Maybe its very permanence, in and through every corrective of advancing knowledge, is a witness to the ultimate quality of the reality in the midst of which man has been set, and which he is intended to know. Our decision on this question will depend upon the philosophy from which, consciously or unconsciously, we start. As theists we are prepared to see in this sense of a will and intention within those events which take up a special relation to the individual's own will and intention, whether as helping or frustrating, a dim and inchoate perception of what has been called the " thou-character " of ultimate reality.[2] When this dim and inchoate perception is enriched with that clearer awareness of God as personal which is given through the social medium, and

---

[1] *Op. cit.*, p. 155–6. Bergson quotes at length the remarkable description of the San Francisco earthquake given by James in his *Memories and Studies*, p. 209–14. In it James describes how this vast upheaval seemed to take on the quality of personal purpose directed to himself.

[2] Heim, *Glaube und Denken* (2 Aufl.), p. 220.

is otherwise cleansed and expanded, there arises the awareness of divine providence active within the believer's own
personal life and answering prayer. We shall come back
to this point again in discussing providence and miracle ;
meanwhile it suffices to point out the direct line of connexion
between the instances discussed by Bergson and the profound
intuitions of God as active in the events of their life which
come to most sincere and prayerful Christians. If we grant
validity to the latter, as we do, then we are prepared to
grant some sort of validity to the former also ; in both there
is a perception of the " thou-character " of ultimate reality,
in the one case primitive, undeveloped, mixed with ignorance, superstition and egotism, in the other case enlightened
and cleansed, not only by scientific knowledge, but also by
the reconciling work of Jesus Christ. It is partly the purpose
of this book to show what is this enlightened and cleansed
awareness of God's activity within events.

Though we have thus treated the social and natural
environments apart from one another, we must insist again
that to do so is to make an artificial abstraction from the
facts. It is in the intimate fusion and co-operation of the
two that the full chord of awareness of God is set vibrating
in the soul. How the one God can thus declare Himself to the
soul of man in and through this dualistic setting of his life,
it must ever remain impossible to say ; how does binocular
vision present us with one world ? All that can be done is
to note how in fact the two factors interact with and inter-
penetrate one another. Of special significance for our
interest in the awareness of God as personal is the fact
already emphasised that both in the social environment and
in the natural such awareness centres in the relation of
events to the individual's own will and purpose. Here we
glimpse the point where the God of conscience and the God
of nature are ready to fuse together in man's consciousness,
the dim awareness of God as personal which nature mediates

being reinforced by the vivid awareness of Him as personal which society mediates, the vivid awareness of God as sublime and awful and mysterious which nature mediates entering into and enriching the dim awareness of Him as sublime and awful and mysterious which society mediates. Thus the way is opened for that which is in some ways the sublimest of the religious intuitions of man, namely, that the God who gives the laws to the vast processes of nature gives also the moral law to the human heart, that the laws in both instances are manifestations of the one Eternal Personal, and are somehow implicated in one another through their common derivation from Him. No finer examples are to be had than those afforded by the pro-phetical writings and the psalms of the Old Testament, though illustrations could be given from other religions. The divine voice which condems injustice is the voice of Him who walks in thunder through the hills, and the plumb-line set against the immoralities of Jerusalem is an infinite perpendicular from the stars. The steadfast faithfulness of God's moral government, the certainty of the fruits of righteousness and the penalties of sin, are seen to be exempli-fied in, indeed as part of, the unchanging orderliness of nature. It is to the hills that the eyes of the oppressed are lifted, and when God's righteous purpose is achieved, all nature will share in its beauty and peace and joy. " The earth is the Lord's, and the fulness thereof ; the world and they that dwell therein. For he hath founded it upon the seas, and established it upon the floods. Who shall ascend into the hill of the Lord ? or who shall stand in his holy place ? He that hath clean hands and a pure heart."[1]

That this fusion of the God of righteousness with the God

[1] Ps. xxiv. Cf. also Ps. xix. Though the two sections of this Psalm must have been originally distinct, the combination of them is still sig-nificant. The editor recognised, and desired to express, the conjunction of natural and moral law. Other examples are plentiful in the Psalms and the prophetical writings.

of nature should be tied up with the impact of untoward or fortunate events doubtless opens up the possibility of grave error. It leads all too easily to the theory, which appears in every religion and lingers on in the minds of many Christians, that such events are always directly planned divine punishments and rewards ; God smites the sinner with lightning and makes the crops of the righteous to flourish. The mistake, however, of such a theory is that it is a theory into which all experience is forced, and by which, therefore, progress in fuller understanding of the ways of God is made impossible. The fundamental religious perception underlying the theoretical construction built upon it, namely, that the events of nature are part of the dealing of a divine righteousness with man's spirit, remains, and marks a real stage in religious history, even though the nature of that righteousness is misunderstood and the misunderstanding becomes fixed in a rigid legalistic theory of rewards and punishments. But so long as the perception remains free from such generalised theories and is kept within the immediacies of the individual's personal situation, there is no reason why God should not at any time speak righteousness to the soul through some unexpected disaster or blessing, " stabbing the spirit broad awake ", as when Luther at Stottesheim was stirred to the depths by the lightning flash that killed his companion at his side, or when Peter cried at the miraculous draught of fishes, " Depart from me, for I am a sinful man, O Lord." To those who deny the reality of a supernatural, personal purpose dealing with man through his world, such reactions are pure superstition ; but to the theist they may well be, even if superstition and error be mixed up in them, a valid dealing with the living God.

Indeed, when once the dim sense of the presence of the divine Thou in nature has been reinforced by, and fused with, the vivid sense of Him in the ethical sphere of personal relations, there is no limit to the extent to which natural

F

phenomena may be taken up into the living sense of God as personal. Light and darkness become poignant symbols for the righteousness of God and the unrighteousness of man ; the beauty of the sky, or the infinite distances of the stars, may prostrate a man with a sense of the narrow and stuffy egotism of his own soul in the sight of God ; the fruits and flowers will be declared, without affectation, to be the gifts of a divine bounty ; the threat of calamity, or the calamity itself, will suddenly become an accusing finger, making the soul aware of its profound estrangement from God in the sphere of the will ; an experience of God's forgiveness will suddenly transform the whole world so that every lovely thing seems in very truth the overflow of the heart of God. And the fact that much in nature none the less remains inscrutable, grotesque, apparently impersonal, will but serve to emphasise that it is God in all His infinite mystery and wisdom who thus reveals Himself, that, though He is assuredly personal, He is just as assuredly no mere replica of man.[1]

Contrariwise, in so far as the awareness of God as personal in the sphere of the conscience and on the plane of personal relations is undeveloped, or for any reason inhibited, it will tend to remain at a minimum in respect of nature. At best nature will become, as for Mr. Julian Huxley, a mere upspouting of some elemental creative something to which in moments of ecstasy we surrender ourselves ;[2] at worst it will become, as for Mr. Huxley's grandfather, an alien cosmic drift to which man in his ethical life and personal ideals puts up a feeble and temporary resistance before he and his race finally disappear.[3]

We may conclude these observations with the suggestion that the separation between the social and the natural environments which modern life tends to bring about affords

[1] See below, p. 282.   [2] *Religion without Revelation*, p. 358.
[3] T. H. Huxley, *Evolution and Ethics*, p. 83.

some evidence in their support.   Those are surely right who trace the weakness of the sense of God in so many people, in part, to the almost completely urbanised life, out of touch with nature save at one or two removes, which they are compelled to lead.   Moreover, even their urban life is in a profound way depersonalised and desocialised.   " The unpolitical, desocialised creature who lives in a modern urban apartment house, in a dwelling full of people but without any neighbours, subsisting upon the proceeds of the labour of others with whom he has not the slightest human contacts, is the pathetic product and spiritual victim of a decadent individualistic culture and civilisation."[1] If there is any truth in the analysis given in this chapter, the " denaturising and desocialising " effect of life in our great cities was bound to produce what in fact it has produced, an apparent lack in vast masses of people of any sensitivity to God other than perhaps occasional feelings which pass swiftly and leave little mark on life and character.

[1] Niebuhr, *Reflections on the End of an Era*, p. 93.

CHAPTER IV

THE WORLD AS SYMBOL

THAT God should thus approach man through the environment of nature and history, through a natural and social world, is intimately bound up with the essentially personal relationship with the spirit of man into which He purposes to enter.

In order to see this, it is necessary to take note of two things which a genuinely personal relationship between God and man would seem to require.

First, if there is to be co-operation, along with tension and resistance, between the human will and the divine —without which, as we have insisted, the relationship would not be personal—then it would seem that there must be a sphere which is neither man nor God but in which their wills meet and achieve, or fail to achieve, an active and creative concurrence with one another. Stating it from the human side, we may say that it is essential to man's status as a personal being and to his sense of the significance of his moral life, that he should be called upon to make choices and decisions which make a difference and are not merely play-acting ; in particular it is essential that he should be able to refuse to do God's will, not merely in the abstract or in imagination, but in such wise that his refusal involves that *pro tanto* God's will is not done. If his surrenders or refusals make no difference to the ongoing divine purpose, then he is merely a straw on the stream and has no true standing in a personal world with God. It would seem to be necessary, therefore, that there should be a world which in some way stands over against both the will of God and the will of the individual, having significance for both as that in and through which real co-operation can be attained, and genuine sonship on the part of the latter achieved. Or stating it from the divine side, we might say that if God's purpose in respect of man was to create creators, who should realise themselves by entering into genuine personal co-operation with Himself, then He was under necessity to set man in a world which in a sense was as yet uncreated, a world in which the full working out of His will would depend on the responses and decisions of man.

It is confirmation of this that those religious philosophies which have failed to insist on the world of nature and history as having significance for, and a relative independence of, the will of God, nearly always end in a thoroughly depersonalised conception of man's relationship to God. Minimise the independence of the world and nothing can save the independence of man. Thus in acosmic pantheism the world loses its independent significance by being regarded as extraneous or foreign to the divine life, partaking of the nature of illusion. In cosmic pantheism it loses it by being completely identified with God ; in its totality the world is an already realised and eternal harmony of being and individual existents are merely adjectives or phases of it. In the one case it is affirmed that there is no world in which anything that might be called the divine will could be done ; in the other case it is affirmed that there is no world in which anything that might be called the divine will needs be done. Indeed in both cases the thought of God as will disappears ; He is conceived in terms of eternal and fully realised being, with the result that the individual himself comes to be conceived in terms of such being also, and not in terms of a will that somehow stands over against God and is called to fellowship with Him in His purposes. The soul comes to be regarded as fundamentally a " bit of divinity," and the way of its salvation is not through a personal union of will in which a oneness in duality is achieved, but in an absorption with the ultimate source of all being, described usually in some such image as the merging of the raindrop in the sea.

Second, it seems clear that if there is to be anything in the nature of genuine personal co-operation between man and God, then God's will must bring man's will into harmony with itself, not by any exercise of *force majeure*, but always by eliciting from man his own inner perception of its righteousness and his own spontaneous surrender to it in obedience and trust. Here again we confront that duality or tension in unity which alone constitutes a relationship personal. As was said earlier, that which distinguishes treating a being as a person and treating him as a thing is that we do not seek to manipulate the will, but to appeal to it through its own insight and consent. In the highest personal relationship the other does what I desire, not because my will has been imposed on his, but because we are in the same world of values, because my insights have become his insights, my meanings his meanings. So it is in God's personal dealing with man ; and because it is so, there is necessitated a world as the medium of the relationship. For a conveying of meaning which is not a mere imposition of it seems to require that it should be mediated through symbols. By a symbol we mean a sign which indicates meaning, and the peculiar quality of a symbol is that it can only enter formatively into the mind of another, and affect his activity, if he in some measure apprehend its meaning and accept it for himself. It is not possible for a symbol whose meaning cannot be read, or being read is not accepted, to enter formatively into the personal life. It has to stay, so to say, on the frontiers of the mind.

The world is God's symbol, God's medium of speech with the soul of man.

It is indeed a highly significant fact that in the main

men are able to communicate with one another only through
signs and symbols. In more lowly forms of life it would
appear to be otherwise. Rivers has suggested that ants
and bees, for example, communicate and co-operate with
one another through a process of suggestion so complete
and irresistible that there arise the almost mechanically
precise cohesion and collaboration of the ant-hill and
beehive.[1] If this be so, it involves that such creatures have
little of what might be called individual psychical existence
at all. Their psychical being flows in and out of one another
like a stream of water flowing in and around porous pots.
There are no frontiers to their mental life, no, so to say,
immigration barriers on the frontiers turning back un-
desirables. But nature seems also to have taken another
line. Along this line mutual permeability of psychical
being has grown less, the frontiers have become more
sharply defined and policed, until in man, in whom alone
appears anything that may truly be designated individuality,
or personal life, the isolation of mind from mind is very great
and is in some ways the most noteworthy thing about him.
Yet the isolation only obtains in respect of that excess of
direct suggestibility which characterises other forms of life.
For man has elaborated a new method of communication,
one which allows a full enough exchange of meaning and
yet respects the frontiers, the territorial integrity, of the
personality, namely the use of symbols, and particularly
the use of language, which is a highly complex and refined
method of signalling to one another. When I speak to a
friend, I cannot thrust my meanings directly into his mind,
however much I may be disposed to think that it would be
to his advantage if I could. I can only come so far as the
frontier and signal my meaning, and the latter can only
become his after he has interpreted the signals and taken
up their significance into his own personal awareness. He

---

[1] *Instinct and the Unconscious*, Chap. XII.

may, however, reject their meaning, but the fact that it was first symbolised is precisely what gives him the opportunity to accept or reject it, to hold it, so to say, at arm's length and consider it. Doubtless we must not exaggerate this isolation of mind from mind even in respect of mere suggestibility. It does not require much observation to note how much people influence one another by suggestion without their being explicitly aware of it ; yet also it does not require much observation to note that it is precisely this open side of our being which is most inimical to the development of character and has to be most watched. It is well known that high suggestibility and low and unstable mental life go together.[1]

All of which illustrates a principle which underlies the setting and circumstance of man's life as these have been ordained and are used by God. The principle is sometimes called the sacramental principle. It is that God deals with men, communicates Himself to them, through symbols. He does this in order that they may have room to grow as persons, and may enter into truly personal relations with Him. Nowhere, indeed, could this be more urgently necessary than in respect of man's relationship with God. R. H. Hutton, speaking of the strange fact that God, the greatest of all realities, is not also the most obvious and impressive, says : "A powerful, massive character, though it be nearly perfect, often positively injures those within the circle of its influence. They lose the spring of their

---

[1] The comparatively rare fact of telepathy, at any rate in any striking and clearly identifiable form, and its dependence on some sort of specially intimate and affectionate relationship between the persons involved, might suggest that powers of suggestibility are meant to be temporarily in suspense in human nature while genuine personal life and relationships are developed. If that is so, it is perhaps not far-fetched to imagine that such suspension is appropriate to this earthly life, and that the life of perfect love, which is heaven, means the regaining of these powers on a higher level. Heaven, so conceived, would be a state of being, at present unimaginable, where personalities are in perfect *rapport* and union with one another, without, however, ceasing to be individuals.

mind beneath the overwhelming weight of its constant pressure."[1] But if that danger exists in respect of human personality, how much more in respect of the personality of God in its relation with finite creatures whom He seeks to fashion into personal life ? Wherefore, in pursuit of that purpose He has withdrawn Himself behind symbols. Neither for man's thinking, nor for his loving, does He present Himself as a single, unmediated, divine object. Jesus said : " It is expedient for you that I go away " ; God said from the beginning : " It is expedient for you that I keep away." So He speaks to man through the world, through the system of society and nature in which He has placed him.[2]

Nature and society are then God's symbols, God's signs, God's language with the personality of man. They veil God, yet also to the hearing ear and the understanding heart they unveil, reveal Him. This does not mean that they are only that, but that they are that so far as they enter into the divine purpose of fashioning man into personal life. Berkeley, as Oman has insisted, pressed the comparison of the created order to language too far. He overlooked, Oman says, the fact " that the universe we perceive is not merely consistent for our thinking, but has significance for itself ; and that if so, this must be between us and the mind of God. Were this not so, the universe would be a very poverty-stricken affair, and objective knowledge an illusion. He rightly thinks it all meaning, but it is meaning in itself and by itself, and, probably to a larger extent than we know, for itself, as well as for us and for God."[3] That the created order is something in addition to being God's medium of speech with the soul of man is, we shall see, an important truth in relation to our understanding of the divine provi-dence. It underlies much of the impression of sheer mystery and even irrationality which it makes upon us. It is not in

---

[1] *Theological Essays*, p. 7.   [2] Cf. Althaus, *Die letzten Dinge*, p. 34.
[3] *Op. cit.*, p. 171–2. I owe much to Oman's discussion.

the least necessary to Christian faith to maintain that all creation should be a means to the end of human personality, but only that it should include all that is requisite to that end and nothing that should make its final achievement impossible.

There is another way in which we must qualify the comparison of the created order, as the medium of God's addressing of Himself to the soul, with human language, if we are not to be led astray. A word is a symbol to which a certain meaning is arbitrarily attached ; it is, that is to say, an extrinsic or conventional symbol. The extrinsic or conventional symbol does not carry its meaning along with it ; it has to be learnt. The word " table ", for example, does not *per se* suggest the object " table ", it could as well stand for " chair " or any other thing ; and the same word in two different languages, or systems of signs, might stand for two quite different objects. There are, however, symbols of a different kind, which may be called intrinsic, or expressive symbols. An intrinsic or expressive symbol is one which is organically related to, and sustained by, the wider and deeper reality which it represents. Its meaning therefore is not one which has to be memorised like the meaning of a word in a foreign tongue ; to the mind which is at all attuned to the reality which it represents, and only to such a mind, it immediately in some degree conveys its message. A symbol of this kind might be compared to a single ray of sunshine which breaks through a grey sky. To the depressed and chilled mortal it speaks of the sun still riding the heavens in fulness of light and warmth ; yet it only does so, because it is itself nothing apart from the sun ; it is itself charged with the virtue and significance of the larger reality it represents.[1]

[1] R. Will, in his *Le Culte*, Tome II, p. 100 f., distinguishes between the rationalist, the magical, and the realist conception of symbols. The first and the third of these, as the names might indicate, correspond with the distinction given above.

So far as our own personal relations with one another are concerned, the most expressive of intrinsic symbols are bodily acts when they are the natural outcome of the invisible states of mind which they represent. Through an act we sense something of the whole range of personal outlook and feeling without which the act would not have been done, by which it is sustained, and with which it constitutes one continuous organic reality. Spoken words are of course acts, but in so far as they take on the expressive symbolic quality of acts, it is because there is added to the merely conventional verbal form which may be found in the dictionary an instinctive and impulsive tone and inflexion which cannot be found in the dictionary or set down on paper at all, and which springs from the total organic response of one personality to another. Actions, we say, speak louder than words, and to say that inflexions and tones speak louder than dictionary meanings, is merely to say the same thing over again. A snarling face or an angry tone directed towards myself does not have to be decoded, however swiftly, into its meaning, but through it I intuit immediately the other as standing in a certain type of relationship with me in a personal order. This is because the man's body is part of himself and his inner life is dynamically present within its actions. It is not correct to say that the man uses his body to express himself ; rather the body's acts are the man in action. They are continuous with his whole personal life, yet they do not contain his whole personal life ; hence they serve as intrinsic or expressive symbols.[1]

[1] See above, p. 17. This has some connection with the question of ritual in worship. The justification of ritual is that acts are more immediately and effectively expressive of feeling and will, that is, of the whole personal attitude, than words to which something of the artificiality of their origin always attaches. But that involves that the most effective ritual is that of which the meaning is intrinsic and self-interpreting, and not extrinsic, needing to be learnt like a code. Thus the bowed head and the bent knee are a perfect piece of ritual symbolism.

Applying this to the thought of the created order as God's medium of speech with the personality of man, it is obvious that the comparison breaks down if we think exclusively of verbal symbolism, which, as we have said, is to so great degree conventional and extrinsic. God's symbols must be intrinsic symbols which carry their meaning along with them, otherwise the awareness of God through them could hardly get started at all. They are to be compared more with the expressive act than with the merely conventional vocable, that sort of expressive act which is so organically continuous with the wider reality it signifies, that it conveys the awareness of a direct personal rapport with it. This, indeed, is how the matter presents itself in the religious consciousness. God speaks, acts towards man through the situations of nature and society ; nevertheless when man hears God speaking he is conscious of standing in an immediate personal relationship to Him as active will and purpose. The relationship is immediate, and yet not unmediated. The environment is felt as standing between the soul and God in such wise that whilst the territorial integrity of the personality is preserved and its will left inviolate, direct rapport between them in the dimension of personal relationship is not prevented.

The triadic relationship of God, man, and world, involving that both man and his world should have significance for God and a relative independence over against God as well as over against one another, involving also that man would know God through the world yet not be separated from God by the world, is doubtless very mystifying for the reflective mind, especially when the religious man goes on to affirm that none the less all things live and move and have their being in God ; yet in the Christian faith, as in any which consistently affirms the personal nature of God's relationship to man, it is, for all its mystery, axiomatic and unavoidable. We shall need to return to the point again later.

CHAPTER V

REVELATION

IN nothing does the essentially personal quality of the religious apprehension of God come to clearer expression than in the fact that belief in revelation, in one form or another, seems to be characteristic of all religion. Yet the closeness, and the precise nature, of the connection between the awareness of God as personal and the idea of revelation are not always clearly understood.

We may start with the distinction between *revelation* and *discovery*. These two words, though in common speech not always properly and consistently differentiated from one another, certainly do not at bottom mean the same thing even for the undiscriminating popular mind. There are occasions when we instinctively and naturally speak of revelation and avoid the term discovery, as there are when we instinctively and naturally speak of discovery and avoid the term revelation. The distinction was recently well illustrated in the newspaper. The police had arrested a man of whose complicity in a crime they had much evidence. It was said in the paper that they had *discovered* certain facts about the man which pointed to his implication in the alleged crime. There was not, however, sufficient evidence to fasten it finally upon him. So they went to work upon him with several hours of continuous questioning, until at last he broke down and confessed. In his confession, said the paper, he *revealed* to the police certain things which they had not *discovered*, which, indeed, almost certainly they

77

could never, without the suspect's aid, have laid bare
at all.

So used, the distinction between the words leaps to the
eye. Both words refer to the apprehension of truths, facts
of our world. But in discovery there is activity on the one
side only ; the facts are there, static, quiescent, unknown,
and they remain unknown until someone searches them out ;
they never do anything to present themselves to the
enquirer. But where there is activity on the other side, an
activity *of* impartation directed *to* impartation, another
word is required, the word revelation. All of which is
obvious. Pursuing the analysis further, however, it becomes
clear that an activity directed to, and not merely
incidentally involving, impartation of truth to our minds,
implies and presupposes as the source of the activity a person
who in one way or another, through some sort of medium,
enters into rapport with us and conveys to us what we have
not discovered, and in some cases could not discover, by
our own unaided activity. When the detective is seeking
clues, it never enters his head that they will rise up and call
attention to themselves ; but when he is seeking a confession, he knows that unless this object which he calls the
prisoner chooses to speak, he will probably never get to
know what perhaps he most wants to know ; hence his
technique of enquiry is entirely different. In the one case
he is out for a discovery which depends on his own activity
alone, in the other case he is out for a revelation which in
the end depends on the activity of another person capable
of speaking a language he can understand. In the one case
he is working in an impersonal medium, in the other in a
personal.

In popular speech, of course, words seldom retain precise
meanings, especially when they refer to the same general
class of facts. Thus a detective might say : " I have
discovered a clue which *reveals* to me so-and-so " ; or he

might come away from the prisoner's confession and say :
" We have discovered so-and-so ", when what he means is
that the prisoner revealed it to him.⊚ But aside from the
uncertain fringes, the distinction is in general clear and
unmistakable. Pre-eminently the word revelation, even in
popular speech, is appropriate to a two-term personal
relationship where one actively imparts to another through
a medium of communication, through speech ; pre-
eminently the word discovery is appropriate to our dealing
with impersonal objects which do not in that sense actively
convey themselves to us at all.

The relation of this to what was said earlier concerning
the basic elements in the awareness of others as personal
is obvious. The sense of the other as an inaccessible source
of activity which is potentially co-operative in its resistance
and potentially resistant in its co-operation is clearly at a
maximum in the relation of active self-communication
through speech or through some other medium. In some
way the other has to speak, else he remains an impenetrable
mystery, if indeed he can be recognised as personal at all.
Much information, useful in its own sphere, might doubtless
be gathered by examining his psycho-physical reactions
with the same detached, impersonal methods as are used in
researching into the ways of frogs or beetles ; but it is not
possible to know *him*, as personal, unless he chooses to unveil
his inner life, to reveal himself to *you*, as personal, by
talking to you, and that not as a mere echo of your words
and thoughts, but himself taking the initiative, thrusting
his mind communicatively and resistantly into yours, his
values and purposes amongst yours, in respect of what is
in some degree a common life-situation.

It is important, however, before we proceed and for reasons
which will appear later, to note that though popular usage
thus often clearly indicates the personal reference of the
idea of revelation, none the less the word is sometimes used

without the clear sense of a personal activity on the other side. Two such usages must be mentioned. First, the word revelation is often used of any acquirement of knowledge which is, or seems to be, disconnected with our own efforts of research and discovery. Usually also an element of suddenness or unexpectedness is included in this usage of the term. Thus a man may ponder long over a problem and when he is doing, or thinking of, something else, the solution flashes into his mind. Its coming appears to be unconnected with his mental processes, though, of course, there is in fact some relationship. In such circumstances he will often say that it came to him like a revelation, or even that it was a revelation.[1] Second, there is a use of the word which has nothing to do with the manner of acquiring knowledge, but arises from the fact that man's mental constitution impels him to try to get below the flux of merely surface impression which his world makes upon him to what he conceives to be a deeper, more permanent and more orderly underlying reality. Thus a philosopher might say that the ultimate reality of the universe is revealed in the phenomena of time and sense ; or a scientist might say that the law of gravitation is revealed in falling apples and stones, and like phenomena. Or it might be said, as it has been recently said, that the essential law-abidingness of a people is revealed only at times of economic tension and stress ; at other times it cannot be known with certainty, being hidden behind the merely surface appearances of conventional behaviour There is much to be said for the view that both these usage are derived from the religious usage of the term, with, however, the sense of an activity on the other side so attenuated as almost completely to have disappeared.

When we turn to the religious usage of the term revelation we find that quite central in it is the living sense of God a

---

[1] An advertisement in *The Times* recently exhorted the reader to try a certain article and " the result will be a revelation to you."

entering into personal rapport with the soul, the living
ase, that is to say, of God as active personal will approach-
the individual in his own immediate situation in absolute
mand and final succour.   The religious man, at the
ment of living awareness of God, does not feel that he has
ppened upon God, as upon another object in his environ-
ent which it would be interesting to investigate further ;
her he apprehends God as actively approaching him, as
tering, of His own initiative, resistantly and savingly into
s personal life.   The only possible word to express this is
elation, the word discovery, with its predominant conno-
tion of activity in man and quiescence on the other side,
ing woefully inadequate.

It is, indeed, sometimes said that in the last resort, in
espect of religion, " no valid distinction can be drawn
between discovery and revelation."[1]   But this leaves
unexplained the fact that such a distinction has been per-
sistently made all down the history of religion.   It is a
truism that a revelation, in order to be received, must be
actively attended to, and no truly religious mind ever overlooks the fact that he must seek God with his whole heart.
What comes to expression in the distinction between discovery and revelation is not so much a difference between
activity and passivity on the part of man, but a difference
in the kind of reality, which, whether sought or unsought,
presents itself to his apprehension in the religious awareness,
and in the kind of relationship with him which it initiates.
It is precisely the difference already indicated, namely that
between a reality and a relationship which are not personal
and a reality and a relationship which are.   Doubtless,
also, it may be argued by a theistic philosophy that all
human activities, even the activity of exploring and discover-
ing the truth about atoms, are rooted in, and, for their

[1] So H. L. Goudge, article " Revelation," *Encyclopædia of Religion and
Ethics*, Vol. X, p. 746.

G

success, presuppose an ultimate reality of a personal kind
that the effort to attain truth in any sphere would not
successful " unless the one Source of truth were willing
reward it."[1] Yet the fact is, the thought of the ultimate
personal only became available for philosophy thro
religion, and in religion it is not discovered by argume
but is given by what is felt to be a direct encounter
personal kind with an ultimate holy and succouring purpo
To overlook this fact is to confuse, as is so often done,
philosophy of religion, or rather a religious philosophy, w
religion itself.

It is, indeed, fresh evidence of the loss of the sense
God as personal in these days, and the obsession of me
minds with what is in reality a monistic system of thoug
that even when the word revelation is used in respect of th
knowledge of God, the thought of God's personal activity
is often not present, or, if present, is so in such an attenuate
form that the word discovery would be just as appropriate
The two popular non-religious uses of the term, noted above
in which the sense of an activity on the other side is omitted
seem, in fact, to have worked back into religious though
with very unfortunate results.

Thus first, in respect of the use of the word revelation in
connexion with any sudden and apparently unconnected
increment of knowledge, we have many consciously o
unconsciously echoing Schleiermacher when he says, i
effect, that the bearers of revelation in religion are simpl
the great men of religious history, who by a unique gif
perceive something new and introduce it into man's religiou
outlook, so that all thereafter are enabled, in greater or les
degree, to share in it.   Revelation in religion thus become
merely the high moments of religious discovery, the grea
revealers, so called, in religion being compared, in fact, b
Schleiermacher to the great pioneers in science and art

[1] H. L. Goudge, *op. cit.*

need not be denied that the facts warrant to some extent
way of looking at things. There are outstanding,
ical figures in the history of religion on whose soul some
awareness of God's demanding and succouring dealings
men breaks, and through whom, as part of the his-
ical process, God speaks to others. But this way of
ting things is unfortunate for at least three reasons.
st, by attaching the word revelation exclusively to
ments when something original and touched with genius
urs in religion, the fact is obscured that all religious
erience, if it is living and formative, has the quality of
elation in it, has within it the sense that the divine Thou
kes Himself known to man in his own personal situation.
ond, it tends to obscure the fact, to quote Häring, that
the believer has quite a different sort of earnestness about
e reality of God " from that which the artist or the
cientist has when dealing with that aspect of the world
which interests him. And, third, it is apt to give the
rdinary believer a wrong estimate of his own religious life.
Instead of realising it to be a continuous intercourse with a
iving, revealing, divine purpose he is apt to regard it as
omething merely parasitic to the insights of others, or, at
most, as a matter of merely occasional, and all too rare,
exalted feelings. It is often said : " Oh, I have had no
revelations " ; yet, if week by week, in the worship of the
Christian fellowship, ordinary folk apprehend anew, in
relation to their own individual situation, the challenge
and the forgiveness of God, that is every bit as much
revelation as ever came to the most gifted prophet or seer
in history.[1]

Second, in respect of the use of the word revelation which
refers to an order underlying, and being known through, the
phenomena of nature and history. Here, even more clearly

[1] See Häring, *The Christian Faith* (Eng. Trans.), Vol. I, p. 52 f. ; also
Titius, *Natur und Gott*, 2. Aufl. p. 738.

there is something akin to the specifically religious usage
the word, for the religious awareness of God is an awaren
of an ultimate reality which is above and beyond and wit
the immediate environment by which man is surround
Religion is nothing if it is not an apprehension of a real
underlying, and more permanent than, the mere flux
changing and evanescent events; yet always it is
apprehension of something which is felt as purposive a
personal and addressing the soul in and through such even
When, however, the scientist or philosopher speaks of
underlying order being revealed in the events of nat
and history, he consciously or unconsciously leaves out t
religious thought of an activity on the other side. Th
perhaps, is of no moment in itself, but it becomes of mome
when the usage works back into theology and into me
whole approach to religion. Thus it is common to hea
people say, in a general way, that they believe in a revelatio
of God in nature and history, and when questioned it appear
they mean one of three things: either that there is a
underlying unity or order of some sort, about which we ma
expect to know more as human knowledge and huma
faculties expand; or that they have occasionally fel
mystical feelings of unity with this underlying, inclusive
order, which they then proceed to describe, in vaguely ideal-
istic and very abstract terms, as an order of absolute values
such as truth, beauty, and goodness; or, finally, if the
do picture this ultimate reality to themselves as in any
sense personal, that is explained away as being due t
the inevitable anthropomorphism of human thinking and
not to be taken as a report of it as it actually is. Seldo
do the words appear to express a pungent and living
sense of divine purpose or will actively dealing wit
them so insistently and directly that they can no mor
disregard it than they can someone hammering at th
door.

It is not unimportant to realise that to speak of a general revelation of God in *all* nature and history is, from the point of view of the truth on which we are insisting, almost a contradiction in terms. For revelation, properly understood, is, as we have said, a category of personal relationship ; and God cannot be related to a man personally through *all* nature and history. A personal relationship between God and man means God meeting the individual with an immediately relevant insistency of value and proffer of succour, commanding here and now obedience and trust, and that could only be in and through the man's own concrete, personal situation, which so far from being general, is peculiar to him and sets an immediate responsibility of action upon him alone. All nature and history cannot be such a real, existential situation to anyone, being, in fact, a highly generalised and abstract idea. If we speak of a general revelation of God in nature and history, the most we can mean is, positively, that God may make any situation, into which any man may come at any time, the medium of His revealing word to the soul ; and, negatively, that even those situations where He does not appear thus to speak to the soul are not apart from Him and do not separate from His overshadowing wisdom and love. But these convictions are not given through the contemplation of all nature and all history, which in the nature of the case is impossible ; they are judgements of faith evoked by God's revealing Himself in the particularities of the individual's personal life. The content of the revelation, inasmuch as it concerns God, of necessity concerns all nature and all history in principle : but the medium of it is the soul's own immediate situation as part of its own unique life history.

It will be clear from this discussion why the religious mind has always tended to insist that the knowledge of God has fundamentally a different character, and depends on

guaranteeing in and through such asking the soul's ultimate
succour, there is revelation. The essential content of
revelation is, therefore, rightly said to be God Himself, and
not general truths about God or the universe or immorta
or the way of duty ; though such truths are implicit in
divine self-giving, as this is mediated ever more richly
the responsive soul in the changing situations of life, and
capable of reflective formulation. And the proper respo
to revelation is rightly said to be faith, faith being not
intellectual assent to general truths, but the decis
commitment of the whole person in active obedience
and quiet trust in, the divine will apprehended as rightfull
sovereign and utterly trustworthy at one and the same tin
Faith, like revelation, to which it is correlative, is therefo
also a category of personal relationship and presuppose
the duality of personal relationship ; it cannot be " pumpe
up ", if such a phrase may be permitted, by the isolated se
from within itself, but must be evoked by the other presen
ing itself as trustworthy. Hence faith, while always man
deed, always sees in God its giver. The same is true o
human relationships. A child's trust in his parents is their
greatest gift to him, for it is evoked and sustained in him
only by their continually presenting themselves, revealing
themselves, as trustworthy.

It follows from this conception of revelation that not all
situations are equally calculated to be a medium of it,
though any situation may become such, owing to a peculiar
relevancy to the individual's life-history, which it may at
any moment assume. Unless a situation is such that it
calls for decision and obedience, and for a new self-commitment to the divine overshadowing providence in that
obedience, it can hardly mediate that vivid awareness of
personal rapport with God which is what revelation is
Revelations in this sense are always points of tension in the
soul's history, and therefore points of crisis, where the soul

must take either a step forward or a step backward in understanding of God and in stature as a child of God.[1] We do not mean by this that the living awareness of God personal can only arise in situations of unusual stress and [confl]ict. That would be palpably false. It may take pos[sessi]on of the soul through the solemn beauty of a summer [even]ing, or in the quietness of worship and prayer, or in [the] sense of the wonder and responsibility of a first-[born] child. Yet in so far as the living awareness of God as [per]sonal does enter into even such situations, it always [pr]oduces an element of challenge and tension which would [no]t otherwise be there, for such awareness is not possible [un]less and until the individual is confronted, in some [m]easure, by the absolute demands as well as the bounty and [be]nediction of God. If such an element is not introduced, [it] is doubtful whether the living awareness of God is present [at] all; at best there is only a reflective superimposition on [a] situation of a quasi-philosophic or poetic idea that all [goo]d things are from above. Every situation in which God [r]eveals Himself to the soul is a crisis calling for obedience and trust; it may begin or end by being such, but such at some point and in some degree it must be. The relative prominence of the element of demand and the element of succour in the total awareness of God may, however, vary considerably according to the situation. Sometimes the soul at its crisis needs more the sense of the comforts of God than of His demands, but even then the latter is only in the background. *Alle Gabe ist Aufgabe.*[2]

---

[1] This is apparently what Herrmann means when he insists throughout his *Offenbarung und Wunder* that a genuine experience of revelation involves that the individual should not merely hear about new ranges of spiritual reality and experience, but should himself begin to live in them and so move forward to a new level of being himself.

[2] Cf. 2 Cor. i. 4: " Who comforteth us . . . that we may be able to comfort them which are in any trouble "; 1 John iii. 1-3: " Behold what manner of love the Father hath bestowed upon us . . . every man that hath this hope purifieth himself even as he is pure."

The notion that faith should be able to discern the active
presence of God in all events and all situations is merely
pietistic ; it is neither supported by experience nor necessitated by the thought of God and His intercourse with
Rather the reverse would seem to be true. Much of m
life of necessity runs in a routine of daily tasks which
the better done for receiving undivided attention
disturbed by the explicit awareness of God ; and there
many decisions to be made and acts done which inv
nothing of crisis in the soul's life, but require only so
experience and common-sense. And even in those situatio
where the soul cries out for an assurance of the living Go
the revelation may not be immediately given. Hunzing
suggests that when this happens it is the result of sin,[1] an
it cannot be questioned that this is a vitally importan
factor, as we shall see ; yet it may also be due to t
relative weakness and immaturity of a growing perso
life, which will be more truly succoured by God's wi
holding a present revelation and requiring rather a stea
fast walking forward in the faith that the divine love an
power, which have assuredly at other times spoken to the
soul, are also present now. Thus in a sense the silence itself
becomes a divine, challenging word. As we shall maintain
in the discussion of providence, in God's education of
the human spirit into a rich personal sonship to Himself
there is a place for darkness and mystery. What is
required is not that God should reveal Himself *in* all situations, but sufficiently *for* all situations, and that we may
believe He does.

Yet to distinguish between situations in which God
reveals Himself in a direct and living rapport with the soul
and situations where the mind is rightly preoccupied with
other things is not to reduce life to a disjointed alternation
of religious and irreligious moods. The living awareness of

[1] *Das Wunder*, p. 60.

God given in the moments of revelation abides in the whole
set and direction of the life, and in the soul's capacity in
⟨an⟩y situation, by a moment of recollection, to become again
⟨awar⟩e of the living God.[1]

⟨A⟩ word may be added concerning the Bible considered as the revela-
⟨tion o⟩f God. In the light of the principles set forth in this chapter it is
⟨clear ⟩that the Bible *per se*, i.e. considered simply as a written text is not,
⟨and n⟩ever can be, a revelation of God. It becomes revelation only as God
⟨spea⟩ks through it relevantly to my situation, and it becomes unique
⟨reve⟩lation only as He speaks through it relevantly to something unique
⟨in m⟩y situation. It is as mediating Christ the Reconciler to my basic
⟨nee⟩d of reconciliation in my present historical circumstance that the
⟨Bib⟩le becomes a unique source of God's revealing word to the soul. But
⟨I, o⟩r someone, has to bring it into my present situation, make it part of it,
⟨bef⟩ore God can speak livingly through it. Thus if we use the term " the
⟨W⟩ord " in the sense of God's living speech with the soul, it is true to say
⟨th⟩at the Bible is not the Word of God, but the Word of God is in the Bible,
⟨and⟩—in the categories of this chapter—the Bible is not the Revelation of
⟨Go⟩d, but the Revelation of God is in the Bible.

CHAPTER VI

PROVIDENCE

It has been said that faith in providence is religion its
and, again, that the denial of providence is the denial
all religion.[1] This is undoubtedly true if by faith in pro
dence is meant, not a quasi-philosophical affirmation of
ultimate harmony in things, but a confidence that man
personal life is the concern of a wisdom and power high
than his own; and if by religion is meant living an
spontaneous religion as it rises in the heart of the comm
man. Faith in providence is, in other words, anot
aspect of that awareness of God as personal which, we ha
maintained, lies somewhere at the root of all man's religi
history.

This is evident, indeed, from the analysis already given
of the essential factors in the living awareness of God as
personal. In such awareness, we have seen, the thought of
God as absolute demand and the thought of Him as final
succour are inseparable from one another, and if the
idea of providence has always seemed to centre in the
latter rather than in the former, that is because of
the proneness to think of God primarily in eudæmonistic
terms, as the giver of good things, which is characteristic of
the natural man, and from which even Christian thought on
these matters does not always succeed in guarding itself.[2]
Yet the idea of God's judgement upon, and punishment of
disobedient and impious men is usually never wholly absent

[1] Häring, *The Christian Faith* (Eng. Trans.), Vol. II, p. 514.
[2] " Provisions " in common speech means exclusively " things to
eat ".

rom the thought of providence, even though it often falls
nto the background. That faith in providence and the
awareness of God as personal are indissolubly involved in
ne another is further evidenced by the kind of problem with
vhich that faith always wrestles, alike in reflection and in the
ractical life. It wrestles with the problem of evil in its
ual aspect of suffering and wickedness ; yet in the main it
nly feels these as problems at the point where they seem
o be peculiarly challenging to, and destructive of, that
ignificance of man's personal being which is inseparably
ound up with his sense of God.[1]

To take each point in turn :

First, the problem of suffering.

It is obvious that much of the pain of life does not
onstitute a problem either for theory or for the practical
usiness of living, and never has been considered as so doing
y healthy human nature. Unless we are going to ask for
world so utterly different from the one in which we find
urselves alive that it is impossible to form any conception
f it, it seems clear that life could not persist, nor could it
levelop, unless on the one hand it could suffer the dis-
omfort of at least temporarily dissatisfied desire, and
inless, on the other hand, it were set in a world sufficiently
table and regular in its behaviour to negate, even painfully,
ny desires which in effect presume it to be other than it is.
A living creature with no inward sting of want, and no
utward discipline of an environment sternly requiring
djustment to itself, would in fact not be " living " in any

[1] Strictly speaking, there is no special problem of evil save for the
man who is trying, consciously or unconsciously, to interpret the world
n terms of an ultimate purpose interested in persons. There may be a
ractical problem how to deal with (say) an earthquake when it arises,
ut if the desire to interpret the universe in terms of the values of in-
ividual personality be completely set on one side, an earthquake is no
nore of a problem than the fall of a leaf ; it is, for reflexion, just one
iece of the jig-saw puzzle along with others, and it is of no special con-
equence that we do not happen to like its ugly colours or jagged shape.

sense in which we can understand the term. It would be indistinguishable from a stone. Certainly anything in the nature of rational consciousness and self-direction could not arise. It is therefore idle to speculate whether a world had been possible wherein life generally, and personal life as we know it in ourselves in particular, could have developed without pain of any sort whatsoever. At some point or other we have to cease speculating on abstract possibilities and accept the given. Nor, in fact, does normal man feel it necessary to discuss the matter, at least in respect of much of the discipline of his life. He not only accepts without question these basic conditions of his life, but also positively rejoices in them. He delights in measuring himself against difficulties and hardship, and if sufficient opportunity is not offered, he will create it in games and self-imposed tasks of various sorts, such as climbing Everest or seeking the Poles. No one in his senses would vote for a painless world for a world in which there were not real tasks, tasks, that is wherein there is an ever-present possibility, and on occasion the actuality, of frustration and defeat. Even frustration and defeat are found to be opportunity for new virtues and accomplishments.[1]

How then do pain and frustration become a problem for

[1] Cf. Lessing's oft-quoted dictum that had he to choose between truth and the search for truth, he would choose the latter. Aldous Huxley (*Brave New World*, p. 283) has put the point vividly in the passage where the savage voices his rebellion against the perfect Utopia into which he has been brought: " ' But I like the inconveniences.'—' We don't,' said the Controller. ' We prefer to do things comfortably.'—' But I don't want comfort—I want God, I want poetry, I want real danger, I want freedom, I want goodness, I want sin.'—' In fact,' said Mustapha Mond ' you're claiming the right to be unhappy.'—' All right, then,' said the Savage defiantly, ' I'm claiming the right to be unhappy.'—' Not to mention the right to grow old and ugly and impotent ; the right to have syphilis and cancer ; the right to have too little to eat ; the right to be lousy ; the right to live in constant apprehension of what may happen to-morrow ; the right to catch typhoid ; the right to be tortured by unspeakable pains of every kind.' There was a long silence. ' I claim them all,' said the Savage at last." Pascal has the same thought (*Pensées* Ed. Brunschvicg, p. 389.)

the religious mind, and indeed for the mind of man generally ? They become a problem precisely at the point where
they seem no longer to serve the high ends of zestful
endeavour and a strong personal life, but rather to run
counter to them ; that is to say at the point where they
seem to negate human personality rather than to minister
to it. The frustrations of life take on this dysteleological
quality in relation to human personality along three lines.

First, there are happenings, such as, for example, earthquakes, typhoons, floods, etc., which in their uncontrollable,
wholesale destructiveness irresistibly convey the impression
that man's world is at bottom indifferent to, and therefore
ultimately destructive of, the values and achievements of
human life. A challenge by the environment may be met,
and even welcomed, if it be not incommensurable with man's
powers, but when it is of a kind which reduces him and his
fellows to the status of a bundle of straw tossed in the wind,
it seems in a radical way to depersonalise him, and thus to
threaten the very foundation of his being and the sources of
all his endeavour. In more recent times this impression of
a certain ruthless indifference in the natural order to the
personal values of man's life has been reinforced by the
picture of nature as a blind concatenation of mechanical
cause-effect relationships, with which science has familiarised
the popular mind.

Second, there is the fact that altogether apart from such
lurid interrogation marks which nature again and again
seems to set against the significance of his personal life, man
finds within his own being factors which seem to render him
something in the nature of a permanent misfit in his world.
And yet these factors are precisely those which are essential
to his having any personal life at all. We have gone into
this at some length elsewhere.[1] The permanent dissatisfaction which seems to lie at the heart of even the highest

[1] *Experience of God,* Chap. III.

human achievement, which seems indeed to be that which
alone makes his highest achievement possible, has been a
commonplace on the lips of those who have been ready to
reflect on these matters, all down the ages. And it is
precisely in relation to those yearnings which have been
bound up with his awareness of God that this unending
disquietude has been most acutely felt. Always man's
reach seems to exceed his grasp ; he solves one problem and
another rises in its place ; from the midst of one satisfaction
another dissatisfaction is born ; like Moses on Mount Nebo
he views the promised land and then inevitably hears the
chilling words : "I have caused thee to see it with thine eyes,
but thou shalt not go over hither."[1] This, in view of what was
said above about the zest of pursuit might be regarded as
not altogether a disadvantage, yet pursuit which seems to
contain within it no possibility of arrival, of permanent
accomplishment, has no real zest at all. A harvest without
ploughing would degrade human personality to the level of
a fed beast ; but a ploughing without harvest would degrade
it to the level of impotent and irritated imbecility. Yet
something of that quality does seem to attach to human
life, and most of all in its highest reaches.

Third, and bringing to a tremendous focus all these other
things, there is the fact that man is conscious of being under
sentence of death. Death, so inevitable, so final, so much
a matter, apparently, of chance, challenges and negates with
irresistible force man's sense of his own significance as a
self-conscious personality. This is felt most poignantly in
that relationship in which the awareness of personality as
a unique, irreplaceable, intrinsically valuable thing reaches
its maximum intensity, namely, the relationship of love.
Doubtless few avoid feeling the challenge which death offers
to man's sense of the worth and meaning of his own being,
forcing him to ask the question, even though he immediately

[1] Deut. xxxiv. 4.

verts his mind from it, what is the significance of his
ersonal life when a streptococcus can snuff it out in delirium
nd agony—is it, after all, only a " tale told by an idiot,
ull of sound and fury, signifying nothing " ? But the
hallenge becomes more than a challenge, becomes a
rightful frustration in the central places of the personal
eing, when one beloved vanishes into the abyss. To quote
what we have written elsewhere : Love is, of course, a very
omplex thing, but " at the heart of it and giving it its
eculiar human quality is a more or less conscious apprehen-
ion of the loved one as a distinct self or individuality
apable of entering into peculiar ' rapport ' with the self or
individuality which loves. The relationship, being between
selves ', is a unique relationship, as unique and unre-
eatable as the two distinct personalities which enter into
. Hence if a man loses his wife or child, he loses some-
hing which quite literally cannot be replaced. It is difficult
o believe that an animal losing his mate could be conscious
f irreparable loss in anything like the same degree, for not
nly is individuality not so highly developed, but the
ppreciation of it, the valuation of it, as involving selfhood
is in the nature of the case impossible."[1] Cutting right
cross, then, the most intensely personal of human relation-
hips, there is apparently a complete negation of it.

Second, the problem of wickedness.

Like the fact of suffering, the fact of wickedness, from
ne point of view, does not constitute a problem for the
ligious mind, or indeed for mankind in general. It is
ound up with the fact of freedom, without which anything
the nature of a truly personal relationship is unthinkable.
Whatever may be the problems which the idea of freedom
ises for philosophy, it raises none for the practical life and

---

[1] *Experience of God*, p. 53. For a powerful statement of the peculiar
ustration involved in the death of an individual who is truly loved see
aillie, *And the Life Everlasting*, p. 59 f.

H

least of all for the religious man as he is aware of himsel
standing in a living relationship with God. That it shoulc
be possible for men to be disobedient even to the require
ments of God is essentially bound up with the fact that Goc
presents Himself as will, for will can be known only in sc
far as it stands in tension with, and is in some sense limitec
by, another will. A demand to which there were only on
answer would cease to be a demand in a personal sense a
all ; it would be merely a stimulus comparable to tha
which produces the knee-jerk. The religious mind ha:
therefore never been disconcerted by the phenomenon o
the wicked or impious man as such.

The phenomenon becomes disconcerting, once again, a
the point where it seems to become part of the genera
indifference of the world to the issues of personal life
particularly as these are grasped in and through th
religious awareness. When wickedness is seen to work or
apparently unchecked, the wicked prospering, the innocen
suffering, its consequences being wrought out indiscrimi
nately over the whole area of human life, then, like th
earthquake or the flood, it seems to lend to man's whol
world the appearance of brazen indifference. That Goc
should demand so absolutely the obedience of man, an
yet appear to be so little concerned with his disobedience
that man should be permitted to interrupt and frustrat
the purpose of the most High without immediate an
obvious disaster ; that the pious man's life should o
occasion give no more evidence of the personal succour c
the Eternal than the impious man's or sometimes eve
than that of the beasts in the field, these are problems th
challenge of which cannot lightly be set on one side, as th
Psalms, the Book of Job, and indeed the whole of the Bibl
not to speak of other literature all down the ages, mo
poignantly show. The question which underlies them all
whether the awareness of God as absolute demand an

nal succour is veridical, whether man is, after all, only as
he beasts that perish, or one who is really called by the
Eternal Personal to take a personal place in His sovereign
nd triumphant purpose of good. To believe in providence
s to commit oneself, despite all the appearances, to the
atter alternative. To deny providence *is* to deny religion.

It is impressive witness to the compulsiveness of the
ouch of the Eternal Personal upon the human spirit, and
o the profound way in which man's whole sense of the
vorth and significance of his own life is bound up in it, that
aith in providence, the belief that all things are held in the
rasp of an eternal purpose which is concerned with men
ind women and their history, maintains itself against these
o fierce challenges. Some such faith, vague and inter-
nittent, scarcely rising perhaps above the dim confidence
hat there is an ultimate decency in things and that some-
iow " we shall muddle through ", seems to be that on
vhich most people unconsciously rest, even though other-
vise they make no conscious profession of religious belief.
Explicit teaching, expressed in so many terms, that every-
hing is the result of impersonal fate, or blind mechanism,
ir sheer chance, has never really grasped and held the minds
)f men for long ; such teaching is usually the outcome of
)ure theory, or of a despair which marks the beginning at
east of a failure in the life impulse itself.

The religious mind has always sought to find some
lleviation to these challenges of suffering and wickedness
o its fundamental convictions by interpretations and
explanations of various sorts. Indeed the history of
eligious thought is in large measure the history of theo-
licies. In particular it has been forced, at least in so far as
t has remained true to its fundamental awareness of God
is personal and has not lost itself in abstract theorising of
i monistic type, to some sort of eschatological faith, some
sort of faith that the ultimate justification of the ways of

God with man lies in an eternal realm which, withou
ceasing to be personal, transcends this present life alto
gether. Some consideration of solutions to the problem o
evil which have been offered at various times, and ir
particular of the meaning of eschatological faith, its danger
and its profound implication in the experience of God a
personal, will be given when we come to discuss the Christiar
experience of reconciliation in relation to these matters
Meanwhile we content ourselves with noting that, when al
is said that can be said, the religious affirmation of provi
dence remains, and must ever remain, the affirmation of a
mystery, so far as the manner of its working out in and
through the infinite complexity of events in this universe i
concerned. It is an affirmation of faith and not of sight ; i
arises primarily out of the deep insights and necessities o
the soul of man as God calls it into awareness of Himself and
of its own significance, and not from any observation o
the general course of external events.

It must indeed be once and for all admitted that it is no
possible for our minds to grasp how it should be possible fo
all events whatsoever to fall within the scope of the divin
providence and be made ultimately subservient to Hi
purpose. The mystery of it is inscrutable enough even to a
monism which seeks to see everything as the result of the
direct, unmediated activity of God, or as phases of the
Absolute ; but for theistic faith of the kind we are discussing
which is bound, as we have seen, to attribute to man and
his world a relative independence of God, it is even more sc
That events should be really the result of the interplay c
intramundane causes, including the choices of beings wh
are free to resist God, and yet also be controlled and directed
by His manifold wisdom and sovereign will ; that God has
purpose which He is working out in history, so that men ca
have genuine co-operative fellowship with Him here and
now, yet which, being God's purpose, transcends history

altogether so that man cannot interpret it adequately in terms of this life ; that in spite of all the confusion and heartbreak and frustration of life, the sins, follies, accidents, disasters, diseases, so undiscriminating in their incidence, so ruthless in their working out, every individual may, if he will, not in imagination but in fact, rest upon a love which numbers the very hairs of his head—that is a conception before which the intellect sinks down in complete paralysis. It is only possible to maintain because in the religious awareness something deeper than intellect is involved. Such a conviction is primarily given, as we have said, through the primordial rapport of the soul with God, and it is developed and deepened as that rapport is cleansed and enlarged into true sonship to God through the Christian experience of reconciliation.

The danger in the reflective exposition of the thought of providence is always either that the thought of providence will swallow up the thought of the relative independence of man and his world, landing us in monism again, or that the thought of independence will swallow up the thought of providence, leaving no basis for trust and peace. Somehow the two thoughts have to be held together. They are as a matter of fact not difficult to hold together in the moment of living and serious awareness of God, when the latter presents Himself at one and the same time as absolute demand and final succour, the absolute demand having no meaning apart from the independence of man, the final succour having no meaning apart from the sovereign providence of God. Thus the Apostle can cry, with apparently no consciousness of saying anything paradoxical, " work out your own salvation with fear and trembling, for it is God that worketh in you both to will and to do of His good pleasure." It is when the intenser mood of religious awareness gives way to reflection that the sense of paradox, even of downright contradiction, arises. Then the mind confronts the problem with which philosophy has wrestled throughout the ages and never satisfactorily solved, the problem of the one and the many ; yet coming at it through the living awareness of the Eternal, it is not greatly perturbed that there is apparently no philosophical solution of it, but is content to accept the apparent contradiction and even rest on it. For in its awareness of God it is aware of apprehending a dimension of being which transcends, whilst being intimately bound up in, the dimensions of time and space in which human life is being wrought out, and with which alone human intellectual processes are qualified to deal.

Following some suggestions of Heim,[1] we may perhaps dwell for a little on this matter of dimensional distinction and its relation to the thought of Providence, not indeed in the hope of positively illumining the mystery of God's providential control, but in order that we may be able in some measure to grasp reflectively why such a mystery should appear in the heart of the religious life and, despite its insolubility, be accepted by it, not only without discomfort, but with positive joy. For genuine religion has always rejoiced in the mystery of God, and been ready, like Paul, at the end of his very inconclusive discussion of the divine providential dealings with Israel, to utter not a cry of despair, but a pæan of praise : " O the depth of the riches both of the wisdom and knowledge of God ! how unsearchable are his judgements and his ways past finding out ! For who hath known the mind of the Lord ? or who hath been his counsellor ? Or who hath first given to him, and it shall be recompensed unto him again ? For of him, and through him, and to him, are all things : to whom be glory for ever."[2] *Deus cognitus, deus nullus.*

The simplest example of dimensional distinction is that

---

[1] *Glaube und Denken, passim.*
[2] Rom. xi. 33–6.

etween the dimensions of space. A two-dimensional being,
ving within a flat surface, could form no notion of the third
imension, and his spatial world would seem to him to be
overned by certain necessary relationships of a self-
vident and exceptionless kind. Thus it would be self-
vident to him that only one line can be drawn at right
ngles to another at a given point. If, now, such a creature
ere suddenly to become aware of a third dimension, then
he necessities of its previous two-dimensional experience
vould instantly appear to be, in a sense, broken through.
t would now, for example, be possible to draw a second
ine at right angles to another at any given point. Yet, in
nother sense, the necessities would not be broken through,
or it would still be self-evidently true that in a two-
limensional surface only two such lines could be drawn.
That which, viewed from within one dimension is impossible,
s actual and obvious when viewed from the standpoint of
nother. It is important to note that when a new dimension
ias opened up to awareness, it does not annul the previous
limension, though it does seem to break through its
pparently irresistible logic; rather does it take it up
nto itself, in a permanent and inescapable relationship.
Thus it is impossible for creatures such as ourselves to
get back into a two-dimensional world. We can indeed
make an abstraction and formulate a plane geometry, but
ilways we are aware when we contemplate a surface that
every point within it is, as it were, at the end of a line
perpendicular to the surface running up to the stars, or out
o the horizon. Every surface is for us the surface of a solid
oody, even though its depth is infinitesimal, and we choose
for certain purposes to disregard it. Yet, the truths of
plane geometry remain. The point can perhaps be made
even clearer by conceiving that there is a fourth dimension
of space, of which at the moment we are entirely unaware.
To us it is self-evident that there is no way into, or out of,

a hermetically sealed chamber. We are either inside
outside and there is no passage from the one to the othe
On this obvious necessity of our experience a great man
detective stories have been built up. To a creature, how
ever, to whom a fourth dimension was open such detectiv
stories would be intelligible, but quite pointless and un
interesting, because the principle on which they rest has fo
him been transcended. He could appear in, or disappea
from, such a sealed chamber at will. To a three-dimension
being in the room the appearance of a fourth-dimension
visitor within it would seem a materialisation out of nothin
too utterly contradictory of the manifest possibilities of th
situation not to be dismissed instantly as the figment of
disordered mind.

It is suggested that some such dimensional relationshi
lies behind the paradox of the religious perception that a
events whatsoever lie within the providential ordering o
God, yet without ceasing to be the result of intramundan
activities, including the activities of free moral agents. T
the religious mind another dimension, the dimension of th
Eternal Personal, has opened up. There is the dimension o
the temporal, the world of nature and history, and there i
the dimension of the eternal and the divine, and every even
in the former lies also in the latter, just as every point in
plane surface is at the end of a perpendicular to the stars
Nor can the relationships of an event in the one dimension
be expressed in terms of its relationships in the other. Such
relationships can only be set side by side in a proposition
which even to religious faith never loses the quality o
mysterious paradox, and to the irreligious mind may eve
take on the appearance of downright contradiction. Thu
when the religious man cries, with Job, at the death of
child, " the Lord gave and the Lord hath taken away
blessed be the name of the Lord ", it is not necessarily
pious affectation, though it may be ; and, in so far as it i

sincere, it by no means constitutes a denial that viewed from within the dimension of the temporal series, it was a human procreative act that " gave ", and the activity of a diphtheric germ from a bad drain that " took away." The two statements do not contradict one another, for they are incommensurables, as relations in different dimensions are, and supremely so when one of the dimensions is that which stands over all other dimensional distinctions whatsoever, namely the dimension of God.

The same considerations apply to those events which break into life with all the appearance of sheer accident. A tile blows off the housetop, seriously injuring me and upsetting all my plans. This, so far as my own purposes are concerned, is an unlucky accident. What then is it so far as the divine purpose is concerned ? It is difficult to attribute it to a direct act of will on the part of God, as though He deliberately planned it and brought it to pass ; it seems rather to be the result of the interplay of forces in a relatively independent world. Yet also as a religious man I am bound to affirm that the event does not fall outside the scope of the divine providence, and to say humbly ' God's will be done ". Shall I then say that God permits it, but does not will it ? That is of help in that it allows me to relate it to the divine will without in principle so merging everything in the latter that there is no independent order of nature left. Yet, plainly, for reflection that only pushes the mystery a little farther back, for, unless I am to go too far towards the other extreme and so affirm the independence of the world that the divine control in effect disappears, there still remains the question how providence could allow for contingency in human life in such wise that His purpose is nevertheless achieved, making wind-blown tiles, and even the wrath of man, to praise Him. A contingency so qualified would appear to be hardly contingency at all. We are in fact brought back to that unavoidable antinomy which always appears when two dimensions are set in relation to one another.

The utterance attributed to Joseph in the Book of Genesis expresses the issues in a concrete way. When he revealed himself to his brethren, he said : " Be not grieved, God sent me before you to preserve a posterity in the earth. So now it was not you that sent me hither, but God." And again : " As for you, ye thought evil against me, but God meant it unto good, to bring to pass, as it is this day, to save much people alive." Yet into the complex chain of events which had that issue had entered the fierce jealousy of his brethren, his chance visit to them in Dothan, the chance passing of the Midianite merchants, the evil passion of a woman, the crimes and dreams of a court official, the unexpected failure of the crops—events physical, spiritual, accidental, diabolical, and yet somehow, according to Joseph, all events providential. Did God, then, cause the jealousy, the sensuality, the famine, and all the rest ? Or was Joseph wrong in talking of providence, having fallen into the common error of improvising a belief in an invisible ally within events directly things turned out unexpectedly well ? We are, however, not shut up to these alternatives. There is a third possibility, namely that God did not directly cause the separate events, but none the less Joseph was right in seeing them as lying within the overshadowing power and wisdom of God. We can figure this possibility to the mind only after the analogy of dimensional distinctions, and we may suppose that it is precisely the privilege of an obedient and trusting spirit like Joseph to discern the dimension of God with a conviction and a peace not open to other men.[1]

---

[1] Yet as was suggested in Chap. III to any man there may come a dim and fleeting perception of will involved in events which are peculiarly relevant to his own personal situation and destiny ; such a perception is, so far as it goes, a true apprehension of the dimension of God.

CHAPTER VII

MIRACLE

THE experience which finds expression in the idea of miracle is a special form of that which finds expression in the idea of revelation, and like the latter, therefore, it lies very near the heart and centre of living and spontaneous religion. It is for this reason that belief in miracle seems so indestructible; despite all the intellectual difficulties inherent in the idea, and all the attacks made upon it from various angles over many centuries, it still persists wherever religion ceases to be a merely religiously tinctured system of philosophical ideas and becomes a lively and formative and prayerful experience of the living God. Whatever of vulgar superstition may find place in the content of the idea, the persistence of the idea cannot be set down to the mere tenacity of vulgar superstition even in an enlightened age; rather it must be due to something fundamental in the religious life which it must be the first task of the thinker to understand. Wendland has pointed out how even cautious liberal theologians like Harnack and Troeltsch, who, out of deference to the supposed requirements of scientific principles, would expunge the word miracle entirely from the vocabulary of the religious man, none the less " are involuntarily driven to use expressions corresponding to the conception they have rejected, if they are to do justice to their sense of the living action of God."[1]

The fatal mistake is to begin the consideration of miracle from the angle of a scientific or philosophic concept of

[1] Wendland, *Miracles and Christianity* (Eng. Trans.), p. 13.

natural law. Miracle being fundamentally a religious
category and not a scientific or philosophic one, the proper
place to begin is within the sphere of living religion itself
To define miracle *in limine*, for example, as an event
involving suspension of natural laws is to begin in the
wrong place. We must first ask what is the significance of
miracle for religion ; we must define and evaluate it, seek
to understand the indispensability of it, within that context
and universe of discourse. Thereafter we may go on to
enquire how the religious thought of miracle may best be
related to those other aspects of the world presented to us
through other than specifically religious channels. This
does not mean that we wish to isolate our religious judgements from anything that is comprised within our experience
as modern people, least of all from the discoveries of science
when these are well attested. But the final judgement on
a religious matter must be a religious judgement ; that is to
say, it must be one such as the deeply religious man cannot
help making and acting on when he is most livingly aware
that God is dealing with him and he with God, as, for
example, when in a critical situation he is on his knees a
prayer.

To begin, as so many do, by defining a miraculous event
in terms of its relation to the system of nature, instead of in
terms of its relation to the religious life, affords another
example of the dangerous facility with which the abstractions of rational thought can be substituted for, and obscure
the realities of living religious experience. Whatever the
word miracle signifies religiously it certainly indicates something which evokes a profound feeling response akin to
wonder and awe, as the etymology of the word shows. Yet
the definition of miracle as an event involving the suspension
of law by omnipotent might leaves this entirely out of
account. Nay more, it definitely runs counter to it, and
makes it seem out of place. For the possibility of miracle

so defined becomes merely part of the rational meaning of
omnipotence, and in itself it no more evokes wonder to
contemplate omnipotence suspending laws than it does to
contemplate impotence submitting to them. The *mirabile*
in the *miraculum* must therefore have another source than
the mere thought of the suspension of law by God, and
what that source is can be understood only by approaching
the whole question from a different angle, from the angle
of the religious life itself.[1]

Starting, then, from this angle, the first thing to be said is
clear enough, namely, that a miraculous event always
enters the religious man's experience as a *revelation* of God
in the sense in which that term has been expounded in the

---

[1] The history of the doctrine of miracle in Christian theology since
Thomas Aquinas set the fashion of approaching it through the type of
definition indicated, bears witness to the unfortunate consequences of so
doing. Protestant theology, partly doubtless because of its desire to
discredit alleged miracles in the Roman Church, could not long avoid the
conclusion which was in any case implicit in the definition from which it
started, the conclusion, namely, that miracles do not now happen. For
if miracles are by definition events involving the suspension of law by
omnipotence, then nobody is in a position to know when they happen if
they happen at all. For who can so know all the laws of the universe that
he can say positively that this or that event involves a suspension of them ?
An event is not constituted a divine suspension of law merely by being
extraordinary. It may be extraordinary merely because we are ignorant
of its true causes, as Augustine insisted ; or because, as the scholastics
argued and popular superstition at the time firmly believed, demonic
forces of wizardry and witchcraft are at work ; or because somebody is
telling lies about it, as some Protestants were ready to affirm concerning
certain alleged Roman miracles. For obvious reasons, however, it was felt
to be necessary to retain the Biblical miracles. But why accept in respect
of the long-distant past that which no longer happened in the present, or
if it happened, could not be certainly known to happen ? The answer
given was that the Biblical miracles are guaranteed by the authority of
the Christian tradition, as enshrined particularly in the Scriptures. The
question was then unavoidable why miracles happened then if they do
not happen now ; and the answer was that they were given to substantiate
and certify the saving truth which was being revealed—an obvious circle,
the miracles guaranteeing the authority of the revelation, the authority
of the revelation then guaranteeing the miracles. To the question how,
if miracles are in principle unrecognisable, the Biblical miracles were ever
recognised as such so that they might fulfil their evidential function, the
answer was that with the miracle was given to certain folk, through the

last chapter. Whatever else it may be, it is an event or
complex of events through which a man becomes aware of
God as active towards himself in and through his own
personal situation. It is God acting relevantly to a man's
individual situation and destiny ; speaking through events
because He is active in events ; confronting the soul as
personal will and purpose in that immediacy of relationship
which is nevertheless mediated through the environing
world.[1] Unless an event has this quality in some degree
to someone it is not, in the religious sense of the term, a
miracle. Miracle, therefore, is not an external attestation
of divine revelation, but is that in and through which the
divine revelation is given ; it is the intrinsic symbol which
at one and the same time is constituted, yet also transcended,
by the reality it mediates. It is, in Hunzinger's phrase,
" the phenomenal form (*Erscheinungsform*) of divine
revelation."

If this be so, then all that has been said previously
concerning the essential elements in the living apprehension
of God can be transferred straightway to the meaning of

Spirit, the power to discern its miraculous quality ; yet one would have
thought that God could as well have bestowed the power to see the truth
of the revelation which was being certified. In any case there was no
enquiry into the fundamental question whether, and in what sense, the
saving truths of Christianity can be externally certified, if they are not
capable of shining in their own light—the challenging refusal of Jesus to
work miracles with that purpose being overlooked. Roman theology, on
the other hand, has maintained that miracles in the sense of divine suspen-
sions of natural law do still happen, and has endeavoured at times to
demonstrate, in respect of particular alleged miracles, that no other
explanation of their abnormal quality is possible than that God has acted
in this way. Yet, clearly, it is not possible logically to demonstrate such
a universal negative.

[1] The miracles to which the Jewish people looked back, such as the
deliverance from Egypt, might appear to be events through which God's
activity towards the whole people, rather than to the individual, was
apprehended. Yet only as the individuals identified their own personal
destiny with that of the whole people could such events take on that
quality of intense relevance to a personal situation which is essential to
the awareness of miracle.

miracle. Miracle, like other terms, is often loosely and even flippantly used, but if we wish to keep close to the central and serious realities of genuine religion, then we must say that no man has any right to call an event a miracle who does not apprehend in some measure through it both the absolute demand and the final succour of God, and feel his spirit moved to that response of obedience to and trust in the divine purpose which is what we call faith ; for unless these are present it is doubtful whether there is any of that living apprehension of God through an event or events without which there can be no revelation, and therefore no miracle, according to the use of the terms we propose.

Now this use of the word miracle, which enables us to say that *all* miracles are revelations, undoubtedly covers without strain much of the meaning with which the religious mind has at various times and in different terminology invested the term. We shall see later that it does not cover all that is usually intended when the word miracle is used in its most pregnant meaning, but it certainly covers much.

Thus, first, the assimilating of the idea of miracle to the idea of revelation provides for that element of awareness of the supernatural which is undoubtedly included in it. As we saw, the primary religious significance of the super-natural is not the idea of the contranatural, but rather the idea of the ultimate as personal ; it indicates a reality which is not part of the natural order, nor yet separate from it, nor active only in suspension of it, but *above* it, in the sense of ruling it to the ends of a personal kingdom in which man is called to have a part. The experience of revelation is the becoming aware of the supernatural in this sense, and the experience of miracle, therefore, in so far as it is rightly assimilated to the experience of revelation, includes the same awareness.

Second, the assimilating of the idea of miracle to the idea of revelation preserves that awareness of God as active will

operative in events which is an essential part of the religious
meaning of miracle. Revelation means God actively thrusting His purpose of absolute demand and proffered succour
into the sphere of the individual's own preferences and
desires in relation to a situation in the real world ; it is
that meeting of will with will without which, as we have seen,
a personal reality is not known, and it involves that the
world has significance for God's will as well as for man's.
God's activity within history is thus involved in the very
idea of revelation as we have expounded it, and the same
thought is manifestly present in the idea of miracle.

Third, the assimilating of the idea of miracle to the idea of
revelation provides for the element of wonder and awe,
which, as the etymology indicates, is perhaps the most
obvious thing in the religious man's awareness of the
miraculous. For there can be no genuine awareness of
God's approach to the soul in what we have called revelation
without something of that reverberation in feeling which
is akin to wonder and awe, and which in default of exacter
terminology must be called wonder and awe, but which none
the less is *sui generis* and arises only in this relationship.

It is not unimportant in this connexion to insist on the
point just mentioned, and refuse to be led astray either by the
etymology or by the popular use of the word miracle. Some
writers, apparently unaware of the inevitable artificiality
and inadequacy of lumping together such finely graded
things as feelings under general, abstract terms, equate the
element of wonder in the apprehension of miracle with
the same element in non-religious experiences ; that is to
say, they relate it merely to the surprising and startling,
or the mysterious and inscrutable, quality of the supposed
miraculous event. Now it must be granted that a miraculous
event in the religious sense always has an arresting quality
to the one who experiences it ; it is an event which detaches
itself from the usual run of things. Also it has a mysterious

and inscrutable quality ; it is apprehended as springing from a reality which transcends human knowledge and control. But the important question is, what sort of arrestingness, and what sort of inscrutability, constitutes an event miraculous to the religious mind ? Plainly not any sort of arrestingness, for then any startling event would be a miracle, which is plainly not the case, even to the primitive mind ; and a miracle repeated often enough would cease to be one, which again is not the case—no Christian, for example, ever loses the wondering sense of the miracle of the divine pardon and leading, no matter how rich in these his life increasingly becomes. Plainly, also, not the mystery and inscrutability attaching to any event which at the moment transcends our power to explain it in terms of natural causation, for then any event of whose causation we are ignorant would be apprehended as miracle, which is not the case even in primitive minds ; and an event so apprehended would lose its miraculous quality in proportion as the natural causes involved were explored, which, again, is not the case—no genuinely religious mind could ever lose the sense, if he ever had it, of God's providential direction of events in relation to the crises of his own personal destiny, no matter what research might later reveal concerning the different series of natural causes involved. What sort of arrestingness and inscrutability then ? We can only say the arrestingness and inscrutability of *God*, that is to say, an arrestingness and inscrutability not definable in terms of, nor dependent on, our knowledge of natural processes and relationships at all. It is the arrestingness and inscrutability of *revelation*, as we have expounded that term, of an event or situation, which, without ceasing to be part of the natural continuum, is discerned as lying also within a dimension of the supernatural, as mediating the approach of the Eternal Personal to the soul. And the response in feeling is not just gaping

I

astonishment at the unusual or mysterious, but the wonder which is appropriate and peculiar to the apprehension of the divine.[1]

Fourth, the assimilating of the idea of miracle to the idea of revelation makes clear why it is impossible ever to establish by intellectual proof that quality of an event which makes it miraculous to the religious mind. For revelation, we have insisted, is God speaking to the individual personally, that is to say, in a way which is relevant to, and only understandable in terms of, the individual's own concrete situation ; and not only is God in the nature of the case, intellectually indemonstrable, but also it is impossible to take up a personal situation into a general proposition or syllogism without its concrete, historical, livingly personal quality vanishing in a cloud of abstractions. Each man's situation is entirely his own, and nobody else can ever be in it and make it his own in exactly the same sense.

[1] Cf. Heim, *Glaube und Denken* (2 Aufl.), p. 259. There is a sense in which the religious awareness of miracle, so far from being an awareness of the inexplicable and the inscrutable, is exactly the reverse. The religious man claims to know a good deal about that which lies behind the events in question, namely, that no less than God, the Eternal Personal is behind them, and through them is entering into relation with his situation and destiny. The miracle is not so much a mysterious inscrutable as a great illumination. It is a revelation, a " μυστήριον " in the N.T. sense. Wendland (*op. cit.*, p. 284) rightly insists that there is always an inexplicable in events even from the point of view of science, namely, the convergence of the different causal series, and this is important when we seek reflectively to relate the religious concept of miracle to the scientific view-point. But he is misleading in arguing from this to the element of mystery and inscrutability in the religious awareness of miracle, as though the specific inscrutability to which the mind wonderingly responds in the latter is precisely that which is involved in such limitation of scientific knowledge. The religious mind in its awareness of that which it calls miracle is quite remote from such an abstract philosophic idea ; it is filled with a living sense of God, and the element of mystery and inscrutability is that which is involved in all such awareness. Wendland himself says that the inexplicability of the convergence of causal series attaches to all events ; yet not all events are miracles. There must therefore be another element of mystery and inscrutability in the miraculous event. It is, we repeat, the mystery and inscrutability of God, as He makes Himself known to the soul of man.

Hence each man's revelation and miracle must be his own also, and no amount of argument will ever suffice to convince others of the reality of his transaction with God through them. To the rationalist this indemonstrability of miracle is sufficient to put the whole matter out of court as unworthy of consideration ; to the religious mind, when it understands itself and the sphere in which it moves, it is precisely this indemonstrability which is part of the certification that it is a genuinely personal dealing with the living God. Thus our Lord clearly realised that the most marvellous works were not effective to evoke in all and sundry a living and awed sense of God. On the contrary, His works of healing could be, and were, attributed to Beelzebub, and concerning some folk He said that they would not believe though one rose from the dead. In other words the power of an event to reveal God is a function, not of some general quality which can be established beyond the reach of cavil or question, but of its relevance to, and relationship with, at that par- ticular moment, the personal history and spiritual condition of the particular individualities contemplating it. What is a miracle to one is not to another. " Only those who believe through the miracle can believe in the miracle " ;[1] to all else it remains, no matter how unusual or mysterious, opaque, and its unusualness and mystery can without the least difficulty be explained away. An important illustra- tion of the same point is the impossibility of demonstrating that any prayer has ever been answered. The man who has prayed in any complex and difficult situation and then finds events so co-operating and converging that the way is opened up before him, has an awed and humbled sense of God at work in his life ; yet if the sceptic cares to say that it is all merely coincidence, it is not possible to give him a demonstrative proof to the contrary.

We may say, then, that all miracles are revelations, and

[1] Hunzinger, *op. cit.*, p. 45.

all that is essential in the meaning of the latter can be transferred to the former. Why, then, it may be asked, is the word miracle retained at all ? The answer is that the religious mind seems to need the word miracle to indicate a special type of revealing event ; so that whilst all that has been said so far covers much of what is intended by the word, it does not cover all. We may say that whilst from the religious angle all miracles are revelations, not all revelations are miracles. What then are those further qualities which distinguish some revealing events from others and constitute them specifically and pre-eminently miracles ?

We said above[1] that the relative prominence of the element of demand and the element of succour in the total awareness of God may differ according to the situation, though neither is ever wholly absent. Now, it seems to be generally true of those revealing events which the religious mind is disposed to designate pre-eminently miracles that in them the awareness of God as actively succouring human life tends to be dominant. The redemptive aspect of religion and the idea of miracle lie very close to one another. We do not mean to suggest that a clear-cut and consistent usage of the term miracle in this sense can be traced throughout the history of religions ; nothing is as clear-cut and consistent as that, least of all in religion. The idea of miracle as it emerges from the confusion of primitive beliefs in demons, magic, sorcery, into something specifically and identifiably religious, that is to say, into an idea having a special meaning in relation to *God*, is exceedingly difficult to trace in detail ; but the broad tendency is unmistakable. Whatever ambiguous shades of meaning may continue to attach to the word, speaking generally a miracle for the religious mind is pre-eminently an event in which God is apprehended as entering succouringly into a situation. Miracles may still be attributed to demons and sorcerers, but

[1] See p. 89.

entirely different manifestations of power are expected from the gods ; the latter are regarded, however dimly, as representatives of that more permanent order of the world on which human well-being rests, and as the protectors of the pious from the unholy tricks of demons, or even from the wickedness of evil men. In Christian usage, particularly as exemplified in the New Testament, this tendency culminates in an almost complete identification of the idea of miracle with the idea of redemption. The wonderful deeds of Jesus, and those His disciples are expected and empowered to do, and, back of these, God's supreme deed in sending Jesus and raising Him from the dead, are all regarded as manifestations of a new messianic age breaking in upon history, an age wherein those who respond in faith are released by the divine saving purpose from bondage to the powers of this world, and are assured of a part in the ultimate divine victory when all enemies shall be put under His feet.[1]

This description of miracle as an event, or events, in which God so reveals Himself that the awareness of Him as man's refuge and strength is dominant, is, however, still in a measure only preliminary. For it seems clear that not all revealing events of that type would as a rule be designated miracles by the religious mind with quite the same spontaneity and sense of the inevitability of the term. The word miracle is used very loosely even by religious folk, and it is possible to hear it applied in a very undefined, and even casual and unemotional, way to any experience in which the thought of God's succour to man is dominant ; yet whilst it *may* on occasion be used of any such event, there appears to be a certain special type of such events of which,

---

[1] 1 Cor. xv. 25. The whole chapter is instructive in that the thought passes so easily and swiftly, almost confusingly, between the miracle of Christ's resurrection to the ultimate victory of God, and to man's victory God over all his enemies, especially the arch-enemy death. Cf. Hogg, *Redemption from this World*, Chap. I. Hogg, I think, tends to confine the redemptive aspect too exclusively to the Christian conception of miracle.

we might almost say, it *must* be used by any save those who have schooled themselves never to use the term at all. It carries then a concentrated significance and an emotional reverberation which distinguishes it from, whilst it relates it to, the looser and less pregnant uses of the term. It is as though there were concentric rings of meaning to the term, the meaning growing the more focused and intense, the nearer the centre is approached. Or, to change the metaphor, the difference between the general class of events which, mediating the succour of God, *may*, and often are, loosely termed miraculous, and the special and narrower class of event which mediate it so overwhelmingly that they *must* be so termed, might be likened to the difference between a diffused electric charge which perhaps gives a tingle to all the atmosphere and a charge so concentrated that it discharges itself in a vivid flash of light.

The principle upon which this focalisation of meaning takes place is that *the more intensely personal and individual the succour of God is felt to be, the more appropriate and inevitable the word miracle becomes on the religious man's lips*. Rightly understood, in fact, as already said, in the category of miracle the experience of God as personal reaches its maximum concentration. Let us make this clear by examples.

Walking in a garden, or through the fields, a man of sensitive spirit may suddenly become livingly aware, through the contemplation of the beauty and richness and orderly reliability of nature, of the steadfast goodness of God towards man—including himself—in all his weakness and dependency. Such an experience is obviously impossible without some awareness of God as personal. It is an awareness of one aspect of the general providence of God, and in so far as it is a living religious awareness the heart may well be stirred to wonder and praise. Yet the religious man would not spontaneously call such a revelation of God to him at such a moment a miracle ; nor would he use the term of those orderly processes of nature which he apprehends as wonderful manifestations of the bounty and steadfastness and creative power of God.[1] Reference is, indeed, sometimes made to the " miracles of creation ", and we are bidden wonderingly to discern the miracles of God in the most humdrum familiarities of life, the growth of a plant, the pattern of a snowflake. We are far from suggesting that such phrases are improper, still less the sentiments they express ; yet such a usage of the term miracle can hardly be taken as spontaneous and typical. There is an element of philosophic theorising, perhaps even at times of self-conscious attitudinising, in it. That this is so, is shown by the fact that if such a line of thought be consistently carried through, it ends in the view that everything is a miracle, and the term is evacuated of any distinctive meaning at all, except the quite jejune one that there is, despite all our knowledge, a residuum of the mysterious in every event. If there is one thing quite certain in this connection it is that the word miracle on the religious man's lips indicates something distinctive which is *not* applicable, even after reflection, to all events indiscriminately. In other words, the more generalised the awareness of God's goodness and succour, the less the word miracle is applicable. And the reason for this is not, as is sometimes suggested, that apparent rarity or irregularity in an event is necessary to evoke wonder and the sense of the miraculous, as though the quality of the miraculous in events were merely the reflex of our own emotions, but rather, as we shall see shortly, that the more generalised the awareness of God's goodness and succour is, the less intensely individual and

[1] We might suggest, in anticipation and illustration of what is to be said shortly, that if the man had been in a mood of profound despair and anxiety, and crying out for a recovery of faith in God, and if, then, this revelation had come, the word miracle would have been much more likely to come to his lips.

personal it is, though in the nature of the case it can never become completely impersonal.[1]

Again, a religious mind may suddenly become aware of the way in which events, unnoticed by him at the time of their occurrence, have conspired together to equip him for, and direct him to, an opportunity and task, from which now his whole life is seen to derive its significance and purpose. He catches a glimpse of a pattern being woven, and of divine fingers at work weaving it ; or in other words, he becomes aware of " special providences " in his life, and through them of that wider, overshadowing general providence of God which grasps all events in its purpose and is relating them to the individual destinies of men and women, even when they know it not. Now in this case the word miracle is far more likely to come to the lips than in the case just considered, in order to indicate both the sudden supervention of this moment of vision, and, still more, those providential congruencies in events which have now, perhaps for the first time, been discerned. And the reason is precisely that God's concern in human life is now apprehended in a less generalised, and therefore more personal and individual, way. God's activity is apprehended as being, as it were, more focused on, and expressed through, the individual

[1] Stange and others have suggested that it is the mark of the Biblical conception of miracle that the most orderly processes of nature are referred to the direct activity of God and are in principle included under the term. Doubtless for the Biblical writers God's activity is manifested in everything (as, indeed, it must be, in a sense, for any religious mind), but there is no question that there is a distinction drawn between such regularity of creative and sustaining power and specific saving activity in relation to special and unusual situations of need ; nor that, pre-eminently, the idea of the miraculous is attached to the latter. As a rule, reference to the marvels of God's creative and sustaining power leads up immediately to the thought of His specific succours to men and women. The former indicates the necessary presupposition of miracle, namely that God has power over all as Creator ; it is the latter, the fact that He can and does use His power in a redemptive and saving act in response to extraordinary need, which constitutes the miracle itself. (See, e.g., Job v. 9-11 ; Ps. cvii ; Isa. xl. 26-31.)

destiny. Yet here, again, we seem not yet to have reached the most spontaneous, inevitable and typical usage of the word, though we have come nearer to it. Many might thus discern God's providential dealings with them, and rejoice in and wonder at them, without the word miracle coming to the lips at all, and that not because of a shrinking from using the word in any circumstances, but rather because of an instinctive sense of its not being quite appropriate just there. What lies behind this sense of its inappropriateness ? This at least in part, that in such circumstances there is still attaching to the thought of God's providential ordering of human life, something of what may be called unfocused generality. The mind moves immediately from the awareness of divine providence governing a particular disposition of events to the thought of it governing all events, and the "special providence" is perceived as much as an instance of a quite general principle of divine foresight and governance embracing all things as an *ad hoc* immediate adjustment to an individual situation. But this is *pro tanto* to make the word miracle inappropriate, for it implies that rightly regarded all events are miracles, which is, once more, to evacuate the word of any special meaning. How easily the thought of individual providences moves towards a highly generalised and therefore relatively impersonal thought of all-embracing principles of divine governance is perhaps indicated by the way in which Schleiermacher, despite his deep piety, could identify the religious awareness of God's providence with the acknowledgment of a cosmic regularity present in all events.[1] The impersonal pantheism which colours Schleiermacher's thinking is well known, and it is significant, therefore, that he expressly commits himself to the view that miracle is only the religious name for any event.[2]

Where then must we look for those experiences wherein

[1] *The Christian Faith*, (Eng. Trans.) par. 46.
[2] *Reden über die Religion*, 2 Rede.

the word miracle comes with a maximum of spontaneity
and inevitability to the lips of the religious man ? The
answer is, in that relationship to God which we call prayer,
especially as it arises out of a deep sense of need and takes
the form of believing petition. An instance which came
under the direct observation of the writer may perhaps be
permitted.

A mother was informed by the doctors that, so far as
medical science could judge, her baby could not possibly
recover from sickness ; whereupon she called a friend, who,
like herself, was a Christian believer, and asked him to pray
with her that God would restore the child. So they prayed,
and within a few hours the child was on the way to a recovery which confounded all the experience of the doctors,
as they were frank to admit, even including one whose
whole philosophy of life tended to profound scorn of " all
that sort of thing ". Now we are not concerned at the
moment to discuss what such a happening may imply as to
the nature of prayer, its conditions and limits, or how it
may be related to our general conception of the world and
of God's relationship to it. The point at the moment is that
the word which came instantly to the lips of the two people
who had prayed, both of whom were intelligent and cultured,
was " miracle ". They did not say " this is providential " ;
they said, " this is a miracle ", and no other word seemed
appropriate to the awed sense of having transaction with
the succouring will of God in a personal situation of critical
need. Perhaps, then, if we examine this instance we shall
discover what essentially constitutes the religious sense of
miracle when the word is used with its most pregnant and
distinctive meaning.

Three things at least would appear, from this instance, to
be indispensable.

First, there is an awareness of serious crisis or need or
threat of disaster in the personal life, and of helplessness to

deal with it adequately and victoriously through the exercise of ordinary, unaided human powers. Second, there is a more or less conscious and explicit turning to God for assistance. Third, there is an awareness of an *ad hoc* response of God to the situation and to man's petitioning inadequacy in it, so that the crisis is met, the need satisfied, the danger averted, in an event, or combination of events, which would not have taken place had man not so petitioned and God so acted.

We may observe how each of these three points contributes something toward taking the experience out of the realm of the merely general and bringing it within the sharper focus of the individual and personal.

Thus, concerning the awareness of crisis or need or threat of disaster, and of the necessity for divine action if there is to be adequate dealing with these, we may note two things. First, that in situations of this kind the mind of man is concentrated in a peculiarly intense way on his own fate and destiny as an individual seeking a significance for his own being over against those natural forces which seem to have him entirely in their grip. In the ordinary routine of life, when events unfold in a smooth and satisfactory way, there is no special stimulus for man to distinguish himself from nature ; he seems to be part of a beneficent and sustaining and all-embracing cosmic process. The sense of his own personal significance, whilst doubtless never altogether absent, is never so sharply and even painfully focused and defined as when it seems to be about to be engulfed. And this is not less so, when the mind in its prayer for divine aid is concentrated on the need of another person or of a number of others, rather than on its own. Second, when situations of this critical kind arise, there is in the religious mind an awareness of there being at work in them forces which have a relative independence of God. For otherwise it would not be possible to petition God about them. There is a feeling that the situation either is not what God wills, or will not unfold as God wills, if left to the working out of its own immanent processes. Here we confront again, only now within the intimate intensity of personal need, that triadic relationship of God, man, and the world which we saw earlier is indispensable to the experience of God as personal. The all-embracing unity of things must be broken if man's being is to have any genuine significance as personal; God's will must not be a force which runs unimpeded and irresistible through all being, nor man's will be merely a phase of it; there must be independencies and tensions, thus giving opportunity for genuine creativeness and co-operation. In the situation of trouble and the cry to God's succouring purpose, the sense of this duality and brokenness of being, and yet also of a victory over it to be won through a personal (i.e. not monistic) relationship between man's will and God's, reaches a maximum.

This leads to the next point, namely, the turning to God for assistance. Here, even more plainly, we observe the lifting of the situation out of the general scheme of things even a general scheme conceived in terms of divine providence, into something more intensely individual and personal. The prayer to God for assistance implies the belief that God's will is determined in its acting by its relation with my will, and that it is not imprisoned within the mechanical necessities of the physical universe, but can act freely as an operative cause within them and above them. Both these things are of the heart and essence of personal relationship. I can be personally related to my neighbour only if my will is determined by its meeting with his, and is *not* determined by merely mechanical forces; only on that basis, as we saw earlier, can anything in the nature of trust arise. So in the cry to God for help.

So finally, in the intense awareness of an *ad hoc* response of God whereby the situation unfolds in a way that would not otherwise have happened. It is not apprehended as an example of a general system so contrived that in any case everything that happens is for the good of each and all, but rather as an instance of God bringing about what would not otherwise happen and saving me at a time when otherwise I should perish. It is God dealing with a unique and unrepeatable situation in an individual destiny ; it is God knowing me in some sense *by name*. This sense of a direct and individually relevant activity on the part of God is further enhanced by the fact that to the religious mind such divine activity is not an everyday occurrence ; thus again it is lifted out of the merely general. Life is not all crisis, and just as we saw it is not all revelation in the direct personal sense of the term, so even more it is not all miracle. There are long stretches wherein nothing more is required than that men should work with the ordinary forces of nature, using industry, knowledge, and common sense ; and these are as necessary to the development of personality as that they should not be left without resources in prayer and in the divine succour at times of special crisis and need. An adjusting intervention of God at every point would stultify a truly personal relationship to God just as much as a complete refusal to intervene at any point. It is part of the essential personal quality of the awareness of miracle that it should in any one experience be relatively rare.[1]

The word miracle, then, reaches its most intense and characteristic meaning for the religious mind in the answering of prayer for succour in a situation apprehended as being

---

[1] This might be illustrated by the relation of a human father to his child. If he did everything for his child, he could never enter into deep personal relations with it, for it would have no personality to enter into relations with. But equally little could a father who did nothing, not even in a crisis, enter into such relations, for nothing in the way of love and trust and gratitude could develop. There was, therefore, we may suppose, something of genuine religious insight in the view of the older theologians that miracles are *supra et contra naturam*, and yet also rare events. Both thoughts were often unfortunately expounded and supported

peculiarly critical in personal destiny. Some might wish to
extend its meaning to include all answers to prayer, and no
objection could be taken to that ; we have been concerned
merely to discover what is its most pregnant meaning on
the lips of the religious man, what he means to say by it
when it springs almost unavoidably to his lips. From this
analysis we have seen that it is in some ways the most
intensely personal of all the categories of man's personal
relationship to God. This is why, as was indicated in
the introduction, the religious mind has always tended to
cling to the concept of miracle, even when it has not itself
clearly understood the reason, and even been a little shame-
faced about it. It is a clinging to the idea of personality in
God, in face of all those theories which would reduce the
universe to a system of iron laws and banish personality
from the ultimate altogether.[1]

by dubious reasoning, but there was at work the profound religious instinct
so to interpret God and the world that the significance of human personality was unimpaired, and room retained for its highest development.
In the thought of God acting redemptively *supra et contra naturam* it was
insisted that man should not be swallowed up in natural process, but should
achieve a truly personal life in mastery over it through the grace of God.
In the thought of God so acting only rarely and in relation to man's cry
of need in crises of his life, it was insisted that man should not be swallowed
up in God, but should be under the disciplinary necessity of learning the
uses of, and adjusting himself to, a relatively fixed natural order.

[1] Hence those who seek to accommodate the religious belief in miracle
to the demands of science by talking vaguely of miracles as examples of
" higher laws," seem at times to miss the point at issue. If by " higher
laws " are meant laws which are fundamentally of the same mechanical
type as those which supposedly govern the processes of nature, then
nothing that really matters to religion has been conserved. If, on the other
hand, what is meant are laws of a fundamentally different type from such
mechanical inevitabilities, a type appropriate to the spontaneity and
freedom of personal relations, then the main question is still left unanswered, even though it be not unimportant sometimes to insist (as e.g.
below, p. 145) that to believe in miracle is not necessarily to believe in a
capricious universe—the question, that is, whether the two orders of reality
in which are comprised the two sorts of regularity, the lower and the
higher, the mechanical and the personal, can be included without contradiction in a single system of experience and knowledge. See below, p. 157.
Cf. also Tennant, *Miracle and its Philosophical Presuppositions*, p. 29.

The view of the significance of the idea of miracle we have propounded gives a new understanding of the element of wonder which enters into the experience of the miraculous. We said that it is misconceived to relate this merely to the startling quality of the event, or to its supposed infringement of natural laws ; it springs rather out of the awareness of God, and it has that unique quality of feeling which attaches, and attaches only, to such awareness. But now we may discern another factor in it, one which springs out of the fact that there is an awareness of God as personally succouring the individual in his need. The miracle surprises and evokes wonder because it is the manifestation of the active goodness of God to man. Here we touch one of the ultimates of human personality in its responses to another personality. The direct, gratuitous, personal love and generosity of another always come with something of the shock of surprise, and draw forth amazed gratitude, not because of a misanthropic expectancy of the reverse, but because that is how the chords of a human soul not altogether depraved are meant to vibrate in response to this sort of experience in the personal world. To respond otherwise, to take succouring love for granted, is, we feel, a spiritual deformity.[1] The same holds of the soul's response to God in miracle. To the awfulness and wonder of the Eternal there is added the awfulness and wonder of an Eternal who in succouring love condescends to the children of men. The ultimate miracle is the miracle of the love of God.

[1] Cf. Jesus' recoil from the ingratitude of the lepers,—Luke xvii. 11.

CHAPTER VIII

PRAYER

THE discussion of the religious meaning of miracle ha
led us to the activity and experience of prayer. T
the further consideration of the latter we now turn.

If belief in revelation is, in one form or anothe
characteristic of all living religion, so also, and even mo
obviously perhaps, is the activity of prayer. Indeed, it
generally recognised by students of religion that prayer
not merely *a* common characteristic of religion, but rathe
its central phenomenon, " the very hearthstone of a
piety ".[1] All that distinguishes man's specifically religiou
response to his world from his response in morals, science
or art comes to expression in the act of prayer, so that, a
Ménégoz says, " the genius who could write a history o
prayer would provide in so doing an exhaustive history o
religion."[2]

Yet to say that prayer is a universal characteristic o
religion in addition to belief in revelation may be mis
leading, for the truth is that both are rooted in the primordia
religious awareness of God as personal. In the thought o
revelation there is expressed the sense of God's activ
approach as personal to the spirit of man ; in prayer ther
is expressed the answering activity of man, as self-consciou
personality, towards God. The two things are distinguish
able in thought, and both logically and religiously the ide

[1] Heiler, *Das Gebet*, p. 1.
[2] *Op. cit.*, p. 6. For references showing the agreement of scholars o
the substance of this paragraph, see Heiler, *op. cit.*, pp. 1–4 ; supple
mentary references are given by Ménégoz.

of God's revelation is the prior one ; but in the actuality of religious experience they are indivisibly united, though doubtless with varying degrees of emphasis relative to one another at different times. To be livingly aware of God's approach to the soul as personal is not possible without there being some response which is already of the order of prayer ; and to pray a prayer which is in the least degree lifted above the mere mechanical repetition of formulæ is not possible without there being some sense of one's life having significance for an ultimate reality of an actively personal kind. We confront here again that duality or tension which is necessary to constitute a relationship specifically personal. In the soul's rapport with God the duality of "I and Thou" is manifested, in part, in the duality of revelation and prayer.

That prayer is essentially a response of man's spirit to the ultimate as personal is shown by the fact that in its most living and spontaneous utterance, alike in its primitive and most exalted forms, it takes the form of petition. A candid examination of the facts hardly leaves this open to question. The etymology and cognate usages of the word in most languages indicates that if prayer is the heart of religion, then petition is the heart of prayer.[1] But petition has no meaning except as directed to a personal will.

Yet if prayer and petition to the divine will as personal have been historically inseparable from one another, we have to face the fact that it is precisely the petitionary aspect of prayer which, from the earliest times, has called forth question and criticism from reflective minds. By considering these questions and criticisms we shall be able to grasp more fully what the essence of prayer is and how

---

[1] E.g. *beten* and *bitten* in German. In English it is by no means a merely affected manner of speech to say "I pray you" instead of "I beseech or ask you". In Presbyterian Courts the content of a petition is called its prayer.

K

profoundly it is involved in man's personal relationship with
God. Two positions may be distinguished.

(1) First, there are those who reject the idea of God as
personal and either eliminate prayer altogether, or retain
it merely as an exercise in mental adjustment to the world.

(2) Second, there are those who, keeping the idea of God
as personal, retain prayer, but eliminate *either* petition
altogether *or* petition for what is vaguely called " things "
as distinct from " attitudes ".

(1) The attempt made by some to retain a place for
certain states of mind called religious along with a denial of
personal quality in the ultimate has already been briefly
considered.[1] The criticisms which were urged lie equally
against the attempt, made usually by the same thinkers, to
retain a place for the cultivation of such states of mind by
what they call prayer. Perhaps it is in the end purely a
matter of definition of terms, and if anyone likes to dignify by
the name prayer such self-communings to which, *ex hypothesi*,
there is, and can be, no response from beyond the self and its
necessary internal mechanisms, he is entitled to do so. To us,
such a usage seems an almost culpable playing fast and loose
with words. In so far as such exercises are carried through
with a full and explicit awareness that the ultimate with
which man has to deal is impersonal, and that all that is
going on is a process of self-adjustment, then it is *not* prayer
in any justifiable usage of the term ; for, apart from other
reasons, whatever prayer is, it is something which is related
to a spontaneous and unbidden impulse in the average
human heart, whereas such " prayer " has so little relation
to anything spontaneous and unbidden in the human heart,
that very few want to engage in it, or trying to engage in it,
ever make anything much of it. On the other hand, if something is made of it and it becomes real prayer, then that
is because the intellectual conviction that the ultimate is

[1] See above, p. 29 f.

impersonal is no longer explicit and dominant, but has rather retreated before a more primordial, if dim, sense that the personality is *en rapport* with an ultimate reality other than, yet not uncongenial to or discontinuous with, its own deepest life.

(2) The motives which lead some, whilst not denying personal quality to God, to eliminate petition from prayer altogether, are of various kinds and not always easy to unravel from one another. Thus in some instances the position seems to be due, in part, to a " hang-over " of that impersonalistic monism towards which all philosophic speculation seems to have an initial bias ; so that while there is no explicit denial of personal quality in God and much is said that seems to presuppose it, there is none the less an implicit tendency not to take it in a thoroughgoing way. Rather the unconscious tendency is to tone down as much as possible those aspects of spontaneous religion, such as petitionary prayer, where the thought of God as personal comes to clear and emphatic expression.

Leaving, however, this Spinozistic bias of the philosophic mind on one side, there appear to be two main motives at work. There are first motives of a specifically religious kind, and, second, there is the motive to do justice to what are felt to be the inescapable demands of scientific method and theory.

First, then, motives of a specifically religious kind.

The position here seems to be that petitionary prayer is a primitive and even childish form of piety, which it is the mark of a mature and genuinely spiritual religion to leave behind. God is conceived to be the infinite and eternal reality in which all possible riches of being, including personal being, are already actualised. The things of time and sense are already grasped within, part of, this un-imaginable wealth of being, and through them it shines forth, if we can only get our eyes open to see it. The supreme act and achievement of piety is to seek, and enter into, a state of mind in which the eyes are thus open to God, and to surrender the soul so that it rests thankfully in Him, becomes, indeed, itself in a new way aglow with the peace and beauty of the eternal. The highest prayer *is* this state of mind. Sometimes it may be attained through the contemplation of the loveliness of creation. Sometimes a window may open on eternity through the simplest, everyday objects. Or the sense of the Eternal may break through the innermost life of the soul, lifting it to a new level of accomplishment and selfless joy. To the thinker grasping new truth, to the artist fashioning beauty, to the loving spirit giving himself in service to another, there comes a blessed sense of enlargement, of the limitations of the self being transcended, of being one with the source of all life which is God. In the achievement of such states of communion, it is urged, the attitude of demand and petition is an interruption and a hindrance, and must be left behind.

Why, then, is the attitude of petition such an interruption and hindrance? Here the view passes, on the basis of its positive ideals, to negative criticism.

It is said that the attitude of petition is superfluous; God does not need man to tell Him, or to stir Him into bringing to pass, what should be; for every created thing is already grasped within the divine life and purpose which are wholly good and trustworthy. Our part is to open our spirits to His spirit, and to put ourselves in all our living " in tune " with His purpose as it unfolds itself in all the appointments of life. But petition is not only superfluous; it is, it is said, positively impious. It rests unconsciously on the presumptuous idea of a Deity who does not know His own mind, and whose will can be constrained this way or that by ours. Moreover, precisely because it is fundamentally impious, petitionary prayer reacts injuriously on the moral and spiritual life. Thus there is a well-nigh irresistible tendency in it to lapse into the eudæmonism which is so marked a feature of primitive piety ; God becomes primarily a means to our ends, an ally in the fulfilment of our desires. In petitionary prayer, it is said, it is almost impossible to put God at the centre of the picture and not the self. Furthermore petitionary prayer is apt to weaken moral effort. It leads to the expectancy of divine interventions in the normal course of things, and so becomes a substitute for our own endeavours. Finally, it is affirmed, petitionary prayer is not compatible with that poise and serenity of mind which are the outcome of complete trust in God. Petition and trust are, in fact, contradictory terms. The man who asks things, believing that his asking will make a difference, anxiously awaits results ; and if his prayer is not answered, he is beset with doubts whether he has prayed enough, or prayed aright, or even whether the God to whom he has prayed can be real at all. The only way to escape all this is either to eliminate petition altogether, or to confine it simply to asking for help to achieve that blessed state of mind in which it is no longer necessary.[1]

What is to be said to this ? It must be fully granted that on its positive side it emphasizes certain things which are true and valuable elements in the religious life, and that on its negative side it emphasizes certain real dangers in petitionary prayer. Nobody would wish to reduce prayer merely to petition, and least of all to those perverted forms of petition with which most of us are unpleasantly familiar.

---

[1] " Pray till prayer makes you cease to pray "—F. W. Robertson, (*Sermons*, People's edition, 4th Series, p. 32.) On the last point mentioned this school of thought divides. The more thoroughgoing, eliminating petition altogether, would see the highest type of prayer simply in recollection and meditation, so that if it finds verbal expression it is in the indicative rather than the optative mood—" I commit myself to the Eternal Love ", " I open my soul to the Spirit of God ", and so on. Others find no difficulty in asking for the divine help that they may so commit themselves. The former seems the more consistent, the latter less remote from the truth.

The view above stated, however, too lightly assumes that the only thing to do is to eliminate petition altogether. There is another way, and that is to cleanse and ennoble it. We shall try to show, first, that petition is, and must ever remain, the heart and centre of prayer, if the latter is to be the expression of a genuinely personal relationship with God ; that the reason why it appears early in the religious life of mankind, even though it be in crude forms strongly tinged with egotistic eudæmonism, is not that it is childish and must be discarded, like milk-teeth, but that it is basic and must abide all through, like the skeleton on which the body at all stages of its development is built ; that to eliminate it from prayer, therefore, so far from helping man to the proper maturity of his personal life in relation to God is definitely to hinder and prevent it. We shall then try to show in the light of this, that the negative criticisms of petitionary prayer, whilst true of some forms of it, are not necessarily true of all ; yet even those forms of which they are true are by no means wholly bad, being perversions of, rather than total aberrations from, the fundamental truths of man's intercourse with God.

The indispensability of petition is seen so soon as it is realised that petition is an expression within the sphere of the soul's conscious relationship with God of that in which a specifically personal life focuses and unifies itself, namely the will. We have already insisted, from more than one angle, that the awareness of ourselves and of others as personal entities is centred in the consciousness of will, in the consciousness that we are not functions of one another, or of our environment generally, but are in a measure in charge of our own destiny. We are under the continuous necessity of making decisions ; of suspending and controlling impulse and desire in the light of ends with which, as we significantly say, we identify *ourselves ;* of making *history,* our own and that of our society, as distinct from being our-

demands—issues in, and cannot but issue in, petition, even
though it be of a dim and inarticulate kind.

Petition, therefore, lies at the heart of the awareness of
God, and so far from being a primitive immaturity, it is
bound up with man's status as a personal being called to
find his true maturity in the harmonising of his will with
God's. It might be argued, however, that the facts as
analysed would justify only the petition to be enabled to
achieve the true norm of our being which is a righteous life
completely surrendered to God. There is a sense in which
that is so ; for such a prayer, abstractly considered, includes all other prayers. Yet that is precisely the inadequacy
of such a narrowly restricted conception of prayer, namely
that it is so highly generalised and abstract. The yearning
of the soul towards its highest good in God, which is the
fons et origo of all petition, does not as a matter of fact exist
as one interest along with others such as sex, getting food,
attaining knowledge, etc. ; it is only the artificial isolation
of it in thought which apparently gives it that status.
Rather it underlies all other interests, and comes to expression, and seeks its fruition in the binding of them together
in the unity of personal life.[1] We put it another way by
saying that the immanent teleology of human personality
can be realised only in and through the latter's intercourse
with its actual historical environment, and it has no purchase
on that environment save through the multifarious special
interests of our daily life. We put it still another way by
saying that God's will meets ours in absolute demand and
final succour in our present, actual historical occasions ;
thus, for example, God's will is not something which has to
be done in addition to, or by negation of, getting married,
or earning a living, but in and through getting married and
earning a living. Petitionary prayer, therefore, if it is not
to be an unreal, abstract thing, is bound to be continually

[1] See above, p. 41.

expanding and contracting from the general desire to be surrendered to God's will and to be rich in Him, to the particular interests which fill the daily life and in the pursuit of which the larger ends of personality can alone be achieved.

Approached in this way, the criticisms of petitionary prayer set forth above can be seen in their true proportions. To take each point in turn :

The suggestion that petitionary prayer is superfluous inasmuch as God's holy purpose is already directed to our good and is seeking in all things to flow into and take possession of our being, entirely overlooks the possibility that the divine purpose may be such that petitionary prayer is indispensable to its realisation. That it is so indispensable is evident when once the deeply personal nature of God's ends with man is fully grasped. Petitionary prayer is part of the soul's response to God's challenge and invitation to it to become *through* co-operation with Him a personality more and more fitted *for* co-operation with Him ; it is one of the things by which, under earthly conditions, the soul grows in stature as a son of God and in readiness for that which in its consummation transcends earthly conditions altogether.

The suggestion that petitionary prayer is presumptuous, inasmuch as it seeks to constrain the divine will, rests on the same failure to grasp the personal quality of the divine dealing with man and what that of necessity implies. It is indeed difficult to see why it should be reckoned more consistent with the divine honour to be a will which moves in a sort of undeviating, mechanical push to its end, rather than one which, without abating in the least its essential consistency or the assurance of its ultimate victory, can take up into itself responses to the personal needs and petitions of men. Nay, just because the end it is seeking is personal, such personal responses must be included. The essence of a personal relationship is precisely, as has already been said, that one will acts differently from what it would otherwise act because it meets another will, because another will is part of the situation in relation to which it is acting. This alone makes an ethical universe possible. The objection is, in fact, a projection into God of our own egotistic and mechanised conception of will-power as power to ignore or override other wills ; under cover of zeal for God's honour, it depersonalises Him.[1]

The suggestion that petitionary prayer almost of necessity becomes eudæmonistic, making God the servant of our ends, undoubtedly points to a real and insidious danger, of which account must be taken. A careful analysis of the eudæmonistic aspect of prayer, however, shows that it should not be, for all its admitted perversions, dismissed out of hand. If petition be, on its subjective side, the expression of the soul's profound interest in its own highest self-fulfilment—an interest which, we have insisted, is not in isolation from, but is rather the underlying unity of, the more specialised interests and activities of life—and, on its objective side, is the expression of its awareness of God as final succour, then a eudæmonistic element is not only unavoidable, but also eminently proper. Perversion arises when it gets separated from the other aspect of the soul's intercourse with God, namely the awareness of Him as absolute demand. The eudæmonism of the primitive prayer for flocks and crops, etc., can, like its anthropomorphism, be very easily misinterpreted. It is surrounded, and sustained, by the awareness of the god, not as a magnified human being from whom benefits may be " cadged ", as from other human beings, but as—in Ménégoz's words—" a sovereign power radically different from all that is human, yet consenting, nevertheless, by virtue of its own free act, to have intercourse with mortal man. . . . If in so-called eudæmonist

[1] Cf. Stange, *Wunder und Heilsgeschichte*, p. 56.

religion man tends to make his god an auxiliary, or accomplice, in the pursuit of his own vital and ' profane ' interests, it is because, even then, the god is apprehended as logically independent, as actively sovereign, as accomplishing freely a work, according to his own laws—a work perhaps of a very narrow, material, political, fragmentary kind, yet none the less a work which only the god can do, namely one of succour and preservation."[1] Nor, we may suppose, is the awareness of God as absolute demand altogether absent from such prayers ; however dimly, however submerged for the moment in the clamour of personal need, the consciousness is present that man has no right to ask for benefits without offering obedience. To say that the obedience is merely offered as a bribe leaves unexplained why just that sort of bribe should be considered necessary ; plainly there is coming to expression a prior awareness that God is at one and the same time absolute demand and final succour, and that it is precisely this which constitutes him God.[2]

The inescapable eudæmonistic element in prayer is evidenced by the fact that those who would seek to avoid it by eliminating petition and reducing prayer to the cultivation of mystical states of awareness of, and absorption in, the Eternal, themselves in a more refined way tumble into it again. For the seeking of the good things of this world through God there is substituted the seeking of beatific states of consciousness through God, and there is no question that the latter can be just as egotistic, though doubtless in a less naïve way, as the former. To pursue the satisfaction of a state of mind, even though it be through the disciplines of the *via purgativa*, the *via illuminativa*, and the *via unitiva*, is not obviously less eudæmonistic than to pursue the

---

[1] *Op. cit.*, p. 230.

[2] Jacob's vow (Gen. xxviii. 20) has an unpleasant sound, but clearly there is expressed in it, even if in a perverse way, the awareness of God both as succour and demand.

satisfaction of the state of the pocket-book. The lurking egotism of this type of thought reveals itself in the fact that it often issues in an identification of the self with God. We are bidden " sink into ourselves to find God ", " to release the latent divine within us ", " to become ourselves bits of divinity ", and so on.[1]

The problem, then, is not to eliminate the eudæmonistic element from prayer, but to cleanse and elevate it by giving it its proper emphasis in relation to other things and direct-ing it to proper ends. We may lay down the general principle, already hinted at, that the eudæmonistic element in prayer begins to be perverted at the point, and to the degree, that it becomes isolated from the awareness of God as absolute demand requiring that at any cost His will should be done in the world. The primitive eudæmonistic prayer for the good things of life is right in so far as it expresses the conviction that the will of God is directed to man's succour in and through the circumstances of this present world ; it is wrong in so far as, in the clamant egotism of human nature, it too easily identifies the will of God, and the succour which He seeks to bring, with its own desires. The more refined eudæmonistic seeking of a blessed state of consciousness in God is right in so far as it expresses a reaction from such turning of God into an ally of human desires ; it is wrong in that it tends to lose the sense of God as holy will, and of the world as the sphere in which it here and now must be served. The former tends to cheapen God ; the latter to depersonalise Him ; and of the two the latter is the more serious error. In a later chapter we shall try to show how both these dangers are avoided in that type of prayer which arises out of the heart of the Christian experience of reconciliation.

The answer to the suggestion that petitionary prayer is apt to weaken man's own efforts in the management of his

---

[1] I have picked up these phrases from addresses heard at various times.

life, leading him to leave to God what he ought to do for
himself, has already been indicated in what has been said.
The making of prayer a substitute for our own endeavours
arises from the isolation of the sense of God as succour from
the sense of Him as absolute demand, and the avoidance of
it is not in the elimination of petition but in the emancipation of it from such merely egotistic perversion. Moreover,
since petition is part of man's response to the summons of
God to be a genuine personality and to rule his world,
it is, in its most spontaneous forms, always prayer for help
in this rather than for exemption from it. Indeed the
prayer of petition is in a way more compatible with
active endeavour than that attitude of mind which
would see no place for petition at all. For petition expresses
the confidence that the ultimate reality of man's world is
not uncongenial or unresponsive to his life task, wherea.
the petitionless man is always in danger of falling into a
fatalistic despair which sees man, for all his endeavours, the
plaything of forces over which in the last resort neither he,
nor any power the least concerned with him, has any
control.

This leads to the answer to the last criticism, namely
that petitionary prayer and complete trust in God are
incompatible attitudes. The answer is that, whilst this may
be true of certain types of petitionary prayer, it is not
necessarily true of petitionary prayer as such. We would
say, indeed, on the contrary, that in proportion as
petitionary prayer is released from merely egotistic clamour,
the exact opposite is the case. It is an essential element in
a proper trust in, and submissiveness to, God. The man
who is in the habit of bringing petitions to God because he
believes that his heart's desires are of interest to God and
can, through prayer, be linked to a larger wisdom and more
effective power than his own, is in a better mood for accepting whatever may happen than a man who has schooled

himself never to ask for what he desires at all. There is an intimacy, a trustfulness, an essentially personal quality in making known our petitions unto God which moulds the whole character and enables it to accept the untoward event, when it comes, unembittered and unafraid. But the character which is moulded by the other type of prayer is apt to be of a different sort. It is apt to approach to the merely stoical, and at times somewhat egotistically attitudinising, temper of " I am the captain of my soul, my head is bloody, but unbowed ". It is very much to be suspected that those who seek to exercise a purely non-petitionary type of prayer are unconsciously working with a conception of God which is remote from spontaneous piety, and certainly from the Christian conception of Him. The attitude of acceptance of, and surrender to, the divine appointments is a necessary element in all but the most childish prayer, but when it is isolated from petition and made the whole of prayer, the thought of God has taken a shift from that of a personal Father to that of an impersonal cosmic order which may be good, but in which a truly personal relationship with God, of the human will with the divine, can hardly find place. Jesus was not less, but more, able to say " Nevertheless not my will, but thine, be done " because He had previously asked that the cup might pass from Him. The two petitions were part of a single filial relationship of His spirit to His Father.

The second type of motive which impels some to seek to eliminate petition from prayer springs, we said, from the desire to do justice to what are felt to be the inescapable demands of scientific method and theory. This confronts us with the problem which we more than once came in sight of in Chapter VI where we enquired into the significance of the concept of miracle in living religion. The result of our enquiry was to find the essential meaning of miracle in the

answering of petition. The word miracle, when religiously
used, indicates the point where the living apprehension of
God as personal reaches a peculiar maximum ; it springs to
the lips when there is an awareness of an *ad hoc* response of
God to an occasion of need and man's petitionary inadequacy in it, so that the need is met in an event, or
combination of events, which, it is felt, *would not have taken
place had man not so petitioned and God so acted*. That is to
say, the religious awareness of miracle involves an objective
element ; it affirms that events take place through the
initiative of God. Apart from such an affirmation miracle
has no distinctive meaning and petitionary prayer no basis.
But, it is said, does not that involve that the laws, the
immanent cause-effect necessities, of nature are broken
through by God in order to meet an individual need ?

This is a difficulty which weighs heavily on many minds,
and the result is that either petition is eliminated altogether, or it is engaged in with a lurking sense that it is not
quite intellectually respectable, and almost certainly futile
The compromise made by some of not praying for external
events to happen, but only praying for the right attitude to
whatever events may happen, is obviously only a subterfuge
and does not meet the difficulty. For a mental attitude is
an event, and scientifically considered, is as much within
the causal nexus of the natural order as any other. To pray
to God to change our attitudes is as much a request to bring
about something which would not otherwise happen as it is
to pray to Him to change the weather.

It is necessary to consider these difficulties at some length

CHAPTER IX

MIRACLE AND THE LAWS OF NATURE

WE may begin by setting on one side two possible misconceptions. In the first place, to affirm an event to be a miracle, in the sense in which we have used the term, is not to abrogate what is sometimes referred to as the causal principle, the principle, that is, that every event must have a sufficient cause or reason. It is merely to affirm that into its causation there has entered the will of God acting relevantly to a human situation in a way in which it does not enter into the causation of other events.[1] The causal principle, so far from being abrogated, is presupposed. Nor, in the second place, is the principle of order in the universe infringed ; for the religious man never questions that the divine responses to prayer are governed by a consistency of wisdom which may be trusted even when it cannot be fully understood, and which, so far as it can be understood, can be at least partially expressed in the form of a general principle. The point is, in a way, superfluous, for it is impossible to think at all except on the basis of an orderly interrelation of events. It is only necessary to mention it because belief in miracle is at times dismissed out of hand as though it involved such an impossible mental acrobatic feat.

The question, therefore, is not one of causation as against non-causation, or of order against disorder, but whether a certain type of causation and order, namely that involved in the idea of God initiating events in accordance with His

---

[1] This does not mean that there is not another sense in which the will of God enters into the causation of all events.

wisdom in relation to individual situations, is so contradictory of that type of causation and order which science presupposes and investigates that we are forced to choose between them, and believe either in miracle or in science, but not in both.

The answer we shall give is that the work of science, when properly understood, does not require the elimination of the idea of God's personal initiative in events, that answers to prayer might take place and yet the work of science go on entirely unimpeded. Whether God ever does so act, and when, is another question which it is for the religious mind, and not for science, to determine.[1]

The justification of this answer must obviously rest mainly on an examination of what the work of science essentially is, and on an assessment of the status of the general laws which it formulates. But before proceeding to that, it may be well to point out that in our everyday life we are quite familiar with the idea of a volitional initiation of events which without that volition would not happen ; yet it never enters our heads to suppose that the work of science is thereby stultified and thrown into confusion. If I pick up a stone and throw it, it seems self-evident to me at the moment of the act, that had I not done so the stone would have remained where it was ; and it seems equally self-evident that a scientist could do much in examining from his angle what has taken place—the relation of the speed and weight of the stone to the path it describes, etc.— and in predicting what will take place if I again interfere and throw other stones, provided that the general environment,

---

[1] When we speak of science in this connexion we mean that activity which investigates by certain methods the phenomenal world in abstraction from its relation to individual and personal situations and values. If by science is meant the scientific spirit, i.e. a spirit which believes in the ultimate consistency of things, and seeks to think as clearly and as free from prejudice as it can, then the distinction between the religious and the scientific attitudes disappears. Such an attitude of desire and reverence for the truth is an indispensable prerequisite of religious insight.

so far as it concerns the stones and their flight, remains
constant. Man's whole life is built up on this awareness that
he is related to a system which is permanent enough to be
resolved into regularities, and plastic enough to leave at
least some room for his own will to shape it to his own ends.
How this should be possible is a puzzling enough question to
the philosopher, and there have been those who have supposed that I only *appear* to initiate events by will, my
volition being as much determined by all that has gone before
as each succeeding position of the stone is when once it has
started on its flight. The unsatisfactoriness of such a theory
has often enough been demonstrated ; our interest here is
in what is not the least important thing in the demonstration, namely the simple fact that nobody has ever succeeded
in living as though it were true. The power to initiate
events relevantly to ends and occasions is bound up with
the fundamental conditions of our existence, and nobody is
in the least puzzled by the fact that the work of science goes
on alongside the daily exercises of that power ; indeed the
experiments of science are one example of the exercise of it.
If, then, what is familiar in man's relation to his world is
declared, on theoretical grounds, to be impossible when it is
transferred to God, it may be presumed that theory has
somewhere got wide of the facts in a way that it should be
possible to lay bare.

The first thing that needs to be made clear in assessing
the work of science is that the phrase " laws of nature ",
which is so often applied to its generalisations, may contain,
at least in relation to the work of science, a serious *suggestio
falsi* ; this may take one of two forms. On the one hand,
the word " laws " may suggest an external lawgiver who
requires in advance that all events, which, so to say, cross
the frontier from the possible to the actual, shall obey all
his enactments, and will brook no disobedience of any kind.
" Laws which never shall be broken, for their guidance He

hath made ". Doubtless from the angle of theistic faith and philosophy there is a sense in which the character of the universe in general, and in particular the regularities without which it would neither have character nor be a universe, must derive from the will of God, but such a highly general truth obviously gives us no warrant for believing that any regularity we may have observed by our science belongs without qualification to one of the ultimate and unchangeable constancies. It may do so, or it may not, but we are not in a position to say, certainly not on the basis of scientific evidence and method. An observed regularity in phenomena is merely a regularity as up to that time observed, and it is only of *phenomena* ; yet by calling it a law of nature, we are in danger, if we are not careful, of incorporating into it something which has not been observed, and never could be observed, namely an ontological derivation from some ultimate will vaguely and mythologically conceived as requiring absolutely that particular type of obedience from all phenomena of the same order. On the other hand, if this crude mythologising is avoided, the mistake may reappear in a more refined form in the notion that an observed regularity in events is somehow also an observed immutable necessity. But once again, as Hume showed once and for all, an observed regularity is only an observed regularity ; the necessity we read into it, and in strict science we have no right to affirm it to be there. The reason for this " reading in " appears to be a natural, but quite unscientific, confusion between the irresistible movement of our own thought processes in observing events and the movement of the events themselves. We cannot help expecting that a book when it is pushed off the table will fall to the floor ; and the expectancy finds expression in the thought that the book cannot help falling to the floor—a harmless inaccuracy in everyday life, but a dangerous one when elevated without examination into a scientific or philosophic principle. So far as science is concerned the observed regularity of falling books gives no warrant for saying positively that on the next occasion the book will not fly up to the ceiling, though we should all be highly astonished if it did. If science thinks it has such a warrant, it is because it assumes that it has observed a necessary connection, when all it has observed is a regular one, one, that is, which appears to have held up to the present within the limited section of reality so far examined.

Most scientists would agree that these considerations hold of the empirical regularities, to the formulation of which so much of their work is devoted. These regularities are transcripts, made from a certain selected angle, of what hitherto has been found to happen in the phenomenal world. They afford the basis for a judgement of probability as to what will happen in the future, provided the general conditions remain fairly constant ; but they do not warrant any categorical judgements as to what of necessity must happen or cannot happen. From the standpoint of such empirical generalisations *anything* may still happen in the future, however much in practical life we are forced to make our decisions on the assumption that the possibilities lie within the limits indicated by our previous experience. To say that an exact assessment of the empirical laws of science requires the admission that anything may happen, does not mean, however, that we surrender to the idea of caprice, or of events happening which cannot, when they have happened, be related to what has gone before by some kind of generalisation. All events, when they have happened and become part of the continuum of the phenomenal world are amenable, as we shall see, to scientific generalisation. The point is that an empirical generalisation, as made at any one time, can never claim an absolute validity ; if an exception to it presents itself, it will not indicate that a " law of nature " has been suspended, but merely that the generalisation was inadequate to the actual complexity of the universe and must be revised.[1]

There appear, however, to be certain wide generalisations, deeply involved in the work of modern physics, which, when they are once grasped, seem to shine in their own light as final necessities, the violation of which is unthinkable. Such a generalisation is the law of the conservation of energy, when it is properly stated. It does not seem to be a merely empirical law in the sense that, say, Charles's law is.[2] The latter seems to be quite arbitrary, there being no apparent reason why the numerical fraction in it should not be other than it is. But the law of the conservation of energy, though it could not have been formulated apart from empirical evidence, seems to transcend the latter altogether ; it is not reached by a trial and error experimental method, and in the nature of the case could not be, though it may be afterwards in a measure tested by experiment ; it is reached rather by a kind of leap of intuition to something which, in advance of experience, seems to declare itself to be self-evidently and inalterably true. What is the source of this apodeictic certainty which, absent from empirical generalisations, enters into these wider and more abstract theoretical constructions ? Is it because here at last we have the ultimate constitution of the universe in our grasp—" laws which never shall be broken " ? There is apparently much to be said for the view that so far from this being so, such

---

[1] The extraordinarily subtle researches of modern science have revealed the fact that one element can, and sometimes does, change into another, e.g. uranium into lead. To some of the older physicists, with their naïvely simple conceptions of the nature of matter, the assertion that this was possible would have seemed indistinguishable from the bald assertion of miracle ; yet we now know that it does in fact happen and our theories of matter have to be made infinitely more complex in consequence.

" I have many times been witness when the impossible roused itself and happened," says Chan, the detective in one of Biggers' books. (Quoted by Micklem, *The Historical Problem of the Gospels, an Inaugural Address*, p. 4.)

[2] " Every gas expands under constant pressure by $\frac{1}{273}$ of its volume at $0°$ C for each degree centigrade through which its temperature is raised."

laws derive their accent of necessity from the fact that they
are, or include, disguised mathematical identities or truisms,
so that at bottom they belong to the same class of proposition as, say, that A cannot be both B and not-B at the
same time. The disguised nature of these truisms and their
usefulness in their own sphere, arises, according to some,
from the fact that physics elects to deal only with those
aspects of the phenomenal world which can be measured.
Some aspects we measure in one way, others in another way,
and because we measure them in different ways we assume
that we are measuring entirely different things. Laws
governing the mathematical relationships between the
different sets of measurements naturally present themselves, therefore, as necessary relations between the things
measured. But suppose our initial assumption is wrong,
and that what we take to be different things are really
overlapping aspects of the same thing. Then our supposed
laws become merely statements of the mathematical relations
between our different systems of measurement, and partake
of the axiomatic quality which attaches to all such relations
when once they are perceived. Some thinkers conceive that
this is how things are, and that if, *per impossibile*, we could
ever grasp the ultimate nature of the reality with which we
are dealing, we should find that it transcends the abstract
mathematical patterns into which our minds stamp it and
the laws which govern the relations of those patterns to one
another. Such laws, in fact, for all their apodeictic quality,
are not constitutive of nature at all. As Eddington says,
" they are a regaining from nature that which mind has put
into nature."[1]

---

[1] *The Nature of the Physical World*, p. 237 f. Eddington includes in
this type of law the conservation of energy, mass, momentum, and of
electric charge, the law of gravitation, Maxwell's equations. It is perhaps
not unnecessary to add that this view of the status of some of the most
brilliant and inclusive generalisations of physics does not in the least
commit us to a thorough-going subjective idealism, nor does it impugn the

There is, then, nothing in the work of science, when it is properly understood, which warrants us in regarding its generalisations as final laws of nature setting a limit once and for all to what is possible. But important as it is to realise this relativity of scientific knowledge, it is clear that the main problem is still to be considered. Science may admit the relativity of its generalisations as made at any one moment, but it is bound to believe that generalisations are in principle always possible, that there is a real, objective order which may be known and is, in fact, increasingly being known, through its work. The question is whether this fundamental belief on which its work rests would be in any way impugned, if we were to admit the possibility that events might happen through the personal initiative of God acting relevantly to a personal situation. Granting that that which in the light of all previous experience appears highly improbable may at any moment " rouse itself and happen ", must not science maintain that, if and when it happens, it will in principle be possible to include it within the scope of natural laws and relate it to the nexus of causal relationships which it is its business to bring more and more within the scope of its formulæ ? Clearly science must maintain this. Yet, if that be so, what room can it allow for a divine initiation of events which apart from that initiative would not otherwise happen ?

The answer to this question begins in the realisation that science, when rightly understood, can make no claim to give an exhaustive account of the reality with which it is dealing. Indeed on examination the account it gives proves to be very limited indeed, so that whilst science may legitimately claim to give *some* account, in accordance with its own

* value of these generalisations for creatures such as we are, who seem forced thus to apprehend the world piecemeal and to schematise it into measurable patterns. And that the world can thus be successfully dealt with at all seems to indicate that there is some constitutive harmony between it and the mind of man.

methods and categories, of *all* events, it can never claim to give an exhaustive account of any.

Thus, in the first place, as indicated in a previous chapter, the work of science involves a continuous process of abstraction, whereby the richness and particularity of the real world, as it is presented to individual minds in living situations, is deliberately set on one side in favour of a scheme of conceptual symbols and their relations with one another. Such a conceptual scheme must have some relationship of correspondence with the real world for it has been reached by intercourse with it, and is found to be an effective means of dealing with it; but obviously it can make no claim to be exhaustive of it.

In the second place, and this is really a further example of the process of abstraction, science has to accept any group of phenomena into which it is enquiring as a going concern. Every situation is the result of the convergence of a number of different causal series, and science can in a measure disentangle those series in which it happens to be interested, and trace them out a certain distance; but it is in the end quite unable to say why those particular causal series should have coincided and converged together to produce just that situation, and not other ones to produce another situation entirely different. Any attempt to explain that could not stop short of seeking to analyse the state of the whole universe at a given moment and at all previous moments, a task which is not only beyond its power, but also beyond its proper interest; the universe is a " transcendent " which lies entirely outside the scope of its laboratory methods. To use a simile of Beth's,[1] science might be compared to a man tracing out the various coloured threads on the underside of an embroidery. He can tell us a great deal about their different courses, and their relationship to one another, but as to why just those

[1] *Das Wunder*, p. 23.

colours should have been brought together at all on just
that piece of canvas, so that when it is turned over it
displays an exquisite pattern, he can say nothing. The
collocation of threads into that particular harmony is an
inexplicable given, which the analyst is neither capable of,
nor interested in, explaining.

In the third place and most important of all, science can
make no claim, even in respect of those aspects of events in
which it is interested, that it is in any sense laying bare the
ultimate reality with which man has to deal. It " describes "
the behaviour of things as presented to the human mind,
but it can offer no " explanation " in the sense of being able
to relate such behaviour to some final underlying reality
from which it can be seen of necessity to flow. It deals, in
fact, only with phenomena in the strict usage of the term,
with reality as it appears or presents itself to a certain point
of view ; as to what that which so presents itself ultimately
is, it says nothing, and can say nothing, *qua* science. If it
sometimes speaks in a way to suggest that it is revealing
ultimate realities or activities, and not merely describing
their behaviour as it appears to us—as, e.g., when it speaks
of necessary connections, or of an omnipresent ether, or of
a force of gravity pulling the book to the floor—that is
because it has momentarily left its proper sphere and has
yielded unconsciously to the impulse, which lies at the root
of all philosophy as distinct from science, to ask *why* things
behave as they do and not merely *how* they behave.

This point finds expression from another angle in the
suggestion made by a number of competent thinkers that
scientific generalisations, other than those which are disguised identities, are of the nature of statistical averages.
It is well known that those aspects of the behaviour of
human beings which are amenable to statistical treatment
exhibit, when considered in large aggregates, certain fairly
constant regularities, despite the fact that the individuals

comprising the aggregate vary enormously in the quality of their minds, the motives from which they act, and the situations with which they have to deal. On this fact much of economic and social science rests, and without it the imposing structure of modern insurance business would fall to pieces. The statistician who deals with these regularities ignores individual differences as irrelevant to his purpose, though he knows that they are there, and that for other purposes they can and must be taken into account. Now the position of the physicist, when he examines those aspects of nature which can be dealt with by measurement, may very well be the same, except that unlike the statistician dealing with human affairs, he has no means of directly observing the individual constituents, and the ultimate sources of their activity. He ignores them not only because they are irrelevant to his purpose, but because in any case he has no choice. The phenomena with which he deals are mass or macroscopic phenomena ; the noumena which are the ultimate sources of the activity of nature elude his grasp. These may be of the order of life or mind, as some thinkers maintain they are, or they may not : to the scientist *qua* scientist it does not matter one way or the other. His work of enquiry into such regularities as the phenomenal world exhibits can still go on, even if they be only of this statistical sort.[1]

Science, then, can make no claim to give an exhaustive account of the real world ; in particular, the ultimate, ontal factors in natural process, the inner side of it, so to say, for ever transcends its methods of investigation. Even a

[1] Whether the recent researches of physics into the structure of the atom, as expressed in the Principle of Indeterminacy and the Quantum Theory, really mean that we have reached a point, even in respect of matter, where the ordinary principles and methods of science are seen to be inadequate to the ultimates of the real world, coming shipwreck, in fact, on an irreducible individuality and spontaneity in things, I am not qualified to judge. The point is extremely interesting, but does not affect the argument.

scientist like Weyl, who believes that one day it will be
possible so completely to understand the nature of matter
that all the laws governing its behaviour will be shown to
be related together by rational necessity, is constrained to
add that even then we shall not have grasped the ultimate
ground of things.   Many scientists, however, would demur
strongly to the first half of this statement ;   they have
surrendered the idea that science will ever be able to give
a completely satisfactory account of nature even within the
narrow limits which it has marked out for itself by its
principles and methods, though it is bound to carry on its
work on the assumption that such an ideal, though un-
attainable, can be ever more closely approached.[1]

This does not mean, however, that the generalisations of
science may be regarded as being merely mental constructs,
which, though useful to ourselves, report nothing about the
nature of the real world at all. Such pure phenomenalism
not only runs counter to the scientists' profound feeling,
without which his work could not go on, that he is in some
sense exploring and getting to know the real world as it is,
but also is forbidden by the facts ;   for, in the first place,
the scientist's work is controlled by continual reference to the
given, and, in the second place, if the ultimate reality
presents itself to us in a form amenable to scientific generalisation, that must be because of what it essentially is.   That
a reality can present itself to the mind in such a guise is an
indication of what that reality essentially is.   Without
therefore wishing in the least to leave its strictly phenomenal
view-point and to stray into the realm of philosophy or
religion, science has at any rate the right to claim that
however these may conceive the noumenal world, it shall be
in a way that does not leave the work of science, as it were,
en l'air, without any basis in the ultimately real world at all.

Returning now to the purpose of this chapter, it is obvious

[1] See Titius, *op. cit.*, p. 627.

that God's initiation of events relevantly to individual situations, if it be a fact at all, falls within that area of reality which transcends the scientific interest and method. Having said that, it might appear at first sight that so the matter might be left—the divine activity being referred to the more ultimate underside of events which lies ever beyond the scope of scientific enquiry, the generalisations of the latter being referred to the phenomenal aspect of them. Thus religion from its point of view could continue to refer events to the divine action, and science from its point of view could refer them to the interplay of intramundane causes, and neither need have any quarrel with the other. This is a very attractive line of thought, and in the end most reflection on the matter comes back in one form or another to it—to the assertion, that is, that religion in its affirmation of divine activity grasps one aspect of events, and science, in the affirmations which it makes, grasps another.[1] Yet thus baldly stated, it is not altogether satisfying, even though we grant that in the end the question how God controls events both in relation to individual situations and over the whole area of His general providence must in any case run out into mystery, God being God. It is not satisfying because, when all is said, the idea of events being initiated *ad hoc* by the divine will and the idea of them being causally determined by what has gone before in the intramundane situation appear prima facie to be contradictory the one of the other, and the uneasy feeling of contradiction is not assuaged by saying blandly that we are looking at the thing from two different angles. In what sense

[1] It is followed, for example, by Schleiermacher, and, later, by Herrmann, to mention two whose difference from one another is illuminating. Schleiermacher with his pantheistic bias found no difficulty in supposing that the universe should present itself at one and the same time as God and as mechanically determined system of events. Herrmann with his profounder sense of God as personal is painfully conscious of the apparent contradictoriness of the two aspects, but he can offer no solution. The Christian must put up with it as a sort of cross.

can we be said to be looking at the same object, if one of us sees purpose and the other sees mechanism ? It is a little like two witnesses, one of whom says that A is a liar and the other of whom says he is not, composing their differences by saying that they are looking at him from two different points of view ; such a solution would not be very satisfactory to A nor to the people who had to make up their minds whether they would trust him. Unless we can form some conception, however vague, how it should be possible for events to present themselves truthfully on the one hand as the resultant of the *ad hoc* initiative of will, and on the other hand as the resultant of what appears to be the exact contrary of that, namely necessary determination, the mind is left in a state of dangerous instability. There will always be the tendency for the religious point of view to be swallowed up in the scientific, God becoming only another name for the total interrelatedness of things, or the order of nature ; or for the two aspects to be referred to an unknown X which lies behind both, but is neither the one nor the other, both aspects being regarded as subjective, with the scientific aspect, however, ever ready, as usual, to swallow up the other because it seems to deal with more tangible realities, and to be less subject to the vagaries of mere wish-thinking.

It is not necessary for our purpose, however, to attempt to set forth a complete metaphysic, which shall be argumentatively established against all possible demurrers or alternative views. If this were an extended treatise on philosophy, such an attempt would be in place. Our interest is in the Christian experience of God as personal, which in the nature of the case must be self-authenticating and able to shine in its own light independently of the abstract reflections of philosophy, for if it were not, it could hardly be a living experience of God as personal. Our reason for taking up the matter is that so often the soul's deeper awarenesses of, and responses to, the Eternal as personal, and in particular that response which takes the form of petitionary prayer, are deflected and inhibited by wrong notions of what is required by the scientific view of the world. All that is to our purpose, therefore, is to show that it is possible to set the two points of views in some sort of organic relation to one another, even though not all problems can be finally solved ; and in order to do that it is necessary only to sketch one possible theory. It need not be argued that it is the only possible theory, or even that as against all other alternatives it is the best, though naturally it will be the one which in the present state of knowledge appeals to us most and seems most promising of future development. The main thing is to show, if possible, that even for limited human minds the way out of the apparent impasse, which every sensitive mind is bound to be aware of in some degree, is not finally closed, and that in order to enter upon the life of Christian prayer it is not necessary, as Herrmann thought it was, painfully to carry a flat contradiction on the intellectual conscience. If that can be done, then the inward power of the religious life, thus released from a cramping inhibition, may perhaps be trusted to do the rest.[1]

[1] The course of our thought will thus be reminiscent of Kant's in his " Explanation of the Cosmological Idea of Freedom in connection with the General Necessity of Nature " in the *Critique of Pure Reason* (Max Müller's translation, p. 439 f.). Kant is concerned to show that there is at least one way in which the reality of freedom might be affirmed so as to allow " the explanations of physical phenomena to proceed without let or hindrance." He is careful to state, however, that this does not establish the reality of freedom. " That nature does not contradict the causality of freedom ", he concludes, " that was the only thing which we could prove, and cared to prove " (p. 451). We, too, do not seek to establish the theory sketched in the next chapter, the point being that if we can conceive one possible way in which the religious insight and the requirements of science might be harmonised, that should be sufficient to release the former from the inhibitions which otherwise might lie upon it.

CHAPTER X

MIRACLE AND THE LAWS OF NATURE
(*continued*)

LET us begin from within the awareness of God as personal will which, we have maintained, lies somewhere near the heart of all living religion, and which we have sought to analyse in the previous chapters. It has been our contention that there is in that awareness the sense of being in immediate rapport with God in a dimension of personal relationship, such rapport being focused in the awareness of tension, or resistance, or polarity, between the divine will and that of the individual. Now there is in this relationship a peculiar sense of being down on an irreducible ultimate, an absolute in the universe of being.

Thus to consider first the individual's awareness of himself as will: I do not, and cannot, think of my will as something which in reality is other than what it immediately declares itself to be (namely, my will), and which I merely treat " as if " it were my own. Indeed, it is in a sense wrong to talk of it as *my* will, as though it were an object which I attach to myself; it *is* myself, an ultimate, irreducible self-activity, which produces phenomena, but is not itself a mere phenomenon of some unknown reality which is other than I, and which is inaccessible to my control. Doubtless I am aware of myself as a dependent and created being, and as an active self I am limited and restricted by forces whose ultimate nature is hidden from me; but when I exercise will, I am conscious, as it were, of a shaft opening up in the midst of the order of things presented to me, and something ultimate, which is not presented, but is known simply by being it, flowing out creatively into the world through it. These are fumbling metaphors, precisely because we are attempting to describe an ultimate, and for an ultimate there are no images. The best way to bring home to our minds the truth of what is thus obscurely indicated is by the negative consideration that if we could take seriously the thought that the self in its activity is a mere phenomenon of something more ultimate behind, instantly the sense of moral responsibility would depart, and any sense of being a true self, as distinct from a thing, would depart with it. The awareness of moral responsibility, or, what is the same thing, of being free, and the awareness of being in some sense an ultimate in the world of being are indissolubly bound up together.[1]

Second, the same sense of being down on an ultimate appears in the individual's awareness of God as will. The absolute demand which strikes into the soul's life is apprehended immediately as the pressure of the Eternal as will. It is not something which I reflectively interpret as the impact of God's will, or which, for practical reasons, I choose to think of " as if " it were God's will, with the notion somewhere at the back of my mind that it might be something else all the time. Philosophic interpretation is not living religion, nor can living religion long survive the thought that what it takes to be God's will is really only the appearance of something hidden behind, which may not

---

[1] That is why the idea of freedom, so soon as it is analysed, seems to break up into insoluble contradictions. An ultimate cannot be analysed, or expressed in terms other than itself ; it can be apprehended only by in some sense being it, or being constituted by it. Readers will be reminded of Kant's conception of man as noumenally free and empirically determined. Kant's doctrine has been subjected to much just criticism, but there was surely genuine insight in it, and the insight arose from his fidelity to the deliverances of his own awareness of himself as responsible will, as his whole treatment shows. See Ward, *Realm of Ends*, Chap. **XIV**, for a discussion of the permanent truth in Kant's teaching in this respect.

M

be of the nature of will at all. To ask how the ultimate o
divine will can thus present itself to the ultimate of my wil
is a foolish question, for if the relationship could be analysed
further, it would not be an ultimate any longer. To speak
even of the divine will as " presenting itself " may be mis
leading, for it is apt to suggest again that it lies completely
hidden behind a mere appearance. We can only say that
man's will and God's are just " there " in this ultimate and
unanalysable tension of personal relationship, which is
known only in being experienced.[1]

This involves us in the third point, namely that there is
an awareness of an ultimate not only in the fact of my own
will and in the fact of the divine will, but also in their
relationship with one another, not only in the *relata* but
also in the *relatio*. The encounter between the divine will
and my own is felt as something from which I can never
hope to escape to some other relationship less demanding or
less critical for my whole personal destiny. No principle of
relativity is admissible here. In the realm of things it may
be possible for A to be both above and beneath B at the
same time, if seen from different angles. But no change in
the angle of vision, whether of God or man, could ever make
the relationship we are considering appear as other than
that which it is immediately known to be, namely just that
ultimate polarity of wills which is personal relationship, and
in default of which there could not be personal relationship
at all. It is this profound sense of irreducible ultimacy in
the relation of man's will to God's which in part lies behind
the enormous seriousness of all living religion, its trembling
sense that when a man meets God all argument must cease,
that it is impossible to be any other than either with God

[1] This does not set man on a level with God ; however paradoxical it
may seem, man's ultimacy as will is a derived and bestowed ultimacy.
It is this paradox which the doctrine of man's *creation* in God's image, as
distinct from the doctrine that man is an emanation, or manifestation, or
phase, of God, seeks to express.

or against God, that no standpoint can be reached, or even conceived, which would enable a man to be both at the same time.

Yet, we must insist, it is a falsifying abstraction thus to analyse the experience into the awareness of three separate ultimates. All three are really given together in the single awareness of being in an order of personal relationship with God. That is the one inclusive ultimate which is revealed to the soul—the ultimate of a personal dimension in which God has set man with Himself. I become aware of my own will as an ultimate because God enters into this challenging, tensional relationship with it ; I become aware of God as ultimate will for the same reason ; I become aware of the tension itself only as I am in a measure aware of being an ultimate in my own will and dealing with another ultimate in the will of God. All three are given together in a total awareness of immediate, present, personal rapport with God, requiring decision and trust.

The relevance of all this to our problem is that the first step in conceiving how God's initiative in events, particularly in answers to prayer, may be related to the so-called laws of nature is to take these deliverances of the living awareness of God as veridical, as, of course, we have no option but to do, if we ourselves share in it. We must start from the thought that back of all the phenomenal world there is not a completely unknown X, but an ultimate whose essential quality is known in the religious awareness. It is known as will entering into relation with wills. It may be more than that, but it is at least that. The relatively fixed order of nature must then be regarded as somehow derivative from, and only understandable through, its relation to an ultimate so conceived. The argument must not be allowed to slip, as it may easily do, even unconsciously, into the reverse movement, namely that of taking natural law as the prior thing, as somehow essentially constitutive of the ultimate, and then seeking to find place in the latter for will. The effect of that is inevitably to give an irresistible bias towards the religiously impossible conception of a finite God struggling with intractable material or towards an impersonalistic pantheism in which the will of God becomes a mere *façon de parler*, and which is, as Schopenhauer said, really a polite atheism. How then may this derivative relationship of natural law to an ultimate conceived in terms of will be conceived ?

In order to answer this question let us take another look at ourselves as will, as ultimate sources of activity. It is of the very essence of such awareness that we are conscious of, in a measure, shaping the course of events in the world and of not being merely shaped by them ; nor could such a consciousness arise, if our shaping of events were not in some sense an actuality.[1] As I stand at the point of exercising will I am conscious that the future is indeterminate, at any rate within that limited sphere to which my will is relevant. Events may take this direction or that, according as my will says " yes " to this, or " no " to that. This only occurs as I am myself actively concerned in the stream of events ; if I look out on events as a mere spectator, it is not difficult to imagine that they are unfolding according to some cast-iron necessity ; but if I am personally involved in them—be it in never so small a degree or under the most cramping conditions—so that I can will one alternative rather than another, then such an imagination is impossible, except when I look back afterwards and take up, as it were, the role of spectator to myself. Even a man being swept over the rapids, so long as he does not surrender himself

[1] The suggestion that a stone falling freely, if it could be momentarily endowed with self-consciousness, would have the sense of shaping its own course, is misleading because it calls upon us to imagine what is really a *contradictio in adjecto*. It is impossible to see how an entity not shaping its own movement ever could be equipped even with the idea of so doing, still less with that living sense of so doing, upon which self-consciousness depends.

wholly to the physical forces playing upon him, but is ready to clutch this rock or lurch himself away from that, is conscious of a power, however limited, to alter the course of events by his own activity, and bring about that which would not otherwise take place. In much of the routine of daily existence this awareness of power to shape events is latent ; we are content, for the nonce, to let routine take its course, being aware, however, that within certain limits we can at any moment break in, in the light of some larger requirement, and suspend it. In moments of deliberate and reasoned decision, on the other hand, when alternatives are weighed and one accepted to the exclusion of others, the awareness of shaping events is at a maximum. We have already referred above to this commonplace awareness of our daily life,[1] the truth of which may be theoretically questioned, but which is quite unavoidable when we are in the midst of the actual business of living and not merely reflecting on what has already transpired.

But though there is in all such activity the sense of the stream of events being still fluid and indeterminate, there is also the sense that in this fluidity there is involved of necessity a factor making continuously for fixity. This factor has to do with the absolute distinction, which runs through all our experience, between time present and time past. At the present moment, immediately prior to my decision and act, certain possibilities are still open ; but once the decision is taken and the act done, this fluidity has, so to say, congealed once and for all into the fixity of the past. What's done, we say, cannot be undone ; even God cannot make the past so that it has not been. Moreover, what is done is not done with. It has foreclosed certain possibilities once and for all, and so provides permanent conditions, though never final determination, for all future decisions and acts of our will. The present creates the

[1] See above, p. 146.

past ; the past does not *per se* create the present and the future, but abides as a permanent condition of it. This is most plainly to be observed in the fact of memory, and of habit which is one aspect of memory. As our decisions and acts pass over into the past they are not only fixed in the sense that they are gone beyond recall, but also in the sense that they tend all the time, in greater or less degree, to become the settled structure and habit of the organism, whether in its body or in its mind, on which all future activity must in a measure rest.[1]

Now, the suggestion has been made by a number of thinkers that the relation of the fixity of the order of nature, which science observes, to the ultimate creativeness of will, which religion intuits in its awareness of God, is one form of the relation of the fixity of the past to our own present creativeness as this is given to us in the intimacy of our own personal experience. The impression of inalterable regularity in nature is due to the fact that through our senses we are observing the real world all the time, as it were, *post eventum*, in the dimension of time past, as *natura naturata* and not as *natura naturans*, as " *gewordensein* " and not as " *werden* ". The suggestion has been wrought out along two lines.

First—along lines made familiar by Bergson—in respect of the general fact that nature presents itself to us in a form that can be analysed, weighed, measured, and generally split up into entities which by means of abstract concepts can be related to one another in dependable generalisations

---

[1] Cf. the vivid passage in Carlyle's *French Revolution*, Vol. III, p. 22 : " From the purpose of crime to the act of crime there is an abyss ; wonderful to think of. The finger lies on the pistol ; but the man is not yet a murderer ; nay his whole nature staggers at such a consummation ; is there not a confused pause rather—one last instant of possibility for him ? . . . One slight twitch of a muscle, the death-flash bursts ; and he is it, and will for all Eternity be it ; and earth has become a penal Tartarus for him ; his horizon girdled now not with golden hope, but with red flames of remorse ; voices from the depths of Nature sounding, Wo, wo on him ! "

of a causal type. The reason why this is possible is that we are looking all the time at things after they are accomplished by the invisible dynamic agency or agencies which lie behind them, and which are inaccessible to such intellectual analysis. We are looking at " filled time ", and not at the creative sources which are doing the filling, at activity solidified, so to say, in the dimension of time past. We suppose ourselves, indeed, to be looking straight at this present world, and in the sense that we are analysing what is given to our *present* act of perception, we are ; but so far as we are related through our intellectual analysis, not to our own present creativity, but to the present creativity of the world, we are looking back at it all the time. A simple example may serve to make the point more comprehensible. We are told that it is possible that what we discern as a palpitating and lovely star in the heavens may have ceased to exist as a centre of radiation thousands of years ago ; that if such a centre went out of existence now, we should not lose the loveliness of it from the sky until thousands of years hence ; so vast are the distances which the vibrations on which we depend for our awareness have to travel. Yet this is only a magnification of what holds of all our perceptions of what we call the objective world ; between these and the ontal events of reality there is an intercalation of vibrations, and therefore a time interval, however short. The world of nature presented to our awareness is therefore always the accomplished world, and having the peculiar hardness and fixity of the accomplished, it can be measured, weighed, divided up, analysed, schematised into all kinds of abstract conceptual relations. And nothing can become objective, in the sense of becoming object for our senses or for our reflective observation, without assuming the qualities just indicated, without presenting itself as part of a determinate nexus of general relationships capable of conceptual analysis and exposition. To be an

object for us means to have passed out of the indeterminate
present into the determinate past, and to have passed into
the determinate past means of necessity to share in those
structural patterns which it is the business of science to
examine.   Hence even the most unprecedented and unexpected event, when once it has happened, is susceptible of
explanation by science, not in the sense of expounding its
ultimate " why ", but in the sense of indicating the way it
enters in and takes its place in the pattern of filled time.
An event from this point of view might perhaps be likened
to a fly suddenly brought up short in the spider's web ; only
by thus becoming fixed and immobilised in the web and
setting up vibrations in the filaments can it become object
to the spider, who thereupon hurries to the spot and joins
to and around and over the fly the filaments which had
both arrested, and been ruptured by, its flight ;   thus the
fly becomes for the spider part of the web-system and he
can find his way to it again and use it.

The fact that the scientist can in this way measure and explain the fixed, determinate world of objects *post eventum* very
easily leads to the conclusion, the falseness of which Bergson
and others have repeatedly pointed out, that had he known
prior to the event the relationships with the causal nexus
which in fact he has only been able to formulate after it, he
could have foretold what was going to happen with absolute
certainty. This is a *non sequitur*. It is to confuse the in-
alterability of an event when it has happened with a
necessity governing it before it happens. It is also to overlook the highly abstract nature of the relationships which
science formulates, and how little they exhaust, or ever
could exhaust, however multiplied, the concrete, rich,
individuality of events as actually experienced. It is as
though the spider aforementioned, perceiving that the fly
is now part of the structure of his web and the focus of a
network of filaments whose direction and angular incidences

can be exactly calculated, should persuade himself that the
fly is after all only a function of these filaments, and that
had he had enough knowledge at an earlier time he could
have forecast not only precisely where the fly would appear,
but also that it would be a fly and not a gnat or a blue-
bottle.[1]

In the second place, the suggestion we are considering is
wrought out along the lines of assimilating the regularities
of nature to those relative fixities of habit which, in our
experience, the free, creative decisions of will always tend
to form as they pass into the determinate past. This line of
thought is not alternative to the one just given but is a
necessary supplement to it ; for though it may be true that
nothing can become object for us without exhibiting certain
fixed pattern-relationships with all that has already entered
into filled time, yet clearly that does not suffice to explain
all the reliabilities we find in nature. Things mercifully
repeat themselves not only in respect of the abstract relationships which science increasingly reduces to mathematical
formulæ, but also in some measure in respect of their
concrete particularity, so that in our practical dealing with
the world in concrete particular situations we can act at
least with some foresight and consistency of purpose. Thus
we know that if the sun suddenly started taking a zig-zag

[1] Cf. Bergson, *Creative Evolution* (Eng. Trans.), p. 49 : ". . . reality
appears as the ceaseless upspringing of something new, which has no
sooner arisen to make the present than it has already fallen back into the
past ; at this exact moment it falls under the glance of the intellect, whose
eyes are ever turned to the rear. This is already the case with our inner
life. For each of our acts we shall easily find antecedents of which it may
in some sort be said to be the mechanical resultant. And it may equally
well be said that each action is the realisation of an intention. In this
sense mechanism is everywhere, and finality everywhere, in the evolution
of our conduct. But if our action be one which involves the whole of our
person and is truly ours, it could not have been foreseen, even though its
antecedents explain it when once it has happened." Cf. also Heim, *Glaube
und Denken* (2 Aufl.), p. 148 f., (3 Aufl.), p. 116 f., Ward, *Realm of Ends*,
Ch. XIV.

course across the sky, we should be able to relate so unprecedented a phenomenon, when once it had occurred, by
some formula to the precedent conditions ; none the less
we confidently expect that it will do no such thing, but will
rise as usual on the morrow. This expectancy can never
rise to absolute certainty ; but it is soundly based on past
experience of the fact that nature, whilst we have no right
to say that she is governed by cast-iron and always pre-
dictable necessities, none the less has apparently, over large
areas of her activity, relatively settled habits or routine.
Without this element of routine in the dynamic creativeness
of nature, it could have no intelligible meaning, and would
for creatures like ourselves be entirely unmanageable. To
revert to the figure of the spider's web again : the spider
may be assured that any object which becomes immobilised
in the web will stand in a certain type of relation to the
filaments, for only by becoming so immobilised and entering
into that type of relation, can anything become object to
him at all ; yet such assurance would not avail it much in
the business of living if objects substantially the same,
despite individual variations, never came twice. Or let us
imagine a human being so constituted that he can hear
words only when they take a metrical form. Everything
that becomes object to him will enter into certain metrical
relationships with what has gone before, for only thus can
it become object. Yet if no two words ever recur with the
same connotation, the words will never make sense, despite
the formal regularities which of necessity govern them as
objects of hearing.

There are two possible ways in which this type of
regularity in nature may be assimilated to the routine or
habit into which our own activity always tends to pass.
On the one hand, it may be suggested that nature is the
direct expression of the continuous, creative activity of the
divine will, its regularities being then analogous to those

consistencies and reliabilities which the behaviour of a good man reveals to us as it passes over out of the free activity of his spirit into our common world of accomplished and observable fact. The good character is not fettered by such steadfastness of purpose and consistencies of wisdom, nor by the habitual dispositions which these build up in his organism ; rather he sustains and uses them by that continuous creativity which constitutes him a personal will and which itself cannot be made an object of investigation and knowledge. So also, it is suggested, doubtless vaguely enough, though not without meaning, the regularities of nature are the consistencies of God as these are revealed under the aspect of a temporal and created order and in the working out of His purpose with man.

On the other hand it may be suggested, as by Leibniz and by others in different ways since, that nature is not the *immediate* expression of a single creative divine activity, but of an infinite number of entities of a psychical kind in continuous interplay with one another. The ultimate constituents even of matter are conceived to be of the order of life and mind, though on a much lower level than the kind of life and mind which we know in our own consciousness. The relatively settled order of nature, the regularities on which in all our activity we rely, are, on this view, the habits and routines of co-operative behaviour which the constituent monads in their ceaseless activity have so far established, and which form the unchangeable basis, though not the mechanical determinant, of all future creativity. Such habits and routines may present themselves to our minds as statistical regularities, such as always appear within established society, without, however, in any way negating the individual differences and spontaneities of the constituent members.

From the angle of the specific interest of this chapter the second of these two alternatives appears to be preferable.

At first sight the first alternative would seem to have the advantage, for if all the activities of nature are attributed to God's sole creative energy, with secondary causes not involved at all, the regularities being, as it were, a projection on the plane of creation of certain unchanging consistencies and necessities of the divine purpose, then it would seem not too difficult to conceive that God should be able, in response to certain situations and contingencies in human history, to act in a new and unprecedented way, breaking through the routines which He had hitherto followed, so soon as wisdom demanded it. For if the divine will is active in all events of the natural order, then that He should act in this way rather than that in certain situations does not involve any suspension of that order, provided that what He does is always consistent with that ultimate wisdom of which, in any case, the whole creation is an expression. A number of writers who have sought to preserve a place for God's relevant initiative within the natural order have followed this line of thought.[1] Yet the view has certain serious difficulties which the second alternative avoids.

Thus it seems an unnecessary flying in the face of the commonsense apprehension of the world to suggest, as the theory seems to do, that the order of nature has no measure of independent being in and for itself, but is always and only a manifestation of God's direct action. Doubtless any idealist theory of nature, whether monistic or pluralistic, is a flying in the face of commonsense ; but the pluralist hypothesis at least preserves the impression which nature undoubtedly makes upon us, of having a significance in and itself, and as containing, at least in the organic world, a tumult of conative impulses which have in some sense or other to work out their own destiny. In our own being we are constrained to recognise—the more so if we are religious

---

[1] E.g. Wendland, *Miracles and Christianity* ; Hunzinger, *Das Wunder* ; Hogg, *Redemption from this World*.

people with an inescapable awareness of sin as something
the responsibility for which must on no account be put
upon God—an activity which is not the direct activity of
God, namely our own wills, and it seems a little arbitrary to
deny *in toto* to the rest of the created order what is so
central in ourselves. Wendland's statement that " it is a
false view which represents God as working at one time
indirectly, at another directly. The working of God is invariably direct ",[1] taken at its face value seems to provide
no logical stopping-place short of an all-inclusive monism,
in which personal relationships would disappear, and with
them the religious concept of miracle itself. Moreover, a
conception of miracle which makes it merely a new manifestation of a creative will which, equally and in the same
sense, is directly involved in everything else that takes
place, contradicts an important element in the religious
awareness of what miracle is, namely that it is an event
which the ordinary processes of nature would not and could
not have brought forth unaided, an event which in some
way registers a divine deliverance from, or victory over, an
otherwise self-perpetuating hindrance or barrier or inertia
or habit in things. It is difficult to see that this religious
sense could be preserved if all the activities of nature are
attributed directly to the divine will. Tennant is surely
right when he says that Christian theism " must be sufficiently tinged with deism to recognise a relatively settled
order, and an order in which the causation is not immediate
divine creation."[2]

[1] *Op. cit.*, (Eng. Trans.), p. 17.
[2] *Op. cit.*, p. 51. The justice of these remarks may be illustrated by
reference to Hogg's otherwise admirable treatment of miracle in the
book already referred to. The author is keenly aware that religiously the
idea of miracle and the idea of redemption are inseparable, yet philosophically he tries to fit this into a monistic interpretation of nature in
which everything is referred without intermediary to the activity of God.
Hogg says that " the miraculous does not involve any breach of the natural
order itself, but only of a barrier within the natural order . . . within

The second alternative, as already indicated, avoids these difficulties. Though in any complete philosophical treatment of it it has difficulties of its own—the difficulties which always arise in connexion with the relationship of the one and the many—it has at least the advantage of preserving a measure of independence for the created order. If, then, we are prepared to accept it as at least a possible theory,

the phenomenal or created universe there is a partially isolated realm which very inadequately displays [God], and the miraculous or supernatural involves the inruption into this realm of some of the reserves of God's cosmic energy which do not ordinarily have free operation there " (pp. 149–50). It would appear from this that for Hogg the miraculous is in a very real sense a breach of the natural order, and not merely the appearance of such to our incomplete knowledge. For the barrier and partial isolation are themselves part of the order, and when they are broken through there occurs what may not inappropriately be called a suspension of it. Doubtless the existence of the barrier, and the breaking through it under certain conditions, are themselves part of a universal, all-inclusive order, but to affirm that is to affirm something quite jejune, for the conception of universal order, as Bultmann says, " *ist mit unserem Dasein in der Welt gegeben* " (*Glaube und Verstehen*, p. 215). The question still remains what is the real status of the barrier and the apparent settled order which obtains within it. In replying to this, Hogg seems to oscillate between two views. On the one hand he seems to regard the so-called natural order as merely the way in which we roughly interpret the world in order to serve our own practical necessities. It is an artifice or working convention, a dealing with averages and not with individuals (p. 153 f.). God, however, does not work by rules, but by the " living and spontaneous orderliness of a perfect intelligence dealing with each situation ; to our crass minds this self-consistency looks like rules." On the other hand he seems to regard it as " long stretches of monotonous occurrence " which the divine purpose requires in order to achieve its ends (p. 162). In other words, the scientific interpretation now becomes no longer a mere working convention, but an expression of a real order, a real monotony in things. It matters not that Hogg puts this monotony in the divine activity itself. The point is that there is in the divine mind (cosmic order) a real differentiation between long stretches of monotony and, on appropriate occasions, " interruptions of it ". Though later he makes the somewhat astonishing suggestion that " so-called natural events are, as it were, nothing else than God, for the sake of our spiritual education, playing at being a machine, miracles and contraventions of natural law being God interrupting that make-believe and reminding us that really He is something greater and more mysterious than our knowledge has discovered " (p. 166). Surely if a rigorous monism is forced to such a conclusion, it is better to discard it, and start as the pluralist does from the plain fact that nature has a measure of apartness from God. We are aware, however, that this view also has its problems.

our answer to the question of how God might initiate events within the natural order in response to prayer without making impossible the work of science would lie somewhat along these lines.

Following up what was said at the beginning of the chapter, we would suggest that in the ultimate order of things there stand human personalities, as created creators, set in a dimension of personal relationship with the Eternal Personal. Ranging down from the human personal there are other relatively independent creative entities, all of them, even on the very lowest levels, of a fundamentally mental kind, and all of them also in a continuous relationship or rapport with God, though not in a personal way. There may, of course, also be creative entities higher in the scale than man. All these and their relationships to God, and to one another in God, are the ultimates of the real world, and through them the process goes on. Their activity is in what we, who can only think in terms of the time-series, must call the creative present. Nature as it presents itself to us is a sort of *depositum* of this activity as it passes from the creative present into the past and so becomes, on the one hand, phenomenal to our senses, and, on the other hand, a relatively settled routine on which future creativity must rest, but by which it is never completely determined. Now God's problem in relation to such a system of created creators, who have already fashioned a determinate past and a relatively determinate routine character as the basis of their present activity, is to achieve His own purpose, so far as it is concerned with the time-series, in a way that does not negate the system—though that is perhaps a misleading way to put it, for the creation of such a system and the giving to it some latitude to create itself is itself part of the content of the divine purpose, so that the idea of negativing the system is, from God's point of view, self-contradictory. A control of events which does not negate the system and so defeat the purpose in the nature of the case cannot be unlimited ; it will always have to move within the limits set by the routines of the past. Such a direction might be conceived as acting on two levels. On the one hand it might act by some sort of direct rapport, of necessity inaccessible to our observation, with sub-personal entities, a rapport which uses the routines of their activity in relation to a given situation[1] ; a dim analogy to this might be the way in which men on occasion control one another's conduct sometimes deliberately, sometimes unconsciously, by processes of suggestion. On the other hand, where the level of personality is reached, the direction must be of a kind which takes account of will in the full personal sense of that term ; that is to say, it must be conceived as waiting continuously for its fuller realisation upon man's spontaneous alignment of his will with God's as this is revealed to him in the manner analysed in the previous chapters. Doubtless the first method may also be used in respect of man, so that when he refuses to be God's agent he may still in a measure be taken up into His purpose as its unwitting instrument, both for those divine ends which are being wrought out in the time-series and those which transcend the time-series altogether ; but if man's relation to the divine will is to be kept within the sphere of the personal, it must be that at certain critical points the latter chooses to make itself dependent for its fuller realisation upon the co-operation of the will of man.

This, then, is the under, invisible, ontal side of nature and history—the living, creative will of God in continuous rapport with a system of living, creative entities, and waiting, in the case of man, for the personal co-operation of a will which has been given a peculiarly exalted status of independence even over against God. The outward, or phenomenal side is what is presented to us through the senses, as this living

---

[1] Cf. Tennant, *Philosophical Theology*, Vol. II, p. 218 ff.

creative present becomes the past and solidifies, as it were,
into a fixed order ; as such it is amenable to the examination
of science, which in the nature of the case never can penetrate to the ultimate present which lies behind. Now
prayer is essentially a transaction in the creative present ;
it is within the inner " will-side " of events. It is a relation
of the will of man to the will of God, and, through the will
of God, to all the living creativeness of nature. At its
highest it is the throwing of the whole personality into the
creativeness of God. It is not merely man accepting God's
will, but his endeavour to fulfil the place for which he has
been created, the place, that is, of a personal fellow-worker
with the will of God so far as it makes itself known, and is
being wrought out, within the limits of space and time.
The results of prayer, therefore, will not in the least affect
the work of science, any more than in any case what goes
on in the ultimate creativity of the universe affects the work
of science, for science does not and cannot deal with this at
all. Prayer is one aspect, we repeat, of the creative will-
order which underlies the phenomenal world. If God, when
man enters into a right type of prayer-relationship with Himself, initiates events through the rapport which He has with all
His creatures, science will still be able to give an account of
such events in its own way, so soon as they have become
accomplished fact ; nor will it ever be competent to say
whether such a divine activity has been operative or
not. Religious insight can alone determine that, as we
insisted in an earlier chapter.

In conclusion, a concrete illustration may be given.
Let us suppose, for the sake of the argument, that
when the children of Israel crossed the Red Sea, what
happened was that a strong wind drove back the waters just
at the moment of their dire need. Two interpretations of
this conjunction of events are possible. First, that it was a
fortunate coincidence ; the wind would have arisen in any

N

case, and it was sheer good luck that the Israelites arrived when they did. Second, that it was a miracle ; the wind would not have arisen just then, had not a transcendent factor, namely the will of God acting relevantly to that situation and in response perhaps to a prayer of need, entered in. Now the point is that from the point of view of science it is a matter of indifference which of the two interpretations is offered ; neither one is called for rather than the other if the work of science is to proceed. If it were true in fact that God brought about the wind, science could still pursue its enquiries, the wind being now accomplished fact, into the question how it was related to previous meteorological conditions, and exhibited the general regularities (probably of a statistical kind) which govern the pressures and resistances of gases ; for it could not become part of man's phenomenal world without manifesting those relationships and exhibiting those laws. How then could God conceivably so enter into a general meteorological situation that the outcome is different from what it would otherwise be, thus perhaps falsifying the forecasts of the weather experts attached to Pharaoh's court (forecasts, be it noted, which in the nature of the case could never be absolute certainties) ? If we must form a picture, it might be along the lines suggested above, namely that God so uses His all-inclusive rapport with the ultimate entities which constitute the inner, creative, present reality of the natural order, that their various routine activities are not overridden, but used by redirecting them in relation to one another. Just as man brings about effects in nature which would not otherwise happen by redirecting its routines in relation with one another, so does God, except that God acts from the inside, so to say, by inner rapport and not by external manipulation in the gross. Such rearranging and bringing together of different series of routine events would in the nature of the case not be observable by science. In the supposititious case given, the meteorologists might explain the falsification of their prediction by saying that a disturbance arose unexpectedly over the Indian Ocean, that the said disturbance was probably connected with air-currents from the Antarctic, that those air-currents derived from something else, and so on, until in principle the whole universe is theoretically involved, and thus the interest and scope and methods of science completely transcended.

It is perhaps not unnecessary to add that this illustration does not commit us to any particular view as to the propriety of praying about the weather. Indeed, nothing in this chapter commits us to any view as to what the proper objects of prayer are. On that we shall say a word from the Christian point of view later. Our endeavour has been simply to show that if God's free initiation of events were a fact and petitionary prayer were really effective, the work of science would not be made impossible, and that therefore there is nothing from the scientific view-point which would clash with the religious man's assertion that these things are so. There are limits to prayer, the limits set by the will of God, but it is not within the competence of science *per se* to say what these are. That in the end must be a matter for religious insight.

PART II

THE CHRISTIAN EXPERIENCE OF GOD AS PERSONAL THROUGH RECONCILIATION

CHAPTER XI

SIN AND RECONCILIATION

THE questions discussed up to this point have all been approached, it is hardly necessary to say, from the angle of Christian conviction and experience; the conclusions reached, however, have all had a wider reference than to the Christian faith alone. They have been general conclusions concerning the elements in, and the sources of, man's experience of God as personal, concerning, also, the essential meaning of certain categories, such as revelation and miracle, which arise out of that experience—conclusions which in principle hold of most, if not all, forms of living religious faith. The assumption underlying the line of thought followed has been Harnack's dictum that he who knows the Christian religion from the inside is in a position to know something about all religions.

We now propose to pass into, or rather to keep more closely within, the sphere of the specifically Christian faith and experience. We propose to ask the question, what part does Christ play in the Christian believer's experience of God as personal? It has always been the central affirmation of the Christian Faith that the supreme, unique, and in some sense final, revelation of God to men is Jesus Christ. If revelation be interpreted in the manner which has been indicated in the earlier chapters on that subject, then this is tantamount to saying that Christ has a supreme, unique, and in some sense final, part to play in man's experience of God as personal. We might put it another way by saying that it has always been the affirmation of the Christian faith that Christ is the supreme *miracle*, in the sense of being the supreme instance of God acting within history relevantly to a human situation of need ; which again means that His peculiar significance is to be found in the sphere of man's experience of God as personal. The remainder of the book will be devoted to this topic, to which, indeed, all that has been said hitherto is, in a way, only prolegomena. We must, however, limit ourselves, for such a plan, in principle, involves a discussion of every aspect of Christ's work in the life of the Christian believer ; everything that Christ does for a man is a taking of him into deeper personal fellowship with the Eternal. In accordance with the purpose of the book, our main interest will be in the Christian view of providence and prayer, other matters being taken up only in so far as they seem to be essential to the understanding of these topics.

The transition to the more exclusively Christian experience of God as personal is through a consideration of the fact of sin, what it is, and what its consequences are. To this, therefore, we first turn. It is, however, neither possible nor necessary to take up all the difficult questions which are involved either immediately or remotely in the doctrine of sin ; all that is required is that we should see the relationship of sin to our particular interest in the experience of God as personal. This, indeed, takes us to the heart of the matter, for whatever else we may conclude sin to be, it quite certainly means something which happens in the sphere of man's personal relationship to God. It is, in other words, a specifically *religious* category.

This fact is often obscured by popular speech, which constantly uses the word sin, as it does the word revelation, in such a way that the reference to God is no longer present, or, if present, is so in a very attenuated form ; unsatisfactory

actions of all sorts, from serious offences to relatively
trivial failings, are called " sins", and the people responsible
" sinners", sometimes, indeed, with an accent of indulgence,
and even flippancy, entirely remote from the religious
usage of the term. The lawyer should speak only of crime ;
the moralist only of vice ; the religious man, seeking to
indicate something in which the profoundest and most
far-reaching responses of his soul to the Eternal as personal
are involved, must find a category of his own. He speaks of
sin. Of all religious categories, the word sin, with the exception of the supreme category of God, is the most closely
packed with meaning. Only those who find they must use
it, can really know what that meaning is.[1]

The profound and far-reaching meanings and bearings
of the word sin may, perhaps, be best approached by taking
note of three definitions, or descriptions, or interpretations,
of sin which have recurred again and again in the history of
thought, not, however, always in separation from one another.

Thus, first, there is the conception continually to be met
with, that sin is fundamentally something which man does
against an eternal law, or laws, inherent in things. It is
lawlessness of an ultimate kind. Different views may be
held as to the source of the moral law which is infringed.
To the Hebrews the source was a divine law-giver, who,
somewhat in the manner of a human king or legislature,
laid down commandments and statutes for His own purposes
and required obedience to them, attaching rewards and
penalties to observance or non-observance. To the Stoics

---

[1] The tendency of some religious thinkers in these days to minimise
the significance of sin, and even to eliminate the term altogether, bears
witness once again to the depersonalising of the idea of God and the
substitution of philosophic truths about the ultimate and its relation to
man (usually at bottom monistically conceived) for that living awareness
of God which we have been endeavouring to analyse. The religious man,
however, must have a distinctive term for a relationship which, having
as one of its terms the unique fact of God, is, as livingly realised, quite
sui generis. If the word sin is denied him, he must find another.

the law was the law of nature, part of the constitution of the world, derived ultimately from the divine reason, but immanent, as the divine reason itself was vaguely conceived to be, in the essential structure of the created order. The Chinese conception of Tao seems to be along much the same lines. In more modern times the moral laws which should govern men's lives have been vaguely identified with the principles governing the always on-going process of evolution ; man must make the barque of his life move with the stream of progress, with that creative something within nature making for more life—or else perish. Others again continually speak of a moral order which must be fulfilled, eternal principles of justice and righteousness which must be served, come what may. It is not to our purpose to discuss the precise meaning, or the validity, of these variant ideas. The point is that they continually recur in one form or another, bearing witness to a deep-seated awareness in man that there confronts him in his moral sense something which is not primarily an expression of his own nature, or designed to serve his own well-being, but is already " there ", whether he likes it or not, in the essential and inexorable nature of things. It is Law, and if he chose to be lawless, he must take the inevitable consequences.

Second, there is the conception that sin is essentially self-abuse. It is an action, or a way of life, which goes against the true norm of man's own being. This is, in a way, another form of the view just mentioned, except that now the law which is infringed is regarded as primarily written within the constitution of human nature. The one view does indeed tend to pass into the other, as it did with the Stoics, who regarded the law of nature as permeating the being of man, so that man, in conforming to it, achieved his own highest life, not as an added reward, but as a necessary consequence. But such a fusion is not inevitable. Thomas Huxley had, apparently, the highest ideals of what a man can and ought to be in himself, and yet denied that those ideals had any counterpart in the order of the external world,[1] and many of our modern secularists seem to regard morality as fundamentally indistinguishable from hygiene, having no reference other than to the biological requirements of the organism. Whether such views are tenable or not, they bear witness to the fact that it seems to be a spontaneous deliverance of the moral sense of mankind that somewhere in that area of things indicated by the term sin man turns aside from the path of his true development, injures his own being, is not his true self, " lets himself down " as popular speech puts it.

Third, there is the conception that sin is essentially selfishness. It is an attempt to isolate and enclose the self and its ends, a refusal to merge the life in a larger whole. The fact that there are a great number of variant ideas as to what the larger whole is from which the errant man isolates himself only serves to emphasise the sameness of the fundamental idea. At the lowest extreme there is that thin and secular morality which identifies wrong-doing merely with anti-social conduct, and conceives that no one can be condemned for doing what he likes, provided only that he does not disregard unduly the requirements of his community. Then there is the view which on psychological grounds maintains that men's minds are made for fellowship, and cannot be healthy and happy unless they learn to lose themselves creatively in the larger life of mankind. Again, there are the various forms of pantheism—the cosmic variety which discovers the highest bliss in " moments of transcendence," when the personality realises its unity with the whole order of the world and accepts its place in it without regret or wishing it otherwise ; and the acosmic variety which yearns after the complete disappearance of the self in Nirvana, wherein every desire has ceased, including even the desire for any

[1] *Evolution and Ethics*, p. 83.

form of personal existence as a self. Finally, there is the whole Christian ethic of love, the finding of the personal life by completely surrendering it to the will of God in the service of man. And running through all these special expressions of it, there is the deep instinct of the common man to revere above all things else the selfless life and to detest its opposite, so soon, at least, as it reaches a certain pitch of ruthlessness and disregard for others.

Fourth, there is what we indicated at the beginning to be the specifically religious thought of sin, namely that it is something through which a man is set against *God*, the word God standing not for an impersonal Moral Order or Creative Life Force, nor for a man's own Better Self, nor for the Totality of Social Ideals, but for the Eternal as personal will which enters into relation with the will of man in a polarity or tension of personal relationship. As we saw in the previous chapters, the central thing in the awareness of God as the eternal Thou standing over against the will of man is the impact of an absolute demand, which demand, however, is apprehended not as merely demand, but as an expression also of a succouring purpose which, through the demand, is inviting man to tread the way of his highest blessedness. Through this central impact the whole dimension of the Eternal as personal, omnipresent, omniscient, holy Creator is opened up livingly to the soul, not indeed in this analytic and conceptual way, but in a unitary awareness which is just the awareness of *God*, and which cannot be described in terms of any other experience. In accordance with this the specifically religious sense of sin centres in this central impact of the divine will as absolute demand ; it is apprehended as being fundamentally a refusal to respond to that demand, as disobedience, as involving, therefore, a dislocation or rupture or alienation—whatever word may be chosen to indicate that which, being ultimate, is inexpressible—in the most fundamental of all personal relationships in which man stands, namely his relation as will to the Eternal as will. But though the religious sense of sin centres in this, it does not exhaust it, any more than the awareness of absolute demand exhausts the sense of God. All that is opened up to the soul of the reality of God in and through the impact of His will upon man's is taken up into the awareness of being disobedient to, and alienated from, that will. Hence, in a way that is not unimportant to note, the three conceptions of sin first mentioned above are all included in the specifically religious interpretation of it.

Thus, sin, being against God, is felt as being against a law and an order which must somehow run throughout all creation ; it is against that eternal, changeless will of God in which the whole creation lives and moves and has its being, and from which it derives its meaning and character. And, being against God, it is felt as being against the self ; for God is apprehended as having created the self precisely that He might thus address it and claim its whole obedience ; moreover, in so doing He is apprehended as pointing man to his own highest blessedness.[1] Finally, sin, being against an Eternal will which includes the whole of creation in its scope, is felt as being the most radical form of self-isolation, self-inclosure, self-affirmation against the other, which is conceivable, the more so as the divine demand is, as we saw, mediated through, and draws its content from, man's social world and its requirements. In the assertion of the will against God's, all other self-assertion is included. All these are taken up into the religious sense of sin, and are, as it were, overtones within it, sometimes one, sometimes another, being more dominant. Yet the ground-tone, which abides throughout, is the sense of being in conflict, through a refusal to obey, with the Eternal Personal.

[1] See what was said above, Chap. II, concerning the relation of the awareness of God to the immanent norm of personality.

Thus far we have been thinking of sin as something which happens in the sphere of man's personal relationship to God. We turn to other, though not unrelated, meanings and bearings of it when we consider it in relation to the inner life of the individual sinner. We propose in this connexion to ask two questions relevant to our main interest : first, what exactly goes on in the inner life of a man when he sins ? Second, what are the results in his inner life when he has sinned ? Ultimately, of course, these two questions cannot be separated, for what goes on at the moment of sinning depends in part on the consequences of sinning in times past ; but for purposes of exposition they can be considered apart.

First, then, what goes on in the inner life when a man sins ? A simple answer might be that the individual becomes aware of an absolute demand as the word of God to his soul, and then by a free and underived act elects to disobey it. The defect of this answer is not only that it over-simplifies the facts, but also, if it were true, it would deprive the relationship of its personal quality. For if the demands of God are to enter a man's soul in a truly personal way, they must present themselves to his own insight as reasonable and right and relevant to the situation in which he is, otherwise they would have no intelligible meaning, or, having meaning, could only be obeyed as a horse obeys the whip. But a demand which shines, be it in never so small degree, in its own light as reasonable and good, must evoke a certain psychological impulsion of the soul towards it, and therefore disobedience to it can never be simply a matter of negating the demand through some unattached and underived act of freedom directed simply to it ; what has to be negated is in some measure *the propulsion of our own soul towards it*. And again, the awareness of God as personal is bound up, we have seen, with the resistance which the divine demand offers to our own values and preferences ;

that is to say, the impact of the divine will can be known as such only by the conflict into which it enters with certain impulsions already present in the soul. Hence obedience to God can never be simply a matter of affirming His demand by some unattached, underived act of freedom directed simply to it ; what has also to be done is to negate *a propulsion of the soul away from it*. Moreover our awareness of ourselves as personal, as beings who are called to be not mere functions of nature, but in a measure in charge of their own destiny, is bound up with this same fact of being impelled from within in two directions and on two different levels. Only because there are instinctive elements in our make-up which *are* functions of the immediate environment, and another element which is not (namely God's addressing of Himself to the soul in sacred demand), can we discern our proper task and feel it to be a genuine moral struggle, involving the possibility of real achievement and real defeat, and not a piece of play-acting. In an earlier chapter we suggested that the absolute demands of God are profoundly implicated in what we called the immanent norm or teleology of human nature, and this, if it be true, indicates the source of that " psychological pull " which these demands must have if they are to shine in their own light as right and good, and so enter into the inner life in a truly personal way.

If this then is the situation, the question is just how exactly does the freedom of choice between the higher and the lower, towards both of which the soul is internally impelled, enter in ? The answer is that it takes place somehow through the use of the attention. The Greeks held the view that sin is fundamentally ignorance, and that if a man saw the good clearly and fully, he would inevitably do it. This undoubtedly over-simplifies the facts ; but it has this double truth in it, first, that the good (or as we would prefer to say the will of God) has an affinity with a deep urge of

the soul already there, and, second, that the critical thing
is the extent to which the vision of the higher course fills
the mind. Where the view is shallow and wrong is in its
inadequate understanding of man's responsibility for, and
the enormous difficulty of, holding the higher course clearly
and fully before the mind. William James, in a famous
chapter, reduces all acts of volition to acts of attention of
this kind. All ideas, he says, tend to act themselves out,
and the tendency is the stronger the less there is of other
competing ideas in the mind. " Effort of attention is the
essential phenomenon of the will." " The strong-willed man
is the man who hears the still, small voice unflinchingly . . .
holds it fast, in spite of the host of exciting mental images
which rise in revolt against it, and would expel it from the
mind. Sustained in this way by a resolute effort of attention, the difficult object ere long begins to call up its own
congeners and associates and ends by changing the disposition of the man's consciousness altogether. And with his
consciousness, his action changes, for the new object once
stably in possession of the field of his thoughts infallibly
produces its own motor effects. The difficulty lies in
the gaining possession of that field."[1] This, to be sure,
does not cover every complexity of the problem, but it
certainly correctly reports a central fact in experience,
which, if it be a fact at all, could hardly be analysed
further.

Man's freedom, we may say, consists in the power to
suspend temporarily his tendencies to act, and then do
something with his attention. On the one hand he may
insist upon it with himself that he shall look frankly at the
higher course, hold it before his mind, realise its full significance as the word of God to his soul, and so give the deep
urges of his being towards it the opportunity to mobilise
themselves and gain release. If he can do this, the contrary

[1] *Principles of Psychology*, Vol. II, pp. 524, 562.

impulses, being deprived of that occupancy of the mind without which, for all their urgency, they cannot issue in action, die a natural death. On the other hand, he may not look frankly either at the higher course or at the lower in the light of the higher ; if he did, there could be no doubt of the outcome, for it is psychologically impossible for a man really apprehending " the good and perfect will of God " to choose the evil, saying in effect, out of some vacuum of spontaneity, " evil be thou my good ". What he does, rather, is to weave a web of sophistications and rationalisations and self-deceptions over the lower course, making " the worse appear the better reason ", or over the better course, making it appear somehow irrelevant and inappropriate to him at that particular moment. Thus the way of lower desire is given possession of the field, the higher call being deprived of that which, despite its affinity with the deepest things in man's soul, can alone make it effective and triumphant, namely the concentration of the spirit through attention upon it. Yet even then he cannot escape the pull of the higher way upon his soul, for it is indissolubly bound up with the norm of his own being, and he cannot escape himself. So, for peace of mind, the rationalisation and self-deception have to be persisted in long after the actual occasion has gone by. Hypocrisy is said to be the tribute which vice pays to virtue. A deeper analysis might show that it is the tribute which every man at some point or other pays to the inescapable norm of his own being.

That sin is thus at its heart and centre insincerity most sensitive natures have felt. It is going against the light, such light as one has, not in the sense of snuffing it out as a man might a candle-flame between his fingers, for that no one can do, but in the sense of screening it under a veil of excuse and subterfuge. It is " holding down the truth in unrighteousness ". It is for this reason that men have

o

always sensed that sins of passion, in which a man is swept
off his feet by some suddenly and violently stimulated
impulse, are likely to be less significant than sins which are
the working out of quieter and subtler processes of the mind.
The former in comparison with the latter may have in them
relatively little of " tampering with the truth ", of that
insincerity which is the ultimate source of sin's power to
destroy.

Second, what is the result of sin in the inner life of the
individual ? What has just been said has unduly simplified
the matter in that it has offered an analysis of the sinful
response of a man's soul to the impact of the will of God
in abstraction and isolation from his past history and from
his implication in the lives of others. This is artificial,
for the situation in which a man finds himself at any
given moment of decision is always profoundly affected
by his previous sins and failures, and by the sins and
failures of the society which has moulded him from his
birth.

The result of the insincerity which thus turns aside from
the call of God is that the personality, deflected from the
norm of its own being and from the true purpose and uses
of its world, becomes increasingly insensitive to that call.
It grows less and less capable of discerning what the will of
God is, or even that there is a will of God at all ; or if it
continues to speak of God, it is with little living sense of
Him as personal and even at times with an explicit theoretical repudiation of personal quality in Him. Insincerity
swiftly becomes a habit, continually creating fresh opportunity and occasion for its exercise ; until it ends by being
almost a necessity, for the longer this way is persisted in, the
more the monitions of God—if indeed they can break
through the increasing dimness and insensitivity of the soul
—lose their quality of being an invitation to blessedness
and become instead a condemnation threatening the whole

structure of the life in a way too disturbing to be faced. This alienation from God in the mind is, however, not of the mind only. It causes, and is itself caused by, a coarsening of the whole personality, including the will and the feelings and even the physical appetites, for, we reiterate, somehow the norm of the whole personality is involved. Such coarsening may be masked by the refinements of culture and the restraints of civilised manners ; but it is ever ready to reveal itself whensoever personal relations reach a point of unusual strain. The almost incredible callousness and brutality which modern civilised people can display to one another, and the pitiful subterfuges with which they are ready to justify them, even in the name of God, are writ large across the history of the world since 1914. They bear witness to an appalling blindness to the real nature and requirements of the personal order in which God has set men with Himself.

These consequences of sin would be bad enough if confined to the personality of the individual sinner. But just because it is a personal order in which man is placed, it is impossible that they should be so confined. No individual can be judged wholly responsible for the state of darkness in which he dwells. If it is always in a measure the result of his own insincerity, it is also in a measure the result of other people's. For the insincerities of individuals organise themselves into social systems, with their enormous power to shape every new personality which is born into them. Every individual, himself swiftly victimised as soon as born, is soon in turn victimising others, and so the process goes on, until a cosmos, or as Ritschl called it, a kingdom of evil, with a frightful power of self-perpetuation and renewal, is brought into being. The inner life of the individual thus becomes, not a clear-cut issue between the higher and the lower, between conscience and instinct, but a confused cock-pit of forces, some of them unconscious and even uncontrollable, in which

it is impossible to say where personal choice and responsibility begin and end.[1]

If this be in any degree a true diagnosis of the situation,
it is clear what the central problem of man's salvation is.
Somehow the darkness of his mind must be broken through
so that he can at least begin to see things as they really
are—God as He really is, himself as he really is, his neighbours
as they really are, within that whole personal order which
underlies all the circumstances of his life and in which it is
the divine will that he should find his right place. Thus
to break through the darkness of his mind cannot, however,
be merely a matter of displaying the truth about his situation
to him even in what might be supposed to be a lucid and
convincing way, for the problem is precisely man's ingrained
insincerity, which finds it hard to face up to any truth
which has a challenge to his egotism in it, and hardest of
all to face one which is a radical condemnation of his whole
life. The saving revelation must be such that at one and the
same time it shows man the truth and makes it possible for
him to be sincere with it. It must make him vividly aware
again of the searching, holy will of the Eternal dealing with

---

[1] Cf. J. Lewis, *The Lord of Life*, edited by Vernon Bartlet, p. 13:
" A system of interests and values of a perverted sort often appears in
society as a kind of eddy within the general stream of corrupt social life ;
thus we speak quite commonly of the ' Racing World ', the ' Night Club
World ', and so on. It is important to consider how accurate the designa-
tion ' world ' is in such cases, for the personalities who live within such
spheres are themselves the creation and reflection of these perverted
activities and values. Both their individual souls and the objective world
they know and see and believe in and reach towards are of this peculiarly
distorted and unreal character. Finally, even the whole world-order may
' lie in the Evil One ', the whole of human life being honeycombed with
spiritual idolatry."

Fritz Künkel, in his *Einführung in die Karakterkunde*, writing as a
psychologist, shows how the egotism and concomitant blindness of parents,
teachers, friends, the whole system of social relationships into which every
child is born, in varying degree stimulate and confirm egotism and blindness
in him. He puts his finger on the central point when he defines the saint,
from the psychological point of view, as one who has attained the highest
possible degree of sensitivity to reality, of insight into the true nature of
the world, of mastery in the use of proper means to right ends. (p. 9.)

him, challenging him, condemning him, yet in such wise as to enable him not to run away from it, but sincerely and humbly to accept it. In short, it must bring a new manifestation of God as both *consuming fire* and *final refuge and strength*, only now in such wise that the inner darkness caused by sin and insincerity is broken through and the deepest springs of the soul's life reached.

The Christian affirmation is that God has made such a saving revelation of Himself in the personality of Jesus Christ. It is obviously beyond the scope of this book to consider in detail the way in which this saving work of Jesus is wrought out. All that is necessary is to point out two things related to our general interest in the experience of God as personal, and to the line of thought we have been pursuing in this chapter.

First, God's saving revelation of Himself in Jesus Christ fulfils the condition laid down that it should at one and the same time show man the truth and enable him sincerely to face and accept it. It does this because it is a revelation of God as holy love. On the one hand, livingly to apprehend God as love is inevitably to realise the limitless demands of love and the devastating condemnation of one's whole manner of life which such demands carry with them. Yet, on the other hand, there is no need to flee from the condemnation, precisely because it is love which is thus searchingly dealing with the soul. In its utter condemnation, it is intending to succour and save, and its intention to succour and save makes the condemnation the more piercing and irresistible. Thus to apprehend the utter condemnation of God's holy will of love, and yet also to face and accept it without the sophistications and insincerities with which one has hitherto veiled the light, to face and accept it because it is love with which one is dealing—this is to be truly and deeply penitent. But it is also to be forgiven, to be reconciled, to be aware that the fundamental alienation of the whole being from

God is overcome. It is not that we first repent and then something called forgiveness is added. The two things, though distinguishable in thought, are given in a single, inclusive, personal relationship of the profoundest possible kind, the penitence being deeper because the love of God is already seen to be succouring and forgiving, the succour and the forgiveness seeming the more wonderful the more, through penitence, the soul's complete unworthiness is felt. It is not possible to be truly penitent in the presence of the love of God revealed in Christ without experiencing forgiveness and reconciliation. As Herrmann puts it : " When we see the goodness which condemns us and the love which seeks us as the working of the same personal will, we experience forgiveness."[1]

Second, God's saving revelation of Himself in Jesus Christ is given in the only form which, so far as can be judged, can pierce the darkness of man's soul without ceasing to be a truly personal dealing with him.

Thus, in the first place, it is given through a personality moving within the plane of history and manifesting itself in and through the personal relations of man's own life. We have already more than once referred to the impotence of merely abstract truths to touch the will and the feelings and to mediate a living, personal relationship to God. God's method, because it is personal, is to speak to man through this present, terrestrial order in which He has placed him, and in complete accord with this is the Christian affirmation of God's saving revelation of Himself through a historic personality. In the second place, the saving revelation is given through a personality which is completely surrendered to, at one with, indwelt by, that divine holy will of love by which man, in his darkness, needs to be confronted. A personal life itself infected with the darkness, insincerity, and corruption of sin could not pierce through

[1] *Op. cit.*, p. 130.

the darkness, insincerity, and corruption of sin to the inner-most places of man's soul, and act, in all circumstances and every stage of development, as the source and medium of divine light and cleansing within it. In the third place, the saving revelation is given through the Church ; that is to say, through the fellowship, continuing through the ages, of those into whose lives God is entering savingly through Christ.

This last point is of the highest importance and in any full exposition of these matters would require extended treatment. Because of the Church as the society of those who are being redeemed, the revelation in Jesus Christ is far other than a few stories and traditions about a historic figure receding farther and farther into the past. It is a revelation which meets and grasps the soul here and now through a living organism of personal relations of a unique kind, and as such it has a saving and recreating relevancy and power which would otherwise be lacking. This does not in the least imply that the picture of the historic Jesus given in the New Testament can ever be dispensed with. That, for the reasons given, must ever remain the supreme source of light to every new generation of Christian men and women. But only as Jesus is presented and approached through the Christian fellowship can the saving word of God to the soul that is in Him become " quick and powerful ". Because of this even the simplest Christian piety has always been able to grasp, without difficulty, the essential meaning of Paul's metaphor of the Church as the Body of Christ, and to affirm, despite all theoretic difficulties which hover in the background, the unity, within the one eternal, saving purpose of God, of the Jesus of history and the ever-living Head of the Church.

The important point for us, however, is that the saving revelation in Jesus Christ is thus mediated, to repeat the phrase already used, through a living organism of personal

relationships. The Christian faith, in its insistence upon
this, confirms and consummates what has been said in the
earlier chapters. In Chapter III we insisted that the living
awareness of God as personal is not apart from the social
environment—the infinite personal is given through the
finite personal. In the same way reconciliation to God
through Jesus Christ is not, and never can be, apart from the
fellowship of those in whom that reconciling work is also
being wrought out. From this point of view, the statement
that outside the Church there is no salvation is unexcep-
tionable ; it is really only another way of insisting that God
is personal and deals with men always, and not least when
He is saving them from sin, in and through an order of
personal relationships. To be sure, God's saving work in
Christ can be wrought out only as the endeavour is made to
do His will and trust His overshadowing wisdom in respect
of all personal relationships whatsoever, and not merely of
those within the Fellowship ; but the latter has a special
and indispensable function in that its members, through
their common relationship to Christ—their love to one
another in the love of God, constitute an entirely new sort
of spiritual fact, through which God is able to take men far
more deeply into the world of redeemed personal relations
than is otherwise possible.[1]

[1] Therefore, the Christian faith, whilst it insists that reconciliation
with God through Christ is always " personal " in the sense of being
individual, each walking by his own insight and knowing God directly in
the intimacies of his own life, yet also insists that it is not " personal " in
the sense of being private, requiring nothing beyond the soul and its God
for its inception and progress. This last notion is characteristic rather of
mystical piety, which, according to its essential idea, almost inevitably
tends to dispense with the religious society. The point should be borne
in mind in all that follows in this book. We shall approach the topics
taken up primarily through the experience of the individual, for, we
repeat, except such experience be individual, it cannot be personal ; but
that does not mean that we entertain for a moment the impossible idea of
a private and solipsistic Christian, however little explicit reference may be
made to Church as such. Our individual relation to the reconciling love
of God in Christ—in its demand and succour, in our answering penitence

Thus, then, is brought about the new life of reconciliation with God, in which the awareness of the infinite demands and the infinite succour of His love are daily renewed in penitence and forgiveness, as the soul keeps company with Christ in the fellowship of His people. A profound cleansing, illumination, re-orientation of the inner life, a clearing away of the fogs of insincerity, a growth towards the true norm of personal being, begins. The results of this in the whole tone and quality of the personal life can here be stated only in the most general terms. In general we would say that the man who is being reconciled to God through Christ grows more and more livingly aware, first, that his life, over all its breadth, rests on a personal order which derives its being and its character from the holy love of God ; second, that he himself is called upon to serve that same holy love of God in all his dealings with his fellow-men ; third, that he must and can commit himself without fear to that same holy love of God when the way of obedience seems the way of appalling risk and sacrifice, or when disaster and trouble overtake his life, or, even more, when, with increasing knowledge of God, there comes an increasing sense of disloyalty and sin both in himself and in his fellows. This is the life of faith, sustained day by day by the vision of God given through Christ, and supremely through His Cross. In the category of faith, which as we have before insisted is the most distinctively personal of all categories, there is summed up the whole new relationship to God over the whole breadth of experience, to which Christ opens a man's eyes and into the fuller realisation of which He increasingly brings him. It is a total commitment of the self to the Eternal Personal

---

and trust—has always organic, historic, essential relations to other people, the Fellowship, the Body of Christ. Or as the New Testament much better expresses it, it is by being rooted and grounded in *love*, and with *all saints*, that we are able to comprehend what is the breadth, and length, and depth, and height ; and to know the love of Christ which passes knowledge. (Eph. iii. 17–19.)

as One utterly loving even in His most austere demands, wherefore He can be joyfully obeyed ; utterly wise in all the appointments of His providence, wherefore He can be quietly trusted ; utterly forgiving in His ceaseless exposure of and judgement upon sin, wherefore always can a man look up to Him with a penitence that is without self-deception and without fear.

As a man enters more and more deeply into this life of reconciliation through Christ over the whole breadth of his living, the assurance is built up in him, in a way that is proof against every contrary consideration, no matter how challenging, that the ultimate reality with which he has to deal is personal, that he and his fellows in and through God constitute a personal system, which because it is in and through God outlasts the seen and temporal things of man's terrestrial existence. It is not a matter of abstract demonstration, but of so having the eyes opened to, and living in, and responding to a personal world that it increasingly bears witness to itself as real. Nor, perhaps it is not unnecessary to add, is it a matter of becoming aware of God as *a* personality, as a sort of localised, individualised centre, in the way that we are aware of one another. God is never localised object in that way. It is rather that the Eternal as personal, —how can such an ultimate awareness be expressed ?— becomes increasingly the air a man breathes, the ground he walks on, the light he sees by, presupposed and implied in every awareness and in every response, even when the thought of God is not explicitly present to the mind. The fullest conviction of God as personal is therefore not for all and sundry. It is only for those whose eyes are being opened by the cleansing of their inner life from sin.[1]

[1] This gives at least one answer to those psychologists who affirm that the attribution of personality to God, particularly under the image of father, is merely a childish projection into the universe, otherwise hostile and unmanageable, of a protector and friend. Such a theory, whatever truth it may have in respect of certain types of religious belief, is quite

There is, however, one aspect of the life of reconciliation, which, though barely hinted at in the above summary statement of its content, is of such far-reaching importance in it, and therefore in the whole awareness of God as personal, that it calls for full treatment, the more so as the Christian doctrine of providence depends upon it at more than one point. This aspect may be called the eschatological aspect of reconciliation, and to this we now turn.

inadequate to the depth and reach of the Christian awareness of God as personal, as this is cleansed and developed through Christ's reconciling work within the Christian fellowship. The Christian awareness is ethical through and through, full of high and austere demand, and moving on a plane of self-forgetfulness and love in a divine society of personal ends. To compare it even remotely to the phantasy projection of a cowed and disappointed and infantile mind is absurd.

CHAPTER XII

RECONCILIATION AND ESCHATOLOGY

ETYMOLOGICALLY the word eschatology means doctrine about last things, so that any statement about the ultimate destiny of the individual or the world in general might without impropriety be called eschatological. Thus the theories of certain scientists that the universe, because of the law of entropy, is running down to a final state of motionless equilibrium, are eschatological theories in this sense. One author refers to the primitive man's belief in survival after death as eschatological, even though he goes on to assert that such belief is not a product of religious faith, but rather of the crude psychological ideas of the time.[1]

There is, however, a narrower use of the term which, on the whole, is more useful, though the wider use just indicated need not always be pedantically avoided, and that is to confine it to the religious and theological sphere. It then indicates a doctrine of the final destiny of man and his world in so far as this is conceived as dependent upon something other than, and transcending, man and his world, namely God. It is the thought of *God* as determining the ultimate outcome of things, whatever this may be, which, according to this usage, constitutes a doctrine specifically eschatological. Yet even when thus more narrowly defined, there is still some ambiguity. It is possible to believe, as Plato did, in God as the eternal reality upon which all things depend, and yet to believe that this world goes on for ever and ever in recurrent cycles of events. His eschatology,

[1] J. Baillie, *And the Life Everlasting*, p. 74, 91.

in the sense of doctrine concerning an ultimate outcome of terrestrial happenings conceived as dependent upon God, is not eschatology in the sense that it envisages something which is a real end or "eschaton". His doctrine of last things is that there is no last thing. Should this be called eschatological belief ? It would be pedantic, perhaps, to answer in the negative, yet it would probably eliminate some confusion if we did, and if we confined the word eschatological to those doctrines of the end which envisage some sort of real termination of the present world order. This, at any rate, is the sense in which we propose to use the term in this chapter.

Historically, eschatological conviction in this sense has appeared in its purest and most developed form in four religions, Zoroastrianism, Judaism, Christianity and Islam. In these it is found expression in an enormous variety of detailed exposition, some of it of a wildly fantastic kind, but underlying all such there are to be discerned three main ideas which unite them all and make them specifically eschatological in the sense in which we are proposing to use the term. First, there is the thought of the activity of God. The end of the present order will come, not because of the mechanical interplay of mundane forces, but because, in any event, God, in the achieving of His eternal purpose, intends to bring it to an end at some point or other. Second, the end which is thus brought about by God is a real end, in the sense that the present order gives way to, is replaced by, something which so completely transcends it that there is radical discontinuity between the two, and the one cannot be expressed in terms of the other save by inadequate analogies and myths. Viewed from this angle, the scientific theory of an end-state of equilibrium in the universe is seen to be no true end at all ; for the same processes which brought about the equilibrium persist in the maintenance of it, so that it is still in the fullest sense the same world. Third, though there is discontinuity between this world and the world that is to come in respect of essential constitution, none the less there is continuity between them in respect of the fact that they both rest on the divine will which is always consistent with itself. Hence the world which is to come is the end of the present order in the other sense of the word end ; it is the consummation of that divine purpose which created, and is at work in, the present order and in relation to which alone the latter has any significance.

So conceived, eschatological faith has a profound relationship to the experience of God as personal, and particularly to the consummation of that experience in the Christian experience of reconciliation through Christ, a relationship which it is important to understand, the more so as the modern mind is apt to recoil from eschatological ideas. Such recoil is indeed another symptom of its loss of the sense of God as personal, and its obsession with monistic theories. That there is such a relation is indicated by the fact that it is precisely those religions which have most livingly and consistently apprehended God as holy will active towards man and within history—the four religions named above— which have made eschatological faith dominant in their whole outlook. We have, indeed, suggested that all living religions have at the heart of them some awareness of God as personal, and it is in accord with this that in almost all religions at all stages of development eschatological ideas of a life beyond the grave, and of a world one day transformed, make their appearance. Yet such notions are not central and dominant, and they are inextricably mixed up with those eudæmonistic and egotistic ideas which always threaten to corrupt eschatological faith. For the Christian certainly the eschatological aspect of faith in, and reconciliation to, God as personal cannot be overlooked, for it is clearly dominant in the New Testament and goes back to Him who must ever be the source and standard of specifically Christian conviction, Jesus Christ Himself.

What are the circumstances and states of mind out of which eschatological hopes spring ? The answer in a general and preliminary way is clear. They spring out of an intense realisation of conflict between what is ardently believed and sought after and what in actuality appears to be the facts, between what is grasped in the inner life, or rather let us say what is felt irresistibly to grasp the inner life, and what is known and experienced in the outer world. The historical circumstances in which, for example, Jewish eschatology and apocalyptic arose would be sufficient to show this, even apart from the insight which modern psychology has given us into the mechanism of conflict and compensation. It is a commonplace that men are prone to solve their conflicts and compensate their disappointments by brilliant hopes and imaginary satisfactions. Jewish eschatology shows a crescendo of belief as the long years of bitter frustration and disappointment in their national history mount up, showing clearly that the familiar process of compensation which we can observe in other spheres is at work here also.

Nor is it difficult to see that lying at the root of eschatological faith there are two main problems of human life, of which all men are in some degree aware at one time or another, irrespective of their religious beliefs, or, indeed, of their having any explicitly held religious beliefs at all. One is the fact of death, the apparent running out of every individual life, whatever its quality, into complete extinction. The other is the fact that life generally in this world, even apart from death, seems to have permanent elements of ugliness, disappointment and frustration in it, ill according with the ends which man, by his very constitution, feels impelled to seek and without which the very springs of his life would dry up :

> " Ah! love, could you and I with fate conspire
> To grasp this sorry scheme of things entire,
> Would we not shatter it to bits, and then
> Rebuild it nearer to the heart's desire ? "

In Jewish eschatology these two strands—concern about the achievement of an ideal world in which God's will shall be perfectly done and concern about the individual in respect of death—can be clearly discerned ; they meet and intertwine with one another in the doctrine of the bodily resurrection of the dead in order to take part in the glory and joy of the messianic kingdom.

The eschatological solution of these universal problems is, however, not the only one which has been propounded. We are bound, therefore, to ask the question, in what circumstances that particular solution emerges ? What is the inner connecting process which leads inevitably from the common problem to that particular solution ? The inner, connecting link is, as already indicated, the living experience of God as personal, as holy will addressing the soul of man as absolute demand and final succour. We may say that the more this awareness of God is cleansed, and becomes exalted and dominant, in the religious life, the more inevitable becomes eschatological hope ; until, indeed, at its highest, as in the experience of the Christian believer who is being reconciled to God through Christ, it ceases in a sense to be a hope and becomes a certitude in the strength of which a man lives.

To make clear how this is so it is necessary to revert to what was said at the beginning of Chapter IV concerning the necessity to a genuine personal relationship between God and man of a triadic independence of God, man and the world. Both man and the world must be conceived as having significance for God, and as having a measure of independence over against God as well as over against one another. If this is in any way departed from, so that man and his world become merged in one another or in God, then the personal quality of man's relationship to God is sooner or later, explicitly or implicitly, denied. Now solutions to the problem of the unsatisfactoriness of man's life have been offered which in one form or another do this. Thus in acosmic mysticism the world is treated as of the nature of illusion, and the way to rise above its trials and afflictions is to escape from it into an eternal and ineffable world of divine reality. In cosmic mysticism, on the other hand, the world is identified with God ; the way to rise above its trials and afflictions is therefore to realise that they are not really there, what appears to be such to our defective apprehension being in fact, if only we could see them *sub specie æternitatis*, parts of an already fully realised harmony of being. In both, as was indicated in Chapter IV, the ultimate personal quality of man's relationship with God, as a will set over against the divine will, tends to be minimised or denied.

Another solution against which the same objection lies is the comparatively modern optimistic doctrine of progress. We are bidden discern in the present unsatisfactoriness of life but a stage in the fashioning of a world order of truth, beauty and goodness by a creative power immanent in all things, and especially present in the reason of man. It is generally recognised that historically this faith in an inevitable mundane progress, so different from the cycle theory of the antique world, was derived in part from the Christian eschatological faith, being a secularised form of it ; as such it carries with it some of the power of that faith to give men a significant sphere for their activities and victory over the unsatisfactoriness of things as they are. But it has this fatal flaw, that it devaluates the individual himself, and leaves the problem of his own personal extinction, often through apparently irrational and fortuitous causes, entirely unrelieved. He becomes a mere vehicle of the life-process, a transient bearer of partially realised values, which in some mysterious way are handed on to coming generations. To accept this position cheerfully has at first sight the appearance of exalted self-immolation,

P

but it is a mood which is ill-founded, for in the end this devaluation of the individual as an end in himself works back into his conception of the world, and devaluates it. The life-force begins to take on the aspect of an impersonal energy working to some inscrutable end, the impersonal quality of which is but thinly veiled by speaking, as Windelband, for example, does, of eternal values of truth, beauty and goodness. A creative process which does not now value the individual as an end in himself can hardly be conceived as valuing him in the far-off divine event to which it is supposed to be mounting. Thus again the whole thing becomes depersonalised, as is inevitable if at any point the triadic significance of God, man and the world is infringed.[1]

It is the merit of eschatological faith that it provides a solution for the conflicts and frustrations of life which preserves this triadic significance. Hence it is that those religions which have most emphasised the thought of God as personal will meeting man's will in history have, by a sound instinct, avoided in the main any other than this solution.

Let us take each point in turn, commenting first in a general way and then showing the relationship to the specifically Christian experience of reconciliation.

(1) First, in respect of the significance of man. This arises especially in connection with the problem of death. For this problem eschatological faith provides a solution

---

[1] This may be illustrated from Mr. Julian Huxley's *Religion without Revelation*, wherein we are bidden rejoice in our calling as vehicles of a creative power ever mounting up to higher levels of value, and then told that everything may in the end be swept away as the web of a spider is swept away by the broom (p. 358). Thus always the conception of the life-force is on the verge of changing from that of something which the individual may joyfully serve to that of something which is as impersonal as mechanism, freezing the soul in despair. It is interesting to note the way in which the optimistic doctrine of progress of the beginning of the century collapsed into despair after the world war, so that there reappeared, as in Spengler's *Decline of the West*, the ancient doctrine of world cycles. We shall return to this topic in the concluding chapter.

which preserves to the full the significance of the individual
as a personal end in himself, by affirming, on the one hand,
a life for the individual beyond the grave, and by avoiding,
on the other hand, any conception of that life which involves
the absorption of the individual in God. It would be a
radical misunderstanding of this thought if it were supposed
that it is based on philosophical argument, though inasmuch
as it arises in part from the necessity of overcoming certain
contradictions in experience it has a relation to reason in
the broad sense. It is also misunderstood if it be regarded
as merely the outcome of the fear of extinction or desire for
pleasures prolonged, though eudæmonistic corruptions do in
fact always threaten eschatological faith. It is rather that
the living sense of God as personal, as sacred demand and
final succour, contains within it implicitly a denial of the
finality of death, and it requires only the stimulus of
appropriate circumstance to make that denial explicit in a
consciously expressed faith.

To make clear in a general way the deep roots in religious
experience of belief in survival of the individual after death
we need to go back to what was said in Chapter II. There
we saw how the two elements in the awareness of God, the
awareness of Him as absolute demand and the awareness of
Him as final succour, throw the religious subject into a
dilemma precisely because of the fact of death. On the one
hand there is the demand to surrender life itself, if need be—
the possibility of death, in fact, alone making the demand
recognisable as absolute. This incidence of absolute demand,
we saw, is closely related to the achievement of a genuine
personal life in independence of the world. On the other
hand, to die seems on the surface to destroy the self altogether. To develop a true self, one must be prepared in
principle to perish ; yet if one perish, how can it be developed ? The solution of this dilemma might be sought
along lines of purely rational reflection, as for example in

Kant's postulation of immortality in order to make sense of what he took to be the demands of the practical reason ; but for the religious mind the solution is already given in the essential nature of the religious experience itself. For the demand to serve absolute values at any cost is not in fact apprehended in that abstract way at all, but as the impact of the will of God, of an ultimate personal purpose, which is felt as in some way guaranteeing the personal life in the very act of asking the apparent annihilation of it in death.

In all this we touch the deepest sources of the belief in some sort of survival after death, namely the awareness of the will of God here and now resting upon the individual and asking its surrender to itself. The belief expresses the sense of the value of the self, which can be realised only on the basis of the mastery of death. Here also is the reason why the average man instinctively feels that if it were finally demonstrated that there is nothing beyond death, the highest ideals would somehow lose part of their right to his absolute obedience, and the philosophy of " eat, drink, and be merry, for to-morrow we die," would become one which neither in reason nor in practice he could long resist. Such a feeling is the outcome of a grasp, however dim, of the significance of his own being and of the conditions requisite for the fulfilment of it. It is difficult to believe, indeed, despite contrary theories,[1] that even the belief of primitive man in survival did not have at least one root in the religious awareness and in the sense, just referred to, of the signifi-cance of the self which such awareness carries with it. But be that as it may—who can know, after all, what went on in the primitive soul ?—it is certain that the greater clarity and certainty of the conviction of a life beyond death which become manifest at a higher stage were connected with the greater clarity and certainty of the experience of the will of

[1] As, for example, maintained by J. Baillie, *op. cit.*, p. 90 f.

God challenging the individual in absolute demand and final succour, i.e. of God as personal. Von Hügel's words express once and for all the way in which living religion solves the problem of death : " The specifically religious desire of Immortality begins, not with Immortality, but with God ; it rests upon God ; and it ends with God. The religious soul does not seek, find, or assume its own Immortality ; and thereupon seek, find, or assume God. But it seeks, finds, experiences, and loves God ; and because of God, and of this, its very real though still very imperfect, intercourse with God—because of these experiences, which lie right within the noblest joys, fears, hopes, necessities, certainties which emerge within any and every field of its life here below—it finds, rather than seeks, Immortality of a certain kind."[1] The religious conviction, in other words, is always eschatological, in the sense in which we have defined that term.

It is, however, in the Christian experience of God as personal, and of reconciliation to Him, that this certitude of a life beyond death reaches its maximum. Everything centres here in the growing awareness through Christ of God as holy love. In proportion as the succouring and reconciling love of God to the soul is livingly apprehended through Christ, the idea of complete annihilation in death, or after death, becomes unthinkable. Nothing so contradicts the essential nature of love as the extinction of its object, for love is the affirmation of the other in his totality ; to conceive oneself as the object at one and the same time of a redeeming purpose such as is revealed in the agony of the

---

[1] *Essays and Addresses on the Philosophy of Religion*, p. 197. Cf. Ps. lxxiii. 23, 24. Commenting on this passage, Pringle-Pattison says : " In his experience of communion with God, the author of the 73rd Psalm intimates, he has already tasted eternal life. He has been in touch with that from which nothing hereafter can separate him, so that with God his future is secure. It is the nature of his present experience which is the ground of his for ever." (*The Idea of Immortality*, p. 19.)

Cross and of a destructive force such as death at first sight appears to be is, therefore, impossible. The one cancels the other out. The full power of the Christian conviction requires, however, far more than the awareness of oneself as the object of God's succouring love, for that might easily lapse into a form of that eudæmonism which, however refined, always carries the seeds of despair and unbelief in its heart. Indispensable also is the growing awareness of God's love as absolute demand, of the call to share His holy purpose of love in the lives of others. Here, again, the Church enters in as a necessary factor. As the reconciled man begins to love others with something of the love wherewith God has loved him, to see in them beings on whom rests the love of God, and from whom comes forth the austere challenge of God to his own will, so also their extinction becomes unthinkable. Thus the apparent destructiveness of death is repudiated in an affirmation of eternal life which, alike in its origin and in its scope, infinitely transcends merely private and personal desires.

(2) Second, in respect of the significance of the world. This arises especially in connection with the unsatisfactoriness of this present life. Eschatological faith provides a solution for this which does not evacuate the world of its meaning as a sphere in which God's presence may now be known and His will served, even though these will never be perfectly realised. It does this by conceiving the divine kingdom as the end of the present order in the double sense of the word end. Somehow there is at work within the limitations and frustrations of this world a divine purpose which transcends it and cannot be comprehended in terms of it. The consummation of that purpose will therefore at one and the same time mark the end of this world and be the fulfilment and justification of it. And the divine will, which will be fully realised only then, can none the less be served now, even as the far-off ocean may swell the water

of an inland creek and lift the boats of those who have never seen its infinite horizons. Eschatological faith is thus both pessimistic and optimistic in regard to this world. It says yes and no to it at one and the same time. It is God's world and yet it is not God's world in the fullest sense, being only preparatory to it.

Doubtless this outlook may easily be corrupted into a morbidly pessimistic other-worldliness, which sees this world as irretrievably sunk in evil and conceives that the highest service of God is to be detached as completely as possible from it. This is always due to an infiltration of egotistic and eudæmonistic moods and attitudes, which are at bottom more concerned with the contradiction which this world offers to personal wishes and ambitions (even though these may be expressed in religious form) than with the contradiction it offers to the will of God.[1] In proportion, however, as eschatological faith remains true to its origin in the living sense of God as holy will meeting man in absolute demand, which is also his truest succour, in his present historical situation, it is impossible for it to lapse into such morbid preoccupation with another world. It is here and now that God's will requires obedience ; the here and now must, therefore, be significant for God's will ; yet in proportion as the soul realises the divine demand, so it realises how little of God's will can be done in the here and now. Not to speak of the other ills and frustrations to which man is subject, sin remains an ever-present factor, and the more the soul is possessed with the sense of the limitless demands

---

[1] Thus it was with later Jewish eschatological thought, which drove the contrast between the present age and the age to come ever deeper until the former took on the appearance of being almost an atheistic patch in the universe completely under the dominion of satanic powers. This can be traced to the strain of intense legalistic nationalism which entered into post-exilic Judaism, and in which egotism and eudæmonism were often but thinly veiled by professed zeal for the will of God as expressed in the Law. It should be added that apocalypticism was only one element in Judaism and was repudiated by normal Rabbinism.

of God's holiness, the more intensely the corruptions and frustration of sin in human life are felt. Thus the significance of the here and now irresistibly points forward to that which transcends the here and now altogether.

In accordance with this, it is, once again, in the experience of God as personal and of reconciliation to Him, that this certitude of the world to come, which shall both terminate and fulfil this world, reaches its purest and maximal form, free from egotistic eudæmonism and from the false other-worldliness which derives from it. Here also everything centres in the awareness through Christ of God's will as holy love. To apprehend God as holy love is to apprehend his absolute demands as demands for love. Even as God loved us, so must we love one another. But love has no meaning save as it represents a call and a responsibility which confronts us every time we confront another. Wherever there is personal relationship, there the will of God as love meets us, and demands our co-operation with itself. But it is impossible to love a person except by loving him now; a love which proposed to operate a few years hence, or " hereafter in a better world than this ", is plainly not love at all. Nor can love express itself save in relation to the needs of the other's immediate, historical situation—in the giving of the cup of water. Whence it follows that in proportion as the awareness of God as personal is cleansed and elevated into the awareness of Him as love, this present world comes to have the most solemn significance as the scene where the obligations of the kingdom of God in a personal order are already laid upon us and we must surrender ourselves utterly to God in their discharge.[1] On the other hand, the more clearly the will of God is discerned to be love, and to ask nothing but love, the more poignant

[1] This indicates the only right Christian motive for social reform, namely, not that there should be more material comfort and security for everybody, but that there should be right personal relations. The latter might be achieved in an era of general want.

becomes the sense that, in the circumstances of this present
life, it can never be completely fulfilled, but must await
fulfilment in an order of being so radically different from
the present that God alone can bring it into being. This
last point may be illustrated along two lines.

First, in relation to the reconciled man's thought of
himself as a sinner.

The more he becomes aware of the austere purity and
limitless demands of God's love as this shines into his heart
through Christ, the more he realises how deeply inwrought
into his whole being is that which is not of love, and therefore of sin. This of itself would mean naught but disquiet
of mind ; but the vision of the love of God, as we have seen,
carries with it, not only condemnation bringing penitence,
but also forgiveness bringing peace. There is, however, a
contrariety in this experience which irresistibly forces the
mind out of the here and now into the eschatological beyond.
The essence of forgiveness, and the source of all its wonder
and recreating power, is that at one and the same time
there is a repudiation of the sinful man and an acceptance
of him. The only way of grasping this contrariety, in such-
wise that it ceases to take on the appearance of an immoral
condonation of sin, is to bring in the future and to realise
that God's love accepts us as sinners, and we are entitled to
be at peace about ourselves as sinners, only because, in spite
of what we now are, He intends to present us faultless before
Him. Thus inasmuch as His acceptance of us as we are is
the first step in His purpose to make us other than we are,
it contains within it the most active repudiation of sin
conceivable, a repudiation which will not stop short of sin's
ultimate annihilation. But when, where, how, will that
annihilation be accomplished ? Certainly not in this world.
No Christian believer who knows the searching of God's
spirit in his heart can envisage the possibility of walking
this earth a faultless man ; on the contrary, the more deeply

he moves into reconciled fellowship with God, the more sensitively aware he becomes of the sinful lovelessness of his nature and his need for the continuing pardon of God, so that he cries without affectation, " I am the chief of sinners." Sin and the need for pardon seem part of the essential constitution of life in this world. Where, when, how, then, will that which can justify pardon be realised, namely the elimination of sin altogether ? The only possible answer is that the manner and place and occasion lie beyond the order of this world altogether. The reconciled man's life is thus " hid with Christ in God ". Thus an essential element in the whole experience of forgiveness, which lies at the heart of the Christian's reconciliation with God, is eschatological, is a pointing forward to a divine consummation which involves the cessation of the present sinful order in which man now is. As Althaus says : " Without eschatology the doctrine of forgiveness in view of our present abiding state of sinfulness, cannot be saved from falling either into frivolity or into rank scepticism."[1]

The same thing appears from a slightly different angle in respect of the painful problem of compromise. Often the situation created by man's sin is such that that which perfect love requires cannot be done, and God's will for the individual becomes under those circumstances, not the wholly good, but the lesser evil. The secular mind may dismiss this airily with the statement that, after all, life always takes toll of the ideal. But to the Christian mind, filled with the sense of God's absolute demands and of the disobedience of man which has brought about the situation, there is in it a most painful sense of guilt and frustration. For it means that God's will comes to us as that which in another sense is not God's will at all. The Christian has to be reconciled to it, and yet repudiate it. And that sort of thing seems to run through the whole of this present sinful

[1] *Die letzten Dinge*, p. 38.

order. Once again the solution of the contrariety is in an
eschatological confidence ; in the faith, that is, that the
believer's present surrender to the will of God in its com-
promised form is forgiven in respect of the sin which makes
the compromise necessary, and taken up, in respect of the
obedience that is in it, into a divine purpose which, in its
ultimate consummation, will mark the end of the present
sinful order altogether. The believer, in other words,
commits himself, in penitence and peace, to a divine will of
Love, which while it speaks to him through all the imperfec-
tions of this world and requires the utmost setting of his
soul towards obedience to it, none the less wholly transcends
this world.

Second, in relation to the reconciled man's thought of
others.

One of the effects of Christ's revelation of God as holy
love is enormously to sensitise the soul to the tragedy and
heartbreak of human personal relationships, especially as
these are seen over the whole length and breadth of history.
Indeed, the persistent lovelessness and callousness and
cruelty of so many human relationships, all down the ages
even into this present time, becomes so intolerable that the
mind is ever under temptation to repudiate that from which
such painful sensitivity is derived, namely that view of God
and of the meaning of life which Christ embodied. No
proposition, indeed, could at first sight be more completely
contradicted by the facts than the proposition that underlying and overshadowing human history is an ultimate
power and purpose of holy love. And no one could be more
sensitive to that contradiction than one to whom that holy
love has livingly manifested itself in Christ. There is no
way out of this contradiction, no way to be at peace in a
world where personal relationships, despite the presence of
fairer things, are always breaking down into the most
horrible brutality and corruption, no way, amidst the coarse

insolences of so-called *Realpolitik*, to commit oneself without fear and come what may to the folly of love, save in some sort of eschatological faith that the unmeaning chaos of history, the unending ongoing of sin and its consequences, rests on a divine wisdom not to be measured either in its resources, or in the way of its coming, in terms of history at all.

(3) Third, in respect of the significance of God. The eschatological faith is, as was said at the beginning, essentially a faith concerning God. Hence while preserving the significance of the individual and of the world, it never loses sight of the fact that God, after all, is God and that all things depend upon Him. The sense of God dominates everything else, and, once again, it is the sense of God as primarily and centrally holy will. The kingdom of God to which it looks forward is the kingdom of *God* in two senses. First, it is of God in the sense that it is eternal and must therefore transcend this world altogether. The present order, not only because of the way death and sin seem to be wrought up into its very structure, but because it is in any case finite and subject to the limitations of time and space, cannot possibly contain the realised purpose of the Eternal. It is interesting to observe in Jewish eschatology how the thought of God's kingdom gradually expands until the picture of it as being fully contained in some future state of the world becomes impossible ; there will, indeed, be a perfect world, but only for a thousand years—thereafter the earth will pass away and the eternal kingdom in all its fulness and glory be inaugurated.[1] Second, it is of God in

---

[1] The millenarian hope passed into Christianity through the Book of Revelation. In the teaching of Barthian theologians there seems at times to be a confusing intertwining of the two thoughts that this world cannot contain the realised kingdom because it is essentially fallen and sinful, and that it cannot contain it because it is essentially a time process and there is an infinite, qualitative difference between time and eternity. Sometimes sin seems to be regarded as an element which has entered into the time-process, as an addition, so to say, to its essential limitation, and sometimes as a necessary part of its essential limitation. Both strands of thought do, I think, intertwine in eschatological faith, but in systematic exposition they should be set forth in separation.

the sense that its inception is fundamentally due to God's sovereign act, and not to man's upward striving and progress. The emphasis is on God and not on man. This second point is obviously implied in the first. Just because God's kingdom is transcendent, it is not, and cannot be, brought about by man. The eschatological faith, whilst, as we have seen, never minimising the importance of the response of the will of man to the will of God, is always hesitant about speaking, as so many modern people do, of " bringing in the kingdom " ; it is far from what von Hügel once called " the 1851 exhibition idea of God."

This aspect of eschatological faith also enters deeply into the Christian experience of reconciliation. It emancipates the soul from what someone has called " an irreligious solicitude for God." It enables it to look unflinchingly at the most meaningless confusions and disasters of human life, making no attempt to gloss them over with cheap and sentimental theories of progress, or to pretend that they are other than they are, and yet to be at peace. It saves from collapse into despair when things, for which, in the light of Christ, the soul has come to yearn and work more than for anything else, make little progress, or seem even to go down in defeat. Seeing all things as " still lying within the shadow of the final acts of God ", looking always " for a city whose builder and maker is God ", the reconciled man even in his grief has the untroubled heart. This is the peace of God which passeth understanding. Yet, we must strongly insist again, it does not result in quietism and inactivity, for the reasons already given. The whole soul yearns and prays " Thy kingdom come", and the present deed of obedience is, as Schweitzer suggests, the most intense of prayers, the prayer in which the whole personality is concentrated and focused in will and in act. The most energetic, undeviating, steadfast servants of Christ in the present world are indeed precisely those whose eager strenuousness has behind and within it the power and the peace of the world to come.

The eschatological faith is, therefore, closely and indissolubly bound up with the Christian experience of reconciliation. It arises out of the present living awareness of the personal God through Christ, and the peculiarly intense conflict with the ineluctable facts of the present order into which such awareness throws the soul. Such a hope alone makes it possible to be victoriously reconciled to a radically imperfect world, to which, in another sense, we have no right, least of all in the light of Christ, to be reconciled at all. Reconciliation thus has at its heart a present possession and an as yet unrealised hope ; and each of these requires and strengthens the other. No better illustration of this can be found than the New Testament, which is concerned with little else than the Christian's life of reconciliation with God through Christ here and now, and which is at the same time thoroughly eschatological in its outlook.

The New Testament writers, on the one hand, are all aware of being here and now set in a new relationship with God through Christ. Their salvation is a present possession, giving them increasingly over the whole breadth of their experience a present joy, victory and peace. Yet, on the other hand, they are all equally aware that their salvation is not yet in the fullest sense a present possession, but is still to come. It is now ; nevertheless it is not yet. Yet the " now " and the " not yet " are not separate the one from the other. Only because they can see the tasks and challenges of this life in the light of a divine consummation lying beyond space and time are they able to be victoriously reconciled to them. But also, only because they are being victoriously reconciled to those tasks and challenges here and now, through the living awareness of a divine love meeting them in them, is the " eternal beyond " an unshakeable conviction, and not merely a vague aspiration or a feeble hope. They live now in the power of the world to come ; yet they have confidence in the world to come because it manifests itself now in the power to live, in what Paul calls its first-fruits. There is, therefore, in the New Testament no suggestion of mere other-worldliness in the bad sense of that term. It is an otherworldly this-world-liness. The believer rejoices in this life as a sphere in which he may here and now know the love of God and have victory and joy in Him, serving His will. Yet he is only able to do that because it is the love of *God* which is known, the love of One, that is, whose eternal purpose of good this world is too limited and frustrating and sinful to contain. He inherits the earth, and enters into its true uses and joys, because he is a citizen of heaven.[1]

The exposition of the eschatological hope which has been given provides the answer to those who would dismiss the whole thing as a form of phantasy-thinking. We have said all through that eschatological thought is the product of conflict, and we granted at the beginning that the psychological process involved is fundamentally the same as that which in other spheres leads men to seek to " cloy the

---

[1] Hence a theology which is wholly eschatological and reduces the Christian confidence to mere " hope ", as Barth's appears at times to be, is as false to the New Testament as one which, like Ritschl's and that of the liberal Protestant school generally, tends to overlook altogether the eschatological element in the present experience of salvation. (Cf. Althaus, *op cit*, p. 46 f.)

The polarity of the New Testament experience of reconciliation, as above described, appears most clearly in the belief in the second coming of Christ. Christ had already come ; in Him, in His life, death, and resurrection, God's saving purpose had been manifested in history, and was even now at work in the lives of those who were united to Him by faith. Yet He was to come again in a glory and triumph which would mark the close of the historical process and of " the fashion of this world ". For a brief discussion of the eschatological element in the mind of Jesus, see the note at the end of this chapter. As for the rest of the New Testament, it is hardly necessary to cite passages in evidence of what is manifest on almost every page. Rom. viii is perhaps the most revealing. Here the joy of present victory and peace is expressed in almost the same breath with the hope, nay, the groaning, for that which is not yet accomplished.

hungry edge of appetite with the bare imagination of a feast." But does that warrant us in dismissing the eschatological faith forthwith as merely wish-thinking, having no relation to fact or truth ? Plainly not. Such a conclusion overlooks the elementary fact that no mere analysis of a psychological process can determine the truth or falsity of its product. That conflict and the compensatory mechanisms of the mind *may* produce mere phantasy is obvious enough ; but that is no warrant for saying that it *must*. On the contrary it may open the soul to new ranges of truth ; indeed, the evidence shows that it nearly always is conflict of some sort which does this. Whether in fact the compensatory mechanisms of the mind, the urgent necessity to achieve a balance with its world, will lead to a genuine insight into truth or to mere phantasies, depends entirely on the general quality and trend of the personal life in which they occur.

When we view the eschatological hope from the angle of the highest Christian experience it is not difficult to discover a criterion whereby we may distinguish between false eschatology and true, between that which is merely the product of wish-thinking and that which has within it the inescapable compulsion of truth. Wherever there is manifestly present a consuming sense of God as holy will addressing the soul in absolute demand, so that the contrariety is felt to be not so much between the facts and the individual's own desires as between the facts (including, perhaps, the individual's own desires) and the holy will of God, then at once and to that degree the eschatological hope is lifted out of the sphere of mere wish-thinking ; it becomes an element in the austere and challenging revelation of God, part of the essential impact of which is that it checks and criticises all wishes of a merely egotistic and eudæmonistic kind. On the other hand, whensoever wishes of the latter type are dominant, then inevitably and to that degree, as we have already more than once suggested, the eschatological hope tends to be coarsened and corrupted into the hope merely of pleasures and compensations to come. Not that the element of awareness of God as final succour is not also present even in the purest surrender to God's will ; such awareness always enters into the living experience of God. But in so far as it is profoundly and organically bound up with the sense of God as absolute demand, its power to lead the soul astray into egotistic and eudæmonistic phantasies is nullified. The ultimate victory which is affirmed is always the victory of God's holy purpose, and of one's own desires only in so far as the surrender of these to that holy purpose necessarily carries with it participation in its victory. The emphasis all the time is on God.[1]

Some will be prepared fully to grant that an eschatological hope which has at the heart of it a consuming sense of God as holy will cannot be set on a level with one which has at the heart of it obviously egotistic desires, and yet still not admit that the eschatological hope, even in the former more respectable form, is anything but an empty dream. Such a conclusion will spring from an initial scepticism as to the veridical quality of the soul's experience of God as absolute demand and final succour, even in its highest Christian form, i.e., from a rejection of the whole business of religion as illusion. But to the soul that is livingly aware of God such scepticism, save, perhaps, as a transient mood, is impossible. As the life of reconciliation through Christ

---

[1] Thus Jesus bids His disciples endure all the consequences of obedience to Himself, " for great is your reward in heaven ". To suggest that this is an exhortation to do God's will simply in order to obtain the reward is to be misled by a single word, and to miss the whole spirit of the gospel record. The word reward is, in fact, ambiguous. It may indicate the motive which leads to a way of life, or the consequences which flow from a way of life—two very different things. A man may rightly envisage the consequences, and even steady his soul by the contemplation of them, and yet the motive have a deeper and wider reach than merely an egotistic desire to share in those consequences.

Q

is ever more deeply entered into, so, as we have said, the hope of a world to come passes more and more out of hope into a certitude by which the soul lives, a certitude which is none the less sure for being indemonstrable to those who stand outside, and can only deal theoretically with, the things that belong unto Christ.

We have seen that eschatological faith is related on the one hand to the destiny of the individual, and on the other hand to the destiny of the world. In the consideration of the Christian doctrine of providence, first in relation to the individual, and second in relation to nature and history, to which we now turn, we shall find that at more than one point we shall have to refer back to the positions reached in this chapter.

Note on the Eschatological Element in the Outlook of Jesus

The truth of the views above expressed may be tested and verified by the light which they shed upon the problem of the place of eschatological thought in the teaching and outlook of Jesus. We may briefly make comment in respect of three things.

(*a*) First, in respect of the apparent contrariety between what has been called the " Galilean idyll " aspect of Jesus and what has been called the " forked lightning " aspect of Him. On the one hand, He gives the impression of being essentially quiet-minded, ready to enjoy the flowers, the children, the ordinary things of this present life, interested in men and women and their daily affairs, having in Himself the blessedness of the meek who inherit the earth. On the other hand, He gives the impression of being most urgently possessed with a sense of the crisis into which all men are thrown by the will of God as this meets them in Himself, and of the imminence of the divine kingdom. Most pressing and exigent eschatological thought lies, apparently, alongside of what appears to be the exact contrary. Different solutions of the contrariety have been offered at various times. Some seek to eliminate the eschatological elements, regarding them as interpolations from contemporary apocalyptic.

Some seek, on the other hand, to eliminate the " Galilean idyll " aspect, and to reduce Jesus to a pure apocalyptist. Others would distinguish the two aspects chronologically ; the " Galilean idyll " covering the earlier part of the ministry, the " forked lightning " the later part, the transition from the one to the other being through a partial unhingement of Jesus' mind whereby He came to regard Himself in a megalomaniac way as Messiah. The true answer is surely the one indicated in the text, and exemplified throughout the New Testament, namely that rightly understood there is no contrariety at all. The two aspects are deeply and organically involved in one another. Peace in the presence of this world rests on the experience of God here and now as One whose ultimate victory none the less transcends this world altogether.

(b) Second, in respect of distinguishing between interpolated and genuine eschatological material in the gospels. In view of the so-called Little Apocalypse in Mark xiii, it is impossible to deny that there has been interpolation and distortion of eschatological sayings. The question then is : How may the material be discriminated ? In what was said above about the sources of true and false eschatology some guidance is afforded. It was the intense legalistic nationalism which arose among the Jews after the exile which tended to give to their eschatological thought a wrong twist in the direction of egotistic and eudæmonistic hopes so phantastic and undisciplined at times as to bear all the marks of morbid phantasy. Jesus Himself repudiated this legalistic nationalism, and therefore where eschatological sayings are reported which seem more in tune with it than with His mind, they may be legitimately suspected as due to the interpolation or distortion of lesser minds.

(c) Third, in respect of Jesus' conviction of the imminence of the kingdom. All that has been said above concerning the relation of conflict to eschatological conviction is relevant to the understanding of this.

Jesus seems to have begun His ministry not without hope that the Jewish people would respond and that the kingdom might be manifestly and immediately inaugurated. His unique and intimate sense of God's living presence in the world made such a hope and belief natural and inevitable. But as the hope was more and more disappointed, as faith and fact fell farther and farther apart, He was forced to new adjustments, deeper understandings of God's purpose and of His own vocation in relation to it. He came to see His own passion and death as indispensable to the consummation of God's purpose with men. But how exactly ? One may perhaps be permitted to doubt whether Jesus saw how it would work out. Thus to accept the way of rejection and defeat was along the lines of His deepest awareness of God as holy love ; it was indubitably what was required of Him in the way of that loyal co-operation with the holy will of His Father, without which in any shape or form the kingdom could never come. But in what shape or form it would supervene upon His Cross, He did not clearly see. The Cross was the condition of its coming, the condition to be fulfilled within the actual, historical framework of the world, yet it was a plunge into mystery, into the meta-historical, into the transcendent. For, so far as the historical conditions of this world were concerned, the Cross seemed to register the defeat of God's kingdom ; yet somehow it was the condition of its victory. Of what sort, then, was that kingdom which in and through its defeat here could yet be assured of its victory somewhere, some-when ? Out of the tremendous stress of this mystery and contradiction, thus focused in the Cross, there came to Jesus an intenser eschatological vision than perhaps any He had had before. He saw the essential victory which lay beyond the Cross and which depended on the Cross, yet He saw also that in a sense it was not continuous with anything that could be observed in the actual forces which were governing the lives of men. It was a defeat and yet a victory. There was a gap—a gap, as always in eschatological insight, between the inwardly known and the outwardly apparent. The victory of God could not be wrought out from beneath, from within the world, though what men did, and above all what the Son of Man did, was of the utmost significance. It was something which the mystery of the defeat on the Cross plainly demonstrated to transcend historical conditions and merely historical evolution. It could come only from above, from the finger of God.

Thus He came to utter the words which imply the imminence of His second coming. His deep vision and certainty of God's victory in spite of, nay somehow through, His Cross, and yet the impossibility of relating that victory to anything which might happen on the manward side, comes to expression naturally and spontaneously in the picture of the Son of Man sitting at the right hand of power and coming on the clouds of heaven, not in some remote future—that would cast a suggestion of dubiety over what was at the moment a luminous certainty arising out of the depths of the soul—but now, at once, so clear and intense is Jesus' eschatological vision under the stress of His present situation and of the necessity of winning His soul's victory in and through God. Thus, as von Hügel, Althaus, and others have suggested, *Jesus' profound certainty of God's victory and the final consummation of His purpose is conveyed through the thought of its immediacy.*[1]

[1] Von Hügel expresses the point thus : '' The idea of a speedy second coming expresses a deep and abiding right orientation of first-hand and specific spirituality, which quite clearly tends in proportion to its depth and purity to conceive all *sub-specie æternitatis ;* and inasmuch as time is still considered to apprehend such time as at hand and instantaneous. If our Lord did not know the date of His second coming (and this ignorance He tells us was with Him), then, religious genius as He was, He was bound to conceive it as proximate and swift as lightning.'' (*Selected Letters,* p. 159.)

It is important to be thus reminded that Jesus did profess ignorance of the date of the consummation considered from the angle of the time-series. In this He was different from some of His followers who in more recent times have believed in His imminent return. These latter have lacked the profound spirituality, born of intense and distressful loyalty to the love of God, which sees the victory of God as a present fact, and so is lifted above any real concern about its date. The true eschatological faith sees the consummation as it were outside the time-series, and therefore can speak of it as present, or the day after to-morrow, or a thousand years hence.

CHAPTER XIII

RECONCILIATION AND FAITH IN PROVIDENCE

IF Häring's statement, quoted earlier, that faith in providence is religion itself, be true, then it follows that Christian faith in providence is in a sense the Christian religion itself. Indeed, altogether apart from Häring's dictum, it would seem obvious enough that a discussion of the Christian doctrine of providence might expand into a treatise on the whole Christian life of reconciliation without ceasing at any point to be relevant ; for the Christian life is a life of increasing fellowship with God as personal, increasing realisation, therefore, that, in spite of all remaining mysteries, the texture of life is woven of Love, by Wisdom, with Power.

Yet whilst the doctrine of providence thus in a sense touches on every aspect of the Christian life, it has always been given a much narrower reference in the traditional treatments of it. It has been confined in the main to a discussion of the problem of evil, that is to say, as indicated in Chapter VI, to a discussion of those things which in a peculiar way seem to challenge the fundamental religious intuitions concerning the purpose of God and the destiny of man. This also will be our main concern. Nevertheless, the Christian doctrine of providence, when rightly stated, is far from being merely an attempt to provide a negative rebuttal of difficulties. The negative, as always, presupposes and rests upon a positive. In respect of nearly all such problems, the first, and sometimes the only, thing to be done is to state again with greater care, and perhaps, therefore, with greater insight, what the Christian faith concerning God's providence is, seeking to guard against the shallowness, prejudice and misunderstanding to which the mind of the believer, as well as that of the unbeliever, is prone.

In discussing the providence of God from the Christian view-point, it is necessary to be clear in advance about three things.

(1) First, it is important to keep clear what the source of the Christian conviction of the divine, overshadowing providence is.

The New Testament indicates unmistakably what it is. It is the experience of forgiveness resulting in trust, the experience of being reconciled to God through Christ in the personal life. In Romans viii. Paul's sweeping and eloquent affirmations of God's providence spring out of the experience which he describes at the end of the previous chapter, the experience of God's saving and reconciling work in the intimacies of his own being. He sees, as it were, the vast, over-arching firmament of providence reflected in the narrow waters of his own soul. He knows that the wisdom and love which are meeting him so livingly and savingly within the chaos and complexity of his own life, rule over all, and may be trusted to work just as victoriously within the chaos and complexity of universal history. The inference is not a logical one ; indeed it is not an inference at all, but an intuitive certitude which no contemplation of the darkness and mystery of other lives, or consideration of abstract theoretical difficulties, can shake.

This means that it is entirely mistaken, from the Christian point of view, to seek to establish one's confidence in the providence of God by scanning the lives of others, or the course of history, or the order of nature, for evidences of its working. Such confidence is bound to be insecure, for the evidence in the nature of the case can never be other than highly equivocal ; if it seem cogent, it is because there is brought to its consideration a conviction which has its real roots elsewhere. The rationalist theologians conceived it to be possible to demonstrate a beneficent and contriving agency in nature providing for the well-being of all creatures including man, an argument which came shipwreck in respect of its facts on the Lisbon earthquake, and in respect of its logic on the criticisms of philosophers from Kant onwards.[1] Protestant theology was ready to concede some place to such rational argument. It regarded the doctrine of Providence as an *articulus mixtus*, that is to say, as combining truths derived from revelation and truths derived from the natural reason. In accordance with this the doctrine was considered under three heads : first, *providentia generalis*, i.e. in respect of all creatures ; second, *providentia specialis*, i.e. in respect of all men ;   third, *providentia specialissima*, i.e. in respect of believing Christians. Of these, only the last fell within the sphere of specifically Christian knowledge ;   the first two, being a matter of empirical observation and rational reflection, were regarded as having general validity. Such a treatment of the matter we can no longer accept. Not only, as already indicated, is the rational argument for providence unsatisfactory, both in respect of the evidence adduced and in respect of the logic which seeks to argue from such evidence to an eternal and transcendent Goodness, but also because such an external clamping together of natural theology and Christian faith is not true to the organic unity of the Christian experience. It was Ritschl who, perhaps more than any one else, made clear once again the roots of the Christian faith in providence in

---

[1] The profound influence of the Lisbon earthquake on the history of theodicy is to be observed in Voltaire's *Candide*, which still has a value as an antidote to that easy-going confidence in God's goodness which always threatens Christian piety, especially when it is conjoined with economic comfort and privilege.

the Christian experience of redemption, going back past the aberrations of rationalism and Protestant orthodoxy to the clearer insights of the Reformation period and of the New Testament.[1]

This, however, does not mean that the consideration of the order of nature, the course of history, the events in the lives of individuals known to us, have no place at all within the Christian conviction concerning these matters. They have a place, but it is always and only within that whole recreation and re-orientation of the personal life which we have called reconciliation, and which rests on something quite other than such reflection, namely the direct, personal dealing of God with the soul through Christ. If, as Christians, we are in any measure able to read the signs of the divine providence in the world, it is not so much because such signs shine in their own light, but because we bring to them from elsewhere a light by which to read them, and, even then, our reading of them can never carry us more than the smallest distance towards a full understanding. At the most we have a glimpse of the divine fingers weaving the pattern of events with mercy and judgement, but very little is discerned in detail of the pattern which is being woven. The teaching of Jesus seems to accord with this narrowing down of the question of providence to the dealings of God with the individual soul in absolute demand and succour. Though He profoundly believed in God's overshadowing providence, so that He was ready to affirm that not even a sparrow falls to the ground apart from the will of God, and that even the hairs of a man's head are all numbered, yet He refused to be drawn into a discussion of the question whether the fate of the eighteen upon whom the tower of Siloam fell was a punishment for their sins, their own or anybody's else, adding to His refusal

---

[1] Ritschl, *Justification and Reconciliation* (Eng. Trans), pp. 182, 618. Cf. Stephan, *Glaubenslehre*, p. 122.

the warning, "Except ye repent, ye shall all likewise perish."[1]

Nor is this to under-estimate the strength of the case which theism, as a philosophical theory, can make for itself. That case is certainly not without power, as philosophies go ; but then, how far do philosophies go, when looked at from the angle of living religious conviction ? Philosophical argument *per se* can never do more than attempt to show that the theistic hypothesis is a reasonably probable one, covering perhaps more of the facts, when taken in their general tendencies—especially the fact of the emergence of man with his moral and spiritual experience—than any other ; such a probable conclusion, whose broad generalities can in the nature of the case take little or no account of the particular personal situations which constitute the really pressing problems of life to men and women, can never reach that sort or degree of conviction which finds expression, for example, in the Apostle's cry : "I am persuaded that neither death nor life shall be able to separate us from the love of God which is in Jesus Christ our Lord."[2] Indeed the power of the philosophical case for theism even to persuade to the acceptance of its conclusions as probable seems in large measure to depend on whether there is brought to it a prior desire or disposition to believe in God, that is to say, on the extent to which something in the nature of a religious response to the world is already there. From the Christian point of view the main value of the philosophical consideration of theism, and particularly of the problem of evil as

[1] Thornton Wilder, in *The Bridge of San Luis Rey*, puts the point in a vivid way. A priest conceives the idea of trying to show by searching enquiry that there was a providential appropriateness in the death of all the people who perished in the collapse of a bridge. In a measure he succeeds, which suggests that if we could do in fact what is only possible in fiction, namely look into the intimacies of others' lives, we could see the divine reason for much that happens. But the priest, appropriately, was burned for heresy for making the attempt.

[2] Rom. viii. 38.

elated to theism, appears to be twofold : first, it helps to
remove the suspicion which rests upon some minds as an
inhibition of their deeper religious instincts, that theism
cannot survive a frank facing of all the facts as known ;
second, it helps to put facts which seem especially to
challenge belief in God in their proper perspective, and to
rid the mind of obsessions, confusions and irrelevancies
which so often make such facts appear other than they
really are.

(2) Second, it is important in all discussions of these
matters to keep as close as possible to that revelation of
God's nature and purpose, which is the source and norm of
all specifically Christian experience and thought, namely the
whole mind and personality and life and death of Jesus
Christ.

Clearly any understanding of the ways of God with men
must rest upon some awareness of what the divine purpose
is seeking to achieve in human life. If God is seeking one
thing, and man believes that He is, or ought to be, seeking
something else, there can be nothing but estrangement, misunderstanding, and cross-purpose. Now it is part of the
reconciling work of Christ, as we have previously insisted, to
break through the darkness caused in man's soul through
sin and reveal to him what his real needs are, or, in other
words, what God's purpose with him actually is. That
purpose can, in the light of Christ, be briefly stated : it is to
fashion men through freedom into sonship to Himself and
brotherhood to one another, or, more shortly, to build a
kingdom of right and rich personal relationship, that is, of
love—love being interpreted not in any sentimental sense,
but in a sense as austere and demanding as the Cross. This
is God's work in the world, though in its ultimate consummation it transcends the world ; and men are truly reconciled
as they learn to share in that work with every gift and power
of their being. And the providence of God means the

adequacy of God's wisdom and power to the task with which He has thus charged Himself, as this is wrought out under the forms of time and space and in relation to each individual person to whom He has given life. Any interpretation of providence, therefore, which loses sight of, or does not do justice to, this intention to fashion a kingdom of love must be misguided. Yet to lose sight of it, or to do less than justice to it, is fatally easy to minds always prone to interpret the world in eudæmonistic terms and to measure the goodness of God by the extent to which pain and trouble are escaped. The only way to guard against it is to keep close to the mind of Jesus, particularly in its austerer aspects and especially as these come to their awful consummation in the Cross.

The point, elementary and obvious as it is, cannot be too strongly emphasised. It has important bearings, as we shall see, on the question of the right objects of Christian petition, and on the problem of suffering. Nothing, indeed, could be clearer than that the life, teaching, and death of Jesus, as these are set forth in the Gospels and re-expressed through the subsequent New Testament experience, offer a final repudiation of eudæmonism as a fundamental principle for understanding God, or rightly responding to the world He has made. God's purpose is to conform men to the image of His Son, and His Son died on the Cross. To conform them to that image and to save them from trouble, even great trouble, are two contradictory ends which not even the providence of God can encompass at one and the same time. To be sure, it is extremely difficult, and in some instances impossible, with our present knowledge, even to begin to construe some types of human suffering and frustration in terms of the divine end of a kingdom of love. As was said earlier, the Lisbon earthquake and similar things still stand as a final repudiation of all easygoing views of providence, and as a baffling mystery even to those who

re ready, in the light of the Cross of Christ, not to be easy-
going. None the less we are entitled to refuse to be put off
by the fact that such things cause suffering, even though we
cannot see how in the providence of God they will be made
to serve the high ends of His eternal kingdom. A world
with earthquakes in it is an austere world, but that so far
fits the conception of an austere Father of men's spirits,
revealed in One who counselled men to chop off an offending
limb and enter into life with a maimed and broken body
rather than not enter into it at all. This leads immediately
to the third point.

(3) Third, it is important to remind ourselves that we
have no business to expect, even in the light of Christ, a full
illumination on every mystery of life.

It is, indeed, part of Christ's reconciling work that He
brings the soul to see that, paradoxical as it sounds, some
of the greatest revelations of God are in the dark mysteries ;
that darkness itself, when a man is rightly related to it, can
become a form of light ; that, therefore, a full illumination
would be definitely undesirable to such beings as God wills
us at present to be. It is possible to be blinded with excessive
light. Nothing more plainly marks the difference between
the religious and the philosophic approaches to the problem
of evil than this. To the philosophic mind the evils of life,
in so far as they remain unexplained, represent so many gaps,
irreducible dark spots, over which perhaps at best a flimsy
bridge of speculative possibility may be built. But to the
religious mind, so far from being mere gaps, they become
sacramental of deeper trust in, and therefore deeper
knowledge of, God.[1]

Thus, in the first place, it is part of the use of the dark
inscrutabilities of the created order to preserve in the soul,
in the midst of its new-found life of reconciliation with God,

---

[1] Cf. Augustine, *Confessions*, Bk. I, Ch. 6 : "Let us delight to find Thee
by failing to find Thee, rather than by finding Thee to fail to find Thee."

a proper sense of the mystery and transcendence of God. The danger has always beset Christian piety, especially when it is of an intensely personal kind (as indeed all Christian piety in one sense ought to be), of losing the sense of the distance of God in the sense of His nearness. The believer becomes, if the word may be permitted, " pally " with a Deity whose purposes in this world are concentrated in the activities of parish groups, and beyond this world in providing bliss for them. The result is a thin and trivialised Christian life, ill-according with a Saviour who died in agony amidst darkness and earthquake, or with the deep and awe-struck tones of the New Testament writers—as Paul, for example, when he quails before the mystery of Hebrew history and cries, " How unsearchable are His judgements and His ways past finding out."[1]

In the second place, it is one of the uses of the darkness of life continually to bring back the reconciled soul with renewed concentration and dedication to that which is not in darkness and is the only source and centre of all right relation to God, namely the doing of His will as this is discerned in the immediate situations of the hour. Jesus' repudiation of any attempt to explain why the tower of Siloam fell and killed eighteen people, and the solemn added warning : " Except ye repent, ye shall all likewise perish," is relevant here also. It expresses an essential aspect of the reconciled life—to do the will of God where it is known, and so far as it is known, and to stop worrying about it where it is not ; to keep that which is committed unto us, being persuaded that He is able to keep that which amidst so much mystery, we are called upon to commit unto Him. " Peter saith to Jesus, Lord, what shall this man do ? Jesus saith unto him, If I will that he tarry till I come, what is that to thee ? *follow thou me*."[2]

Finally the darkness and perplexities of life are to the

[1] Rom. xi. 33.   [2] John xxi. 21, 22.

reconciled life a continuous and indispensable opportunity for that attitude of trust in God which is both the source and the consummation of a truly personal relationship to Him. A relationship of genuine sonship to God must have this element of sheer confidence in it, without a perpetual demanding of precise explanations and written guarantees against all risks; wherefore a world whose purpose is to fashion into sonship must leave room for such confidence. Jesus more than once called upon His disciples to take up this attitude of personal trust, no matter what darkness of evil and suffering might confront them, as the only way of knowing God, and one source of His reconciling power in the lives of men has been that this attitude was so fully and perfectly His own. " Father, into thy hands I commend my spirit." It is part of the essential meaning of God's fatherhood that He is one into whose hands a man may commend his spirit, and it is part of the essential purpose of this world in relation to man that it should be full of situations where there is no victory save in so far as that commendation is made.

CHAPTER XIV

PROVIDENCE AND THE INDIVIDUAL

BEARING in mind the principles just laid down, we shall consider in this chapter and the next what may be said from the angle of Christian experience and faith concerning God's dealings with individual men and women. We shall first consider what may be said in respect of the problem of evil in its dual aspect of suffering and sin.

It will be evident from all that has been said hitherto that the Christian faith makes no claim to provide an explanation of evil which shall be satisfactory to all and sundry. It is prepared, of course, to insist on those alleviations of the problem, pointed out in Chapter VI, which ordinary rational insight into the basic necessities of sentient existence provides, namely, that the fact of pain and frustration is bound up with some of the highest zests and achievements of human life, and that the possibility of moral evil is bound up with the freedom without which man would have no truly personal life at all. But concerning those darker aspects of evil, wherein suffering and sin seem to take a form, or to produce consequences, definitely dysteleological in relation to human personality, its claim has never been to explain them philosophically, but rather to enable the individual through Christ to have fellowship with the living God in them, in such wise that the necessity for anything in the nature of a complete explanation, in respect either of his own life or of the lives of others, disappears. To the God who is thus livingly known as refuge and strength at those points where the suffering and sin of human history

240

become part of his own intimate personal experience, he is
ready to commit all the rest. This commitment gets taken
up into, and expressed through, what we have called
eschatological faith, the profound conviction, that is to say,
that the divine purpose, which assuredly deals livingly with
men in this present life, none the less in its ultimate consummation transcends this life altogether and cannot be fully
understood in terms of it. This does not mean, however,
that the Christian experience and faith shed no light at all
on the problem of evil, as though it were merely a matter
of being blindly and unintelligently optimistic about
everything. To have victory over evil, through fellowship
with God in it, must mean to understand it a little better
as part of the wisdom of an utterly trustworthy divine love,
even though much still remains in mystery ; certainly it is
to be emancipated from those false interpretations of it which
all down the ages have so easily beset and beclouded the
mind of man. There is light on evil, but it is not complete
light, and it is hardly light at all to any who are not in some
measure living within that world of reconciliation with God
which is its source. The Christian doctrine of providence,
we repeat, and the Christian experience of reconciliation are
inseparable. We state the same thing in another way by
saying that for Christian thought the problem of suffering
and the problem of sin are inseparable ; and of the two, the
problem of sin, the problem of man's estrangement from
God, is the more fundamental. Sin not only causes a great
deal of suffering, but also to the suffering which it does not
cause it lends a power to defeat the soul it would never
otherwise have.

For the purposes of exposition, however, we may begin
with some consideration of the problem of suffering, and
move from that into a consideration of the problem of sin.
What we have to say here may be set forth in three
propositions :

R

First, God succours faith and gives victory over suffering through Christ by making suffering itself the revealing medium of His holy love. This He does supremely through the Cross of Christ as *an actual historical event in the midst of human life*. The words italicised are important and it is of great consequence to understand their importance.

Some sort of faith in divine providence, in a " friend behind phenomena ", in God as final succour, is, we have said, typical of all religion, and the whole virtue of such faith, that which indeed makes it specifically religious, is that it obstinately affirms, on the basis of a primordial awareness of God, that things are not what they appear to be. Yet a faith which is always and only a flying in the face of apparent facts is very insecure, especially when such facts are not merely externally observed, but become part of a poignant personal experience of suffering and frustration. Hence the history of religion affords many examples of attempts to relieve this insecurity by interpretations of various sorts. To the more primitive mind it is sufficient to project into the deity something of its own unstable, emotional life, and to relate the blessings and calamities of life to the more or less incalculable fluctuations of divine favour. A more developed mind seeks to interpret blessing and calamity, as did the friends of Job, in terms of reward and penalty for pious virtue or impious vice, saying, in effect, that the real seeming is not in the beneficence and justice of God but in the characters of men ; the innocent who suffer are not so innocent as they look, and are receiving what they deserve. The Hindu doctrine of Karma is the most impressive instance of this way of alleviating the problem. When this theory seems also to break down on the facts, then refuge is found in the hope of some sort of future compensatory adjustment, either within this life itself, or more usually in a life beyond death. It is clear, however, that such interpretations, though they contain elements of truth[1], do not adequately succour faith. They are too much in the nature of speculative constructs, and have too little basis in verifiable experience to be able to stand up to the challenge they are designed to meet.

It seems clear that there is only one way in which faith in the overshadowing wisdom and love of God can be truly succoured and that is for it to be able to grasp its object, or be grasped by it, out of the heart of those historical happenings which otherwise give it the lie. The revealing medium must be history itself, and it must be history, so to say, at its worst. Only thus can the necessity for a purely theoretical construction, with all the dangers and doubts which must ever wait upon it, be eliminated. In the Christian experience such a revelation is given in the life of Jesus, and supremely in the culmination of it in His Cross. In this climax of His life, both the conditions are fulfilled ; it is historical and it is very evil, including in itself something of almost every darkness to which human life is liable—sin, hatred, physical agony, premature death, the innocent suffering for the guilty, the bitter disappointment of high ideals. Yet because the uniquely pure and revealing personality of Jesus is at the centre of it all, the darkness suddenly becomes full of light ^The discernment is given that as the holy love of Jesus is in the midst of all this evil, so also is that on which it rests and by which it is sustained, namely the holy love of God. The one is apprehended through the other, and both through human history in its most tragic form. Thus we are confronted with what is at one and the same time the supreme paradox and yet the supreme rationality of the Christian's setting of the Cross at the centre of his faith. From one point of view the crucifixion

---

[1] Thus, as we have seen, the Christian view must include the belief that the ultimate justification of the ways of God to men is to be found in the beyond of death. The truth in the doctrine of Karma is that suffering and sin are intimately involved in one another ; the falsity of it is in its legalistic and theoretical assertion of a one to one correspondence.

of Jesus might seem to be the worst item in the indictment which history brings against the love of God. Yet from another point of view the exact opposite is the case ; for only by being first an indictment of the love of God could it ever be an adequate revelation of it. In order to become full of light, it had first to be full of darkness, and, we repeat, it had to be a real historical event. In this paradox of the Cross Christianity differs *toto cœlo* from other faiths. Like them it talks about the providence and the love of God, but unlike them it points not away from history, but to it, and to that within it which, on any estimate, must be accounted its most awful and tragic event. The light which man needs is seen shining out of the midst of those very events which otherwise overwhelm and defeat his soul. How the consummation of the life of Jesus in the crucifixion should thus mediate the assurance of a divine love which, so far from being denied by the dark things of life, is in the midst of them, finding in them its supreme opportunity to reveal its depth and the way of its victory, it is in the nature of the case impossible to say. That God can and does speak to the soul of man through his world, that revelation is a fact, must ever remain an inexplicable ultimate of the religious awareness. We can only take note of it when it happens, and seek to grasp more fully its meaning and its providential appropriateness to our situation of need.[1]

The way in which the light shines out of the darkness of the Cross may be illustrated in relation to what has always been to sensitive souls one of the most painful challenges

---

[1] To the first disciples, of course, the unutterable darkness of Calvary only began to shine with light because of the Resurrection and of the whole new life of fellowship with the Risen Lord and with one another, to which the Resurrection introduced them. Without the Resurrection and all that flowed from it, the Cross both for the first disciples and for us would remain one of the darkest spots in history. Yet even so, what has been said above remains true and important. Within the total context of the Christian experience of reconciliation the Cross ceases to be darkness and becomes light, what the Apostle called " marvellous light ", marvellous because it " shines out of darkness ".

which life offers to belief in the goodness and providence of God, namely the innocent suffering from, and for, the sins of others. It is not to minimise the truly dreadful way in which the sins of wrongdoers are visited upon others, if it be pointed out that this problem, considered in relation to the divine providence, derives much of its sting from a failure fully to realise three things which are plainly at the centre of Jesus' life and teaching : First, that the divine purpose is to fashion the personalities of men in and through their relationships with one another. Such a developing personal order, in which persons are being fashioned through their relations with one another, is inconceivable apart from a profound mutual dependence as well for evil as for good. Second, that, therefore, a strict distributive justice in which reward and penalty are bestowed in exact proportion to virtue and vice, cannot be a rock-bottom principle of the moral order and of divine government. On the contrary, it is precisely the inequalities of life which provide the major opportunities for that generous bearing of one another's burdens without which love cannot be manifested, and a fellowship, which is more than a merely superficial camaraderie, achieved. Third, that in any case the working out of the divine purpose is not confined to the narrow limits of time and history. The dread results, therefore, of man's sin, when it enters into a system of such profound and inescapable mutual dependence, cannot be regarded as final ; they will be redeemingly taken up into that final consummation which transcends time and history and which is the realised kingdom of God. These three truths, which abstractedly stated, have little power perhaps to lay hold of a man at a time of really poignant awareness of the problem, are all focused in the Cross of Jesus, and, so focused, they can become in a new way a living word of God to the soul. In the Cross is discerned a perfect love surrendered to that personal order, ordained of God, wherein righteousness enters into the same condemnation " with malefactors, being crucified with them, one on the right hand and the other on the left." Hence also in the Cross is discerned a righteousness which finally breaks through the categories of distributive justice. It is the supreme example of the innocent suffering for the guilty, so presented that such suffering is seen to be, not the infringement of the moral order, but its greatest glory and the realisation of its deepest meaning. Finally, in the Cross is discerned a complete self-commitment, even in the midst of the profoundest darkness and suffering, to a divine overshadowing providence whose purpose of love, though it is being wrought out through the obedience of His suffering servant in this present awful scene of history, none the less transcends history altogether.[1]

Second, God succours faith and gives victory over suffering by leading men through Christ into a new way of practical living. The Christian disciple begins to know " the fellowship of His sufferings ", becomes increasingly aware of being called to actualise in his own personal relationships the same sort of sharing and accepting and redeeming love which he now knows through Christ to be in God. As he enters into this way of life, he finds two things happening. First, in respect of such suffering and deprivation as may visit his own life, he finds that if he accepts it, not as a meaningless stroke of fate, but as an opportunity to share in the vast fellowship of human pain and to make some contribution to its redemption through patience and self-forgetfulness and love, so the victory over it is achieved ; it ceases to be sterile and becomes a sacrament of higher things both to himself and to others. Second, in respect of the suffering of others, he finds that as he seeks to share its burden and " so fulfil the law of Christ ", so they are put on the road to

---

[1] In the section just concluded I have repeated, with the permission of the publishers, the substance of what I have said elsewhere. (*The Lord of Life*, p. 297 f. ; *Experience of God*, p. 148 f.)

gaining the victory over it. For it is not suffering *per se* which makes men rebel and doubt the goodness of God, so much as suffering in loneliness, suffering in which no one draws near in costing fellowship. The prime source of unbelief is not suffering, but the lovelessness of man, i.e. sin. This brings us back to what was said at the beginning, namely that for Christian belief sin is the more fundamental and the real key to the problem of suffering. So,

Third, God succours faith and gives the victory over suffering by dealing through Christ with the problem of sin. The Christian view-point here can be set forth in two propositions. First, that sin is the chief source of the bitterness and perplexity of suffering ; it throws a shadow across vision, making it appear other than it is. If suffering has an insupportable sting in it, crushing and embittering the soul, it is not because it is, so to say, suffering *per se*, but because it meets and enters into an alliance with the lovelessness of man without, and with a profound disquietude and dissatisfaction with ourselves within, a disorganised and corrupted inner life estranged and alienated from God. Second, that sin is the only disaster which at the end of the day really matters, or, positively, that there is only one absolutely good thing in life, which is to do the will of God and to come to the end of it with a mind " fargone in readiness for Him ". In the discernment of that truth the victory over suffering is won.

When we turn to the question of sin, the problem for Christian faith is, as we saw in Chapter VI, not so much that sin should arise, but what God is able to do about it when it has arisen, and all its evil consequences are being wrought out. Sin must be conceived as an interruption and frustration of the divine purpose of a peculiarly direct kind ; yet God's purpose must be affirmed to be ultimately victorious. The divine providence, in other words, if there is to be any basis for faith, must be affirmed to be adequate to all situations created by sin, yet not responsible for them. How may that be ? What has Christian faith to say concerning the grasp which the sovereign will and providence of God have upon the individual sinful man or woman ?

There are at least three erroneous ways of dealing with the problem of sin as the individual's direct disobedience to, and frustration of, a divine will, which none the less must be affirmed to be ultimately triumphant. They are erroneous because, though they contain elements of truth, they in effect set God's relationship to the individual on a lower level than that of perfect love ; in other words they tend to depersonalise that relationship, for love, rightly understood, is the only relationship which fully grasps and affirms the other as personal.

Thus, first, it is sometimes affirmed that sin, though it is in one sense a frustration of the divine will, yet in another sense never can be that, for the universe in its essential structure is so constituted by the righteousness of God that sin always in the end annuls and defeats itself. Moral laws, on this view, are comparable to the laws of health or the regularities of the physical universe ; if a man will not conform to them, he must suffer, and if he still persists, he will perhaps in the end perish altogether. There is therefore no real problem for Providence, it having been written in the constitution of things from the beginning that there should be no final victory for the evil purposes of men.

It is clear that this expresses an important element in any view which sees in morals more than a set of conventional expediences. Nor is there lacking empirical support for it. In a morally constituted universe there must be, and in actual experience, taken broadly, there certainly seems to be, a principle of judgement at work in life, checking the

wrongdoing of men and defeating their intents.[1] And the
Christian faith in providence, needless to say, takes this up
fully into itself, saying of the evil ways of men that of
necessity " their end is destruction ", and again that the
righteousness of God cannot be mocked, " for whatsoever a
man soweth, that shall he also reap." None the less, from
the Christian point of view, such statements are by themselves far from adequate. This is shown by the fact that
they can still be, and in fact often have been, maintained
even when the thought of God in anything even approaching the Christian sense of the term, is entirely rejected. It
is indeed a fairly typical modern attitude to say vaguely
with Samuel Butler, " that there is something at work in
life, as yet but vaguely understood, making for righteousness ", and there leave the matter.

Wherein then is it inadequate ? It is inadequate in that
it inevitably tends to depersonalise the moral order and the
relation of the divine providence to the individual. It
reduces the whole thing to a quasi-mechanical arrangement
for penalising and eliminating the morally unfit, in which
no regard can be paid to differing degrees of moral responsibility for the past and moral potentiality for the
future. It is enough that a man is here and now at odds
with reality and its inevitable processes. The root mistake
appears to be an entirely false abstraction of the moral order
from the inner life of individual persons. If the moral order
be set over against the individual's inner life, then there is
some point in saying that it has won its victory when it has
defeated the individual's evil purposes and perhaps eliminated him altogether, just as the healthful forces of the body
might be said to have won their victory when they have
eliminated poisons from the blood-stream. But what if the
moral order be, in the last analysis, nowhere save in the
purposes and volitions of persons in relation to one another ?

[1] See below, p. 288 f.

In that case only in so far as those purposes and volitions are not merely checked and defeated, but also recreated into what they ought to be, can the moral order be said to be victorious in any sense that really matters. For only then will it have reaffirmed itself at the precise point where it has been negated and denied. We affirm, then, that a moral order which merely checks and annuls is not one which has at the heart of it an absolute valuation of the individual person as such ; it is not the sort of moral order which is known to the Christian in and through his reconciliation to God through Christ.[1]

The same point can be stated more specifically from the angle of the doctrine of providence. A providence which is content merely to leave sinners to break their limbs on the inexorabilities of the world, or which, like Huxley's chess player, wins its victory by always thinking two or three moves in advance of the strongest player and never on any account relaxing the rigour of the game, may be pictured in personal terms, but it could as well be pictured in impersonal, and certainly it is impossible to predicate of it anything that could be called love. For God merely to checkmate men could indeed be hardly more of a victory than for an avalanche to crush a lizard or an ant ; but for Him to seek and to save the defeated and the lost, seeking and finding individual personal approaches even in the midst of those inexorable consequences of wrongdoing which in any case must belong to a moral universe, that indeed is, to quote

---

[1] The fallacy of abstracting the moral order, so called, from the inner life of persons in relation to one another appears in the attitude of many otherwise well-intentioned people to the punishment of criminals, and in particular to the death penalty. Many in effect commit themselves to the view that the partial elimination of the offender in prison, or the complete elimination of him on the gallows, is itself a vindication of the moral order and a step towards the redemption of society. Yet, plainly, that is hardly distinguishable from the quite impersonal business of killing flies or beetles. It is even more deplorable when the attitude is erected into a cosmic principle and at the heart of the universe there is discerned only the motto " swat that fly ".

Anselm, a task worthy of God ; and anything less than that
is not to treat man in that fully personal sense which alone
is love.

A second erroneous way of dealing with the problem is
akin to the one just discussed, and is subject to fundamentally the same criticism. It consists in making the
category of justice absolutely central in the divine purpose,
so that sin ceases to be a frustration of that purpose precisely at the point where it receives in full its just deserts.
The essential divine triumph consists in the despatch of the
wicked to their place of retribution, the fact that they
remain wicked being, from the point of view of a divine
purpose which is absolutely just, in no wise a qualification
of its victory. The most noteworthy expression of this view
is to be found in the doctrine of predestination in its infra-
lapsarian form. Mankind having brought itself to a situation
wherein it deserves damnation at the hands of a righteous
God, the latter in His mercy chooses some for salvation,
leaving the rest to their well-merited fate. Nor can the
latter complain, seeing that they get exactly what they
deserve. Nor from the point of view of the divine purpose
is the loss of so many souls a defeat, seeing that that purpose
is primarily and centrally directed to justice, mercy being
only an incidental embroidery. Justice, as the old divines
used to say, is *absoluta*, mercy only *ordinata*. God must be
just, though He may be merciful.

Into any detailed criticism of this view it is not necessary
to enter. It is sufficient to point out that it contains the
same element of truth along with the same profound untruth as the view just considered. The element of truth is
that in a morally constituted universe sin must be negated ;
that such negation, if it be real negation, and not merely
abstract and theoretical repudiation, must take the form of
suffering ; that such suffering, in so far as it is apprehended
as flowing from the ultimate as personal will with which

one's own will is at enmity, inevitably takes on the guise of punishment—punishment, unlike the related concept of consequence, being wholly a category of personal relations. The untruth in it is, again, that despite the personalistic terms in which it is expressed, it profoundly depersonalises the whole relationship. The moral order, as inherent in the divine justice, again appears as something standing over against the individual's inner life, capable of affirming itself and achieving its sovereign rights whether that inner life is redeemed or not. This is clearly shown by the fact that some are redeemed by omnipotent grace, and others not, though plainly it would be just as easy for omnipotent grace to redeem all, nor could it but redeem all if such were essential to its self-affirmation. The impersonalistic direction of this whole way of thinking shows itself again in the subordination of love as *ordinata* to justice as *absoluta*. For to grasp and affirm at any cost the whole individual merely because he is " there ", and not because he is deserving or undeserving, is the only way fully to treat him as a person, and that precisely is the definition of love. If such a thorough-going valuation of persons is *absoluta*, then love is *absoluta ;* to make anything else *absoluta* is of necessity *pro tanto* to cease to have a thoroughgoing valuation of persons. This does not mean that love has to be a sentimental thing, with nothing in it of the austerity usually associated with justice. It may take up something of punishment and retribution into its redemptive purpose—though, so soon as it has achieved that purpose, the redeemed man can no longer think of it as retribution and punishment merely ; but it could never stop at mere retribution and punishment. To do so would be in effect to admit defeat.[1]

The third erroneous way is to say that sin is not a frustra-

---

[1] For a useful discussion of the relation of the ideas of justice and love in the Christian conception of that order of personal relations in which all men stand with one another and with God, see **N. L. Robinson**, *Christian Justice*.

tion of God's will at all, inasmuch as man's actions, whether good or evil, are all of them the result of divine pre-ordination and foreknowledge. This thoroughgoing monism, which leaves no problems either for God in His providential dealings with man, or for man in his seeking to understand those dealings, entered into Christian thought in the doctrine of predestination in its supralapsarian form, as, for example, it is expressed by Jonathan Edwards in the concluding summary of his *Inquiry into the Freedom of the Will*.[1]

It is hardly necessary to criticise this view. It suffers, despite the personal categories which it uses, from the defect of all monism, which is that it depersonalises man and his relation to his world in a way that no juggling with the concept of freedom can overcome. It saves the sovereignty of God by giving Him in effect nothing to be sovereign over. It attributes to Him an achieving purpose in regard to man, but in a way that gives that purpose nothing to achieve, and no " man " in respect of whom to achieve it. All that is left is the unspeakably sterile and depressing spectacle of omniscience playing an everlasting game of patience with itself, all possible combinations of the cards being already known by heart.

It would appear from these criticisms that, if we are to remain faithful to the Christian conception of God as holy love, that is, as always dealing with men on the highest conceivable level of personal relationship, we must be prepared to affirm two things concerning His dealing with the individual sinner.

The first is that, without abrogating the inevitable consequences of sin, nay, indeed, often using them, the divine

---

[1] E.g. : " God orders all events, and the volitions of moral agents amongst others, by such a decisive disposal that the events are infallibly connected with His disposal." And again, " All things are perfectly and equally in His view from eternity ; hence it will follow that His designs and purposes are not things formed anew, founded on any new views or appearances, but are all eternal purposes."

providence is always at work in an individual and personal way to bring each individual to the light. This is a belief which in the nature of the case cannot be demonstrated by empirical evidence. The conviction of its truth springs from the Christian's awareness of God as love as this is made livingly known to him in his own salvation. Here we come upon the essential religious meaning of the doctrine of election and predestination, as, for example, it finds expression in St. Paul's epistles. The man who finds himself reconciled to God through Christ is profoundly aware of two things. First, that he has not achieved this new life through his own strength and desert. God in His infinite wisdom and love has wrought this thing in his life and if He had not wrought it, it would never have happened. Second, that this redeeming activity of God springs from His personal, individualising interest in him. It is not that the believer is a small, insignificant item whose redemption happens to be demanded by, and so is incidentally provided for in, some vast cosmic scheme ; but he himself has a place in the divine knowledge and love. And looking back from the standpoint of his present reconciliation with God, the believer discerns with wonder how much events, in ways unnoticed at the time, have conspired to bring about this consummation. All this is expressed in the word " called ", which the Apostle so often uses, and again in the word " predestinate ". The words are primarily religious words, and not the precisely defined theological and philosophical ones which they became with later thinkers ; the meaning they express has a focus of intensely individual awareness, along the lines indicated, of the love of God, and there springs from it inevitably the thought that that same love, which has thus, contrary to all desert, sought and found *me*, must be seeking all. It was only when the thought of election and predestination became part of a hard and precisely defined logical scheme based upon the legalistic conception of God as primarily justice that this further thought, to which the deeper Christian consciousness has always returned, was expressly denied.[1]

This has led us to the second thing which it seems necessary for the Christian consciousness to affirm concerning God's dealing with the individual sinner, namely that not only is He seeking to reconcile every individual to Himself, but also that He will in the end succeed in so doing. For only on that basis can we speak of the ultimate victory of a God who is love. To a God who is primarily justice an irreconcilable sinner despatched to everlasting damnation, or even eliminated altogether, might be triumph, but to a God who is primarily love it could only be the most absolute form of defeat. Thus the profound concern of religious faith for God's ultimate victory seems, in its Christian form, to move unavoidably towards universalism.

The difficulty immediately arises, however, whether such an universalistic faith can be held along with the assertion of the unimpaired freedom of man, without which also there can be no truly personal relationship and therefore no real victory for love. Theoretically it would seem that if man is never to be manipulated and overridden, it should be possible for him to go on resisting even God to the end,

---

[1] Cf. Stephan, *Glaubenslehre*, p. 246 : " *Der Prädestinationsgedanke ist in seinen Anfängen nicht Lehre, sondern Erzeugnis gewisser Inhalte des Glaubens selbst . . . er gerät auch nach seiner ganzen Anlage nicht in Gefahr, zur spekulativen Metaphysik zu entarten, also die Beziehung zur unmittelbaren Frömmigkeit zu verlieren.*"

If we take the course of the Apostle's argument in Rom. ix–xi as a whole, it seems clear that despite one or two expressions (e.g. ix. 18, 21 ff.) which appear to point in another direction, the thought, which almost inevitably arises out of the heart of the Christian experience of salvation, that God's saving purpose is directed to all others as well as to myself, wins the day. How this saving purpose is to be wrought out remains for Paul a mystery. But some evidence he thinks he discerns in the way in which the gospel has reached the Gentiles through the refusal of the Jews ; thus even the latter gets taken up into an inclusive divine, saving purpose. " For God hath concluded them all in unbelief, that He might have mercy upon *all*."

whatever the end may be. Yet, if that be so, what becomes of faith in the divine victory ? The thought that God has all eternity in which to bring men to Himself does not dispose of the difficulty, though it lightens it in that it gives the manifold wisdom of God an infinitely greater scope, under conditions of which we know nothing, than it would have if, as some believe, the soul's eternal destiny is once and for all settled by what happens in this world. None the less the theoretically limiting case of a will which resists to all eternity seems unavoidable.

This difficulty is plainly another form of that ultimate antinomy into which all thought on these matters sooner or later runs out, the antinomy of the one and the many, the sovereignty of God and the inalienable freedom of man— an antinomy which it is ever beyond our minds to resolve into a completely satisfying theoretical unity. Two things may, however, be pointed out.

First, that it is an antinomy which declares itself to, and is accepted without discomfort by, anyone who is conscious of being reconciled to God through Jesus Christ. It seems luminously clear to such an one, as we have already said, that his salvation is entirely of God's achieving and not of his own ; still less does it spring from his own deserving. God has found a way to lay hold of the chaos and corruption of his inner life, and to bring it out of darkness into His glorious light ; yet never is there any awareness of being treated as other than a personal being on whom is laid some responsibility of keeping the loins girt and the lamp lit. But that which has clearly happened to oneself in the providence of God there would seem no reason to deny might happen to all, unless one is prepared to maintain that God elects some to salvation and some not, a view, which, as we have seen, really denies the revelation of God as love which is at the centre of one's own experience of His saving work.

Second, there is perhaps something to be done along the
line of rethinking the idea of coercion in relation to human
freedom. There is, for example, a coerciveness in truth
which is not felt to be an overriding of personality ; rather
we feel that it is part of the very essence of personality that
it can be thus brought under a thrusting and overpowering
impact of truth. We may dislike the conclusions of an
" irresistible logic ", but no one ever proposes to exempt
himself from them on the plea that his personality is being
overridden by such logical argument and not treated with
proper respect. May it not then be possible that God in His
manifold wisdom should in the end bring even the most
recalcitrant spirit to a situation wherein the truth is so
presented that it cannot be resisted any longer ? Precisely
because such a process of illumination must never coerce in
the wrong sense of the term, it may take what we, who can
only think in terms of the time-series, have to think of as a
" very long time ", remembering always, however, that with
God a thousand years are but as one day ; it may also
entail much suffering. But there seems no reason in the
nature of things why it should not be accomplished. The difficulty in arguing thus from the irresistibility of logic to the
work of reconciliation, is that the latter involves the whole
personality, including will and feeling, as well as rational
processes, so that the possibility still seems to remain
theoretically open that the will may perversely continue to
resist even though the truth is now so presented that it
cannot longer be overlooked or denied. Yet perhaps just
because it is merely a theoretical and abstract possibility
we may regard it as not final for our thought. The will,
after all, is not something which functions in isolation from
the rest of the personality, able to do anything which may
be theoretically conceived. The real choices which lie
before it are limited by the specific constitution of human
personality and by the specific situations with which it has

s

to deal. And if God knows what is in man and is sovereign in some way over all situations, it may be that He can bring all human souls to some dread point of illumination wherein they can do no other but surrender and begin to move in another direction.

The objection is urged that even to contemplate the possibility of universal salvation is to take from man's situation as he stands before God, and therefore from the Christian message in relation to that situation, every element of crisis and urgency. It would seem, it is said, that it does not matter what a man does ; for it will all come to the same thing in the end, namely salvation for everybody. The answer to this is that it is not, and never could be, the Christian message to announce blandly a universal salvation. The Christian message, having at the heart of it the Cross, must always be salvation through suffering. There is, in the first place, the suffering of the sinner himself. There can be no cleansing without it. Moreover, as in this world, so in whatever lies beyond it, the reconciled sinner may always carry with him something of the injury and diminution of his personal being which in a real moral order sin must ever bring with it. The joy of heaven, we may surmise, is not in having every conceivable perfection of being in oneself, but in being so related to God and to others in love that every conceivable service open to one in whose past there has been sin is now at last, through much suffering and the forgiveness of God, laid upon the altar of His kingdom. Second, there is the suffering of others. No hope of universal salvation can alter the fact that no man sins unto himself, and that every disloyalty adds something to that corruption and bitterness of life which, whatever be its final outcome, it would have been far better had it never been. Finally, there is the suffering of the divine love as revealed in the Cross of Jesus Christ. It is clear that no one could become in any degree possessed of the truth of a Christian message so presented without becoming aware of the greatest possible challenge and urgency. Anyone who, contemplating the Cross of Christ, could say " that gives me *carte blanche* to do what I like ", would merely declare himself to be still hardened and blind in selfishness ; nor could any preaching of everlasting damnation avail to save him, for it could only appeal to, and so confirm, the very selfishness which is impervious to the challenge of suffering love. But, in any case, we cannot preach a doctrine merely because we think it will get better results. The only justification for preaching a doctrine is that we are convinced of its truth, and our concern has been merely to show that if we feel impelled on Christian grounds not to shut out the possibility of universal salvation, it cannot be urged against that position that it altogether lacks the note of urgency.

CHAPTER XV

PRAYER AND GUIDANCE IN THE CHRISTIAN LIFE

WE turn to a somewhat different—though not unrelated—order of question from that just considered, when we consider the relation of God's providence to the individual who *is* reconciled to Him through Christ, and who, therefore, is profoundly desirous, despite every sin and failure into which he may fall, to know and to do the divine will. We have seen reason to hold to the faith that the austere love of God is inscrutably and savingly at work in every individual life, even the most alienated and rebellious ; moreover every individual life, we must suppose, even in its alienation and rebellion, is taken up into that wider providence of God which transcends the individual altogether, serving unwittingly as His instrument, even whilst refusing to be His agent. There must, however, be a profound difference between the relation of the reconciled man and that of the unreconciled man to the divine providence. The difference is precisely that the reconciled man passes more and more from the status of being the unwitting instrument to that of being the discerning agent of God's will, though to no one is it given to see the full meaning and bearing in God's purpose of what he does. He becomes a co-operator with God, so that through him God gets a purchase on the human scene not otherwise possible.[1]

---

[1] Cf. Oman, *The Paradox of the World*, p. 30 : " All of us alike are God's instruments. By no setting of our hearts on wickedness or doing evil with both hands can we prevent God from using us. Our folly will serve Him when our wisdom fails ; our wrath praise Him, though our wills rebel. Yet, as God's instruments without intention and in our own

The new life of co-operation with God is manifested in prayer, and in a daily activity increasingly informed and guided by the divine Spirit. Each of these two aspects of the Christian experience of God as personal calls for consideration.

(1) First, prayer.

In Chapter VIII we suggested that Christian prayer, prayer, that is to say, which rises out of the heart of the Christian experience of reconciliation, avoids the primitive eudæmonism, which makes God the ally of our unregenerate desires, and the refined eudæmonism which makes Him merely the source of a beatific state of mind. On the one hand, it does not cheapen God, and on the other hand, it does not depersonalise Him.[1] We are now in a position to indicate how this is so.

It takes place through the fact that the supreme pre-occupation of Christian prayer, in accordance with its source in the experience of God's saving and reconciling work in Christ, becomes the furtherance of God's saving and reconciling work in the world amongst men ; or to put it differently, the furtherance of the rule, or kingdom, of the divine will as holy love in the world amongst men. To be sure, an essential element in the Christian awareness is, as we have seen, the thought of the divine kingdom transcending in its ultimate realisation this world altogether ; yet because it is a kingdom of love, it is impossible to be rightly related to it except by seeking to obey its absolute demands here and now in the actual personal relationships in which we are involved. And part of that obedience is the

despite, we generally serve God's ends only as we defeat our own. To be God's agent is quite another matter. This we are only as we learn God's will, respond to His call, work faithfully together with Him, and find our highest ends in fulfilling His."

Cf. also the distinction drawn by Matthews between the man of destiny and the man of Providence, *God in Christian Thought and Experience*, p. 272.

[1] See above, p. 141.

prayer of petition directed to the ends of reconciliation and love.

Petition, so conceived, is immediately set in the way of release from that preoccupation with the self which is the source of all its perversions. The mind is concentrated primarily on the will of God, not on the fulfilment of its own purposes. Nevertheless that necessary eudæmonistic element in all prayer, which springs from the soul's yearning towards its own highest life, is not left out of account. Underlying and informing the whole activity there is the redeemed man's awareness of having been sought and found and reconciled by that same love of God which he now desires to see realised in the lives of others. To that love he commits the fuller realisation of his own salvation, knowing that it is in perfectly safe keeping; and if, like Paul, he declares himself ready to be anathema for his brethren's sake, that is because, paradoxically, he is sure that such a state of anathema would bring him nearer than ever to Him who revealed the heart of God by loving men to the uttermost and giving Himself for them.

Concentration on the will of God, however, does not mean abstraction from the purposes and interests through which alone personal life in this world can be expressed. It is, we repeat, in this world and amongst men that the divine purpose of love has to be served, and its fuller realisation yearned for. Without relation to the purposes and interests of men's daily life, love, whether of God or man, would be nothing but an empty sentiment, lacking all power of expression. Whence it follows that these purposes and interests, so far as they can be related to the supreme purpose and interest of love, become of necessity the subject matter of Christian petition. The general petition that God's will of love may be done, not at large, but here and now through us, breaks up, therefore, in the concreteness of immediate personal relations, into particular petitions for particular persons, and that, too, in relation to the present, pressing, earthly necessities of their lives. Whatever the spirit of love insists that I should try to do in the lives of my fellows, that I must pray for ; whatever the spirit of love insists that I should pray for, that, so far as I have any power, I must try to do. If love calls upon me, for example, to try to heal sickness by medicine, it calls upon me also to try to heal it with prayer, and the two activities can, and should, go on together. It is all one movement of a love which is conscious of itself as having been called into being by the divine love, and has been given the privilege of co-operation with its ever-present succouring and saving activity amongst men.

Some important consequences flow from this way of looking upon petitionary prayer as co-operation with that transcendent will of God which is none the less immanently at work in and through men's relationships with one another.

First, it indicates that the Christian prayer of petition, to be effective, must be more than the mere repetition of a formula however well-intentioned. It must be an expression of a love which is cleansed and enhanced by its own experience of the divine love in Christ ; and it must include that imaginative self-identification with the other man's situation which is the mark of all genuine love. There must be the deliberate effort to enter deeply into his need. To toss off the petition, " O God, make so-and-so better ", is, for example, hardly likely to avail much. But to enter imaginatively into the sick-room, and into the whole strained and anxious domestic situation, linking, as it were, our purpose with God, who is assuredly there already in His eternal wrestling with human pain and defeat—that is another matter ; it is a solemn and joyous responsibility which cannot possibly be sustained in a casual way.

Second, it sheds some light on the question of un-answered prayer. If intercession be regarded as an attempt to get God to do something He is not otherwise minded to do, then the failure of such prayer is a troublesome thing. It suggests that we have not prayed enough, or that God is unresponsive, or that the whole business has been a waste of time. But if it be realised that God is already seeking to succour and bless those for whom prayer is offered, and that by our prayer we endeavour to create that deeper fellowship of persons with one another in God to which God's purpose is directed and on which He has in a measure made its fruition dependent, then the unanswered petition takes on an altogether different appearance. We realise that there must have been other elements in the total situation, which were in the fuller knowledge and grasp of the divine providence and which helped to determine the outcome. None the less we have done our part as co-workers with God, and it may well be that, though the specific prayer was unanswered, yet it played a part in the ultimate working out of the divine purpose of love. The call to work with God, as well in prayer as in deed, is not abrogated by the fact that, in the infinite complexity of His patient and always personal warfare with evil, there are inscrutable necessities, hindrances, postponements which our minds cannot fathom. Rather the call is intensified, albeit never apart from the quiet assurance that His work will go on, if not in one way then in another. Perhaps it was this truth which lay behind Jesus' insistence on importunity in prayer.

Third, it indicates the value of corporate prayer, on which the Christian consciousness has always insisted. If there is an added effectiveness in prayers which, without ceasing to be the expression of the individual's own heart, are also corporate, it is because such prayers are prayers of fellowship, prayers of the Church. They rest on, and carry the power of, at least a partial realisation of that to which all true prayer is directed, namely that membership one of another in the love of God, which is the kingdom. To regard corporate prayer as though it were an addition sum, so that the more people there are praying for anything, the more certain is the result, merely because there are, so to say, more units of prayer-pressure per square-inch being exercised, is, of course, shallow and absurd. More people at prayer means more effectiveness in prayer only if it represents an extension and a deepening of fellowship, a passing of more personalities out of the lower and sinful status of isolation into the higher and redeemed status of loving co-operation in God for the high ends of His kingdom.[1]

Fourth, it indicates the conditions which govern prayer for the success of the Christian's own enterprises in the world. The Christian must bring all that engages his own daily activity to God, and in so far as he can sincerely relate it to what must ever be his supreme preoccupation, namely the work of God in the world, he is entitled to pray for its success. To pray for the success of a business enterprise, wherein methods are determined and success measured purely in terms of dividends for the bank-account, is manifestly a blasphemy too crude almost to be worthy of mention ; but to pray for it, because it is seen, even under the scrutiny of God, to be a service to mankind, and because there is bound up in it the well-being of countless men and women, that is manifestly a different thing. Doubtless the dangers of self-deception in this area are peculiarly great, but *abusus non tollit usum*, and if we were to wait until our motives are perfectly pure before praying, we should never pray at all. Moreover, it is through the endeavour to pray, as well as to work, for our desires that motives are cleansed and ambitions ennobled. The objection sometimes raised that petitions on behalf of our own tasks and enterprises in

---

[1] Matt. xviii–xix : " If two of you shall agree on earth as touching anything that they shall ask, it shall be done for them of my father which is in heaven. For where two or three are gathered together in my name, there I am in the midst of them,"—i.e. the effectiveness lies in the realisation of fellowship with one another in Christ.

the world often contradict and cancel one another, that therefore it cannot be right to present them, is superficial. It seems to rest on a view of God which is at once naïvely anthropomorphic and aridly rationalistic, and to lack a religious sense of the vast mystery of the divine providence and its relationship to the complexities of human history. Here what was said above about unanswered prayer is relevant. The problem of God in relation to men's conflicting prayers is no different from His problem in relation to their conflicting acts ; indeed, in some ways it may be the lesser problem, inasmuch as prayer, in so far as it is sincere, is at least an act in conscious relationship to God, and that may well " let God into " a situation in a way that was not otherwise possible. Yet, of course, when Christian people realise that they are praying for conflicting things, they are under obligation, in the interests of that fellowship without which in the end all prayer is futile, to reconsider what they are doing. There is a greater scandal than praying for conflicting interests and that is to be so secular-minded as not to be ready to pray about them at all.

Fifth, it indicates the answer that must be given to the question whether there are any limits to the things for which the Christian man should pray.

The answer to this question is, in a general way, that decision as to what things to pray for, and what not to pray for, must be left to the divinely illumined insight of the individual as he seeks with all his best powers to serve the will of God in the immediate situation with which he is confronted. From one point of view the religious mind is bound to maintain that all things are possible with God, yet from another point of view nothing could be more irreligious than to say that, for it would seem to deny that God has any specific character and purpose at all. There must be petitions which God can never grant, inasmuch as to grant them would be to deny His nature and purpose, petitions, therefore, which will inevitably disappear from the reconciled man's prayers as he enters more deeply into the life of fellowship with Him. Such limitations on prayer, which spring from the nature and purpose of God and which therefore are not rightly called limitations at all, we must suppose it is given to the reconciled man increasingly to know in relation to various situations in which he is engaged. He will know, with the insight of a love that is being more and more conformed to the image of Christ and the will of God, for what things he ought to pray.

The one thing we must insist on again is that it is for the religious insight to determine what these limits of prayer are ; it is not, for example, for science to say. Thus, if a Christian decides that he cannot pray God to send rain on some famine-stricken area, it must be because he feels convinced that God in His austere wisdom does not do that kind of thing, not because he supposes that science has shown once and for all that that kind of thing cannot in the nature of things be done. For, as we have maintained earlier, science has shown nothing of the sort. Most Christian people do as a matter of fact instinctively set certain limits to their prayers, and always have done so, altogether apart from any knowledge of what science may be supposed to say about the matter. Thus they pray for recovery from pneumonia, but not for the growing of a new limb in place of one that has been amputated. They pray for rain, but not for the sudden upstanding of the crops when once they lie black and dessicated on the parched earth, nor for a multiplication of the half-loaf still left in the pantry. They pray for a loved one's safety, but not for his resurrection from the dead when once he has been killed. They pray for courage to face failure, yet not for skill to write a play like Hamlet or a symphony like Beethoven's fifth. Yet, so far as abstract scientific theory has anything to say about the matter, all these things are equally possible or equally impossible.

The source of these distinctions can be found only in the fact that there is given to mankind, and supremely to the man whose inner life is being cleansed and reconciled to God by Jesus Christ, an insight into those limits which the divine love has itself set, at least for the time being, upon the open possibilities of this world in any situation. There are what may be called hygienic limits to prayer defined by the divine purpose of fashioning human personalities in love, and it is the Christian's calling, through his own increasing self-commitment to that purpose, to be increasingly able to discern what they are in each situation as it arises. A factor in such discernment may doubtless be the knowledge of God's world which science has made available, a knowledge which, as von Hügel loved to insist, can exercise a most beneficent, purgatorial influence upon the religious life, ever ready as it is to lapse into the egotism and indolence of merely magical ideas. Yet the final decision is not with science as such. It is with the insight of the life of piety itself, as it stands within its own historical situation and confronts the call of God in it to the service and the trust of love. Nor is it of great concern that different Christians will draw the limits in different places, provided only that in every case the decision not to pray for this, that, or the other thing is only the negative side of a positive endeavour to grasp every situation in love, and to share, both in heart's desire and in active deed, whatsoever they can understand of God's austere purpose of love within it. The essence of the magical idea, it should be clearly understood, is not in praying for things that will not happen, or which, if we knew all, we should see could not happen, but in praying for things out of a merely egotistic idea of bending the will of God to one's own purposes. We might say, love God and pray for what you like.[1]

---

[1] In this connection we may be permitted a word on the difficult question of the miracles of Jesus. From the standpoint of abstract

Can we, then, say anything as to the way in which the reconciled man grows increasingly to know the mind and the will of God ? What is the manner of the divine illumination and guidance ?

scientific theory the healing miracles are not more credible than the so-called miracles of nature. Concerning neither can science say on general grounds that they could, or could not, happen. What makes many people more ready to accept the former than the latter is, first, that happenings analogous to the former, but not to the latter, apparently happen to-day, and, second, they have a sort of intuitive insight that God does not do things like multiplying bread, though it may be theoretically impossible to deny that He might. It is difficult to know, however, how far the second reason is a piece of genuine insight derived in part from their knowledge of God through Jesus, and how far it is merely a restatement of the first. If there were analogies to the multiplication of loaves in their present experience, would they feel that God does not do that sort of thing ? That it is a piece of genuine insight derived from Jesus might be indicated by the fact that, as the story of the temptation seems to show, Jesus Himself had a very clear insight into what we have called the hygienic limits of the possible from the point of view of God's saving purpose ; it must be granted that a miracle like the multiplication of the loaves before a mob of people hardly looks consistent with the refusal to turn stones into bread, or otherwise give a sign. On the other hand, if it be merely a question of the complete absence of any analogous happenings in our own experience, the uniqueness of Jesus' fellowship with God, and of His vocation, if these be granted at all, might be held sufficient explanation. What was right and possible for Jesus in His situation may be wrong and impossible for me in mine. So far as I can judge, the question of how much, or how little, of the miraculous element in the gospel stories we accept is not of the greatest moment, provided only that the decision springs not from pseudo-scientific dogmatism, but from the continuous endeavour to grasp by every means at our disposal, the mind of Christ, and to live day by day in the service of that saving love of God which shines forth in Him and supremely through His Cross and Resurrection.

Of the events recorded in the gospels and usually classed as miraculous the Resurrection would seem to stand for the Christian believer by itself. This is because, on the one hand, the historical evidence for it is, in a general way, very strong, and, on the other hand, if it be not true in some sense that Jesus was not " holden of death " (Acts ii. 24) but passed through it to an exalted life, then the Christian message and experience all down the ages is left without any foundation save that of pious self-deception and illusion. This still, however, leaves considerable latitude for different views as to the detail of the Resurrection happenings and as to how the exalted state of Jesus and His continuing presence in His Church may in its ultimate theological bearings be best interpreted. In any case, here as elsewhere, the scientist, *qua* scientist, is not competent to say that the event, in the nature of things, could not have happened.

(2) Guidance.

In seeking to answer these questions we do not hope to analyse and explain in detail what must, in the nature of the case, always transcend our knowledge ; our desire is rather to avoid, if possible, wrong answers to them. The consideration of them takes us into the sphere of the doctrine of the Spirit.

The choice before us seems to lie between a conception of the Spirit's guidance which is relatively primitive and impersonal, and one which has been thoroughly taken on to the level of personal fellowship with God through Christ.

In the Old Testament two strands of thought may be observed coming to expression in the use of the category of the Spirit. First, there is the thought that man's personality is, in a unique way, derived from, and sustained by, God. He is specifically man because, somehow, in the underlying deeps, the ultimate affiliations, of his nature, he lives and moves and has his being in a creative, in-breathing, sustaining Power which is none other than the Spirit of the Eternal Himself. Second, there is the thought that any unusual enhancement of a man's powers, whether in physical energy, or creative skill, or prophetic insight and wisdom, is due to an uprush of this same divine spirit, which, however, is still regarded as upholding men in the more normal and humdrum functioning of their lives. Other lines of thought enter in, especially in the prophetic religion of Israel, but these alone are to our purpose as indicating those universal elements in man's religious awareness which have made a separate category of the Spirit inevitable, namely the sense, first, that there are mysterious deeps in the spirit of man underlying the more superficially observable processes of his mind and running away down into the very being of God, and the sense, second, that if God is to use man in any special way for a special purpose, it will be through His flooding up, as it were, through these inner deeps in an unusual degree—or, to change the metaphor in the direction of the original meaning of the word spirit, through His sustaining breath taking the form of a transforming and irresistible " gust " or " afflatus ".

That these are the fundamental and universal religious awarenesses that underlie the usage of the distinctive category of the Spirit of God is evidenced by the fact that even in Christian circles the tendency has continually manifested itself to conceive the guidance of the Spirit exclusively in terms of them. Explicitly or implicitly it has been supposed that the more the self-conscious, self-directing, so to say illuminated, area of man's being could be put into a state of emptiness and passivity, the more opportunity would there be for the divine to break in from the underlying deeps in guidance and direction.[1] Such a view, common as it is, is unacceptable, in that as it reduces the reconciled man to the status of an impersonal instrument in a way that is as repellent in idea as it has obvious dangers in practice. Yet if we reject this way of looking at the matter, we have still to come to terms with the fact that it is a fundamental and universal religious perception that a man's soul does rest upon the deeps of God, and that God's presence in, and guidance of, and activity through it must transcend, in wisdom and reach, the tiny illuminated area of the fully-conscious mental processes. As we have said, it is this alone which makes the category of the Spirit indispensable, and apart from it the idea of Providence seems to be reduced to the dimension of our own thoughts, which is the same thing as to eliminate it altogether. If God is not at work within and through our spirits, even when we are not aware of it, there is little hope. As was said above, even

[1] We have not infrequently heard the prayer in pietistic circles, at the opening of business, " may we have no ideas of our own,"—a prayer which, as a friend once tartly remarked, is only too often swiftly and completely answered.

God's willing agent can never know the full meaning and bearing in God's design of what he is led to do.

The way out of the dilemma is indicated in the New Testament. The New Testament writers carry over the fundamental meanings of the Old Testament usage of the term Spirit, but at the same time they take the further step of virtually identifying the Spirit with the spirit of Jesus Christ. The effect of this is of the greatest importance. It means that the Spirit ceases to be a vague, mysterious, supernatural principle, dimly conceived as a Beyond underlying human nature and manifesting itself through abnormal or semi-occult phenomena like ecstasy or glossolalia, and becomes sharply characterised, its character and direction and ultimate purpose being discerned in the personality of Jesus Christ. The "Beyond which is within", to use Boutroux' phrase, is still the Beyond, the infinite deep of the divine Spirit in which all men live and move and have their being; wherefore it is properly designated the Spirit. Yet in another sense it is now no longer merely " beyond " ; it has received characterisation and definition, and can be put into the brightest focus of man's self-conscious awareness and made the object of his self-directing will; wherefore it is as properly called Christ. The Lord is the Spirit, and the fruits of the Spirit are, in Schleiermacher's fine phrase, the virtues of Christ.

In the light of this we can discern something of the way of God's illumination and guidance of the reconciled man. Never are these apart from what goes on in the realm of conscious insight and self-direction. As the reconciled man deliberately centres his inner life in Christ, "minding the things of Christ", setting "his affection on things above, not on things on the earth", thinking on "whatsoever things are true, honourable, just, pure, lovely, and of good report", "bringing every thought into obedience to Christ"; as in every situation where significant choice and act are necessary he girds up the loins of his mind, seeks to accept, without rebellion, the manifest compulsion of circumstance as part of the appointment, and therefore the guidance of God, summons all his powers and every available counsel of Christian brethren, in order " to prove what is that good and acceptable and perfect will of God "—so, increasingly, he is " transformed by the renewing of his mind " into a genuine agent of God. God, we may suppose, can speak to him and use him for the high ends of His redeeming purpose in the world in a way that is not otherwise possible. Yet though such intimations of, and insights into, the way wherein a man should tread are not given apart from the conscious directing of his thoughts and setting of his will towards the things of Christ, they are not exclusively a function of these things. The continuous interplay between the conscious and the subconscious areas of personality is a psychological commonplace in these days, and if the religious faith in God's providential guidance is well founded, the second must fall within the scope of its working as much as the first. Hence it is that the Christian man often feels the constraint of the divine will upon him in a way which, whilst it is not contrary to his conscious insight, none the less at the moment transcends it ; he is under necessity to walk a step at a time in faith. Looking back afterwards he may see that his decision was wiser and more fruitful than he knew, and that, in Luther's rather exaggerated phrase, God has led him " like an old, blind horse."

It is perhaps not unnecessary to add that whilst we must insist that there is guidance for the reconciled man who is seeking to be God's agent in a sense and to a degree that there is not for the unreconciled man who at best can only be His instrument, none the less such guidance can never be so automatically infallible as to save him from making mistakes. That, again, would be radically to depersonalise the relationship. It is one of the deepest and most necessary exercises of faith in the overshadowing love and wisdom and forgiveness of God which the reconciled sinner is called upon to make, that he should be ready to do the highest that he can see at the moment according to the mind of Christ, committing everything else with a quiet mind to Him. The manifold wisdom of God is fully able to let those who are being saved be not yet fully wise, and to guide them even through their unwisdom at one and the same time into finer character and more fruitful service to His kingdom.

CHAPTER XVI

PROVIDENCE IN NATURE AND HISTORY

THE consideration of the relation of the divine providence to the individual and the consideration of its
relation to nature and history, whilst they may be separated
for purposes of exposition, are none the less closely implicated
in one another in the all-embracing unity of the Christian
experience of reconciliation. We have seen that it is part
of Christ's work in the soul to release it from egotistic and
eudæmonistic preoccupation with its own concerns, and to
make it increasingly sensitive to the concerns of others, or
rather to God's concern in others. God's purpose thus
becomes for it, not merely theoretically, but in a way which
engages the whole being, as wide as humanity itself, as wide
as history. Furthermore, inasmuch as such release from
the self of necessity carries with it a heightened sense, not
only of the neighbour, but also of God, that is, of One who
is the transcendent Creator and Lord of all, One that
"stretches out the heavens as a curtain, and spreadeth
them out as a tent to dwell in ", the awareness of the
divine purpose which is dealing with the soul in its
salvation of necessity expands to include the whole
creation, and this again not theoretically, but in a way
which is capable, at least on occasion, of stirring the
whole personality to its depths. In Chapter III also we
saw how both society and nature enter into the total
awareness of God as personal, and, needless to say, it is
not otherwise in that cleansed and heightened awareness

of Him as personal which is the result of being reconciled through Christ.[1]

To say this does not contradict the principle already laid down that the root of Christian faith in Providence is in God's saving dealings with the individual and not in the observation of external evidences of His working elsewhere. The point is simply that it is an essential part of those saving dealings that a man's eyes are opened to that universal kingdom of love which it is the divine purpose to achieve, and which is the awful measure, on the one hand, of his own insignificance in himself and, on the other hand, of the wonder of his calling and salvation in Christ. The cosmic setting of his life and the significance of his salvation, when clearly realised, inevitably raise new questions and problems, and they are questions and problems from which, even if they can never be fully solved, spring new insights, humbler attitudes, and deeper self-commitments in faith.

(1) Providence in nature.

By nature in this connexion we mean the created order considered as standing as an independent system over against human purposes, as a given which the latter may adapt and use, but which in its fundamental facts and structural principles cannot be altered. We must not, of course, in our thinking separate man from nature so completely that the fact that, in Pringle-Pattison's phrase, man is " organic to nature ", and therefore is a tremendously important clue to its inner meaning, is overlooked. Nor must nature and history be separated too absolutely, for, obviously, the course of history is often determined, in spite of human purposes, by natural circumstance, and, as we

---

[1] So Paul in Rom. viii. 23 speaks of " groaning within ourselves "—anything but a theoretical attitude—and the groaning is for a redemption which includes in its scope the whole creation as well as the " manifestation of the sons of God ".

shall see, in the end the interpretation of history inevitably runs out into considerations of the destiny of the cosmos as a whole. Still, in practice, the distinction between man and his purposes on the one hand, and his environment and its facts and principles on the other hand, is clear enough. Nature is in a measure a " going concern " and pursues its own way, whatever man may do or desire ; doubtless it has in a sense produced man, but it seems to have been there before it produced him, and there is no reason to think that it would not continue to be there even if he vanished from the scene.

Looking over the scene of nature in the sense just given, the Christian thinker is bound to say that there is much of it which it is not possible to construe in terms of a divine providence such as is revealed in his own personal experience of salvation through Christ, even when due weight is given to the elements of austerity and judgment which are assuredly not absent from the latter. Nature from that point of view certainly wears an inscrutable face. There are, to be sure, aspects of it which support a theistic philosophy, and therefore to that extent the Christian faith. That reality, as science is ever more clearly showing, is a close-knit unity of interdependent relationships ; that ever richer forms of organic life have emerged in and through an infinite multiplicity of interacting events, a slight alteration in the configuration of which would, so far as can be judged, have made such an outcome impossible ; that the richest, and most complex, of these organic forms, namely man, has intellectual, moral, and spiritual powers to the exercise of which the universe in its laws and processes appears to be in a remarkable degree adapted—all this certainly points in the direction of a theistic interpretation. It might even be argued that a theistic philosophy, of all possible philo-sophies, provides the most satisfactory synthesis of all the facts as known, though the power of such an argument to convince would doubtless depend on the extent to which there was an initial religious sympathy with such an interpretation. Nevertheless, even if we are prepared to grant that a theistic philosophy can give a good account of itself, there still remain for it, and still more for Christian belief, vast areas of nature which are wrapped in impenetrable mystery.

The incredible and wasteful fecundity of life on this planet alone makes the mind reel, and ask again what can God be at in it all.[1] It appears to be leading to no end beyond the utterly sterile one of indefinitely repeating itself. What an incomprehensibility, so far as any providential purpose which we can even dimly discern is concerned, the enormous busy-ness of, say, an ant-heap is! What mystery looks out through the eyes of a dog! And when to the biological immensities of this little planet are added the overwhelming infinities of the stars, the sense of the abyss of mystery over which everything hangs suspended almost appals the soul. A specially challenging mystery to the Christian mind is the competitive ruthlessness which runs throughout animate nature. The picture of nature as " red in tooth and claw " has beyond question been exaggerated, and much of our recoil from the so-called horrors of the struggle for existence may be due to a naïve and altogether unwarranted projecting of our own sensitive self-consciousness into the lower creation—we imagine ourselves, for example, in the place of the mouse with which the cat is playing. Moreover, even in this area there are gleams and premonitions of better things, as, for example, in that dim foreshadowing of the highest principles of the Christian ethic which is to be found in the mutual dependence of different forms of life upon one another, and in the self-sacrifice of animal parents for their young. Yet, even so,

---

[1] According to Titius over a million species of multicellular animals are definitely known,—*op. cit.*, p. 640.

the other side of the picture is there, and cannot be brushed on one side.

No one has presented this enigmatic quality of the natural order more powerfully and movingly than Mr. Paul Elmer More in his book *The Sceptical Approach to Religion*. The author describes the exquisite beauty and peace of the valley of the Severn as he looks out upon it from some elevated spot. He then proceeds : " my mind turned backwards to the long ages, the incalculable years, of preparation through which the land had passed before it was made fit for this fruitful cultivation :—the fiery convulsions which had tossed up the earth into a sea of mountains, the vast sweep of water that by slow attrition had scooped out this broad channel, and, then, contracting, had left it a fertile champaign. Earth and air and fire and water had all contributed to the fashioning of an almost perfect home for the sons of men. Yet it was not they who did it, these unwitting and, as it were, reluctant elements ; rather, by its own expansive nature and abandoned to its own unchecked action, each of these was an agent of destruction or obstruction. Nor were they, each in itself, capable of learning or of changing their character. They are to-day what they were at the beginning, and at any moment any one of them, if it breaks bounds, may in an hour undo the labour of centuries. Conflagration, deluge, famine, tempest, earthquake, are forever possible and forever threatening.

" And then from these inanimate elements of the scene my thought turned to the creatures that inhabit it, to the plants that cover the ground with a tapestry of embroidered green, and the animals, from the tiny insect scuttling through the herbs to the bird sailing on the thin ocean of the air and the ox grazing stolidly in the field. To the eye it was a wide-spread theatre of joy and a masque of peaceful beauty. Until I thought of what lay beneath the surface.

Here in fact was an army of countless individuals, each driven on by an instinctive lust of life as if engaged in a vast internecine warfare—each blade of grass fighting for its place under the sun and obtaining it by the suppression of some other plant, each animal preying for sustenance upon some other form of life. It is a system of ruthless competition and remorseless extermination. How then out of this weltering conflict has this compromise of organic society been contrived, this ordered polity, in which a sort of balance has been struck, such that the individual strivings for existence become mutually supporting as well as mutually destructive? It was not the common principle of life that effected this harmony, for the law of survival is now, as always, a callous selfishness which teaches the stronger not only to profit by his victory but to take pleasure in the agony of the defeated. Who has not seen a cat toying gleefully with its victim, or a snake gliding exultantly through the grass with a tortured bird in its mouth, and has not shuddered at the gleam of malice in the hunter's eye? Who that has seen a hawk dropping upon its prey, or heard the baying of hounds on the chase, but has wondered at the mingled beauty and hatefulness of life? From every spot of earth rises continually the battle-cry of nature: *vae victis!*"[1]

In the course of Christian history three different lines of thought have, at various times and in various forms, been pursued in the attempt to minimise the otherwise chilling effect upon faith which these facts have.

The first is the simple one of separating the God of creation from the God of redemption; nature looks different from anything that the God who has revealed Himself in Christ might be expected to create because it is in fact derived from a different source. From its first appearance in Marcion, the Christian mind has consistently

[1] pp. 78–80—quoted with permission of the Author and Princeton University Press.

and rightly rejected this as heresy, and has continued to affirm that the God at work in nature and the God and Father of our Lord Jesus Christ are one and the same.

The second is to suppose that the natural order as a whole, and not merely the human section of it, has become involved in some sort of " fall " or sinfulness, and that from this spring those aspects of it which seem to contradict the Christian conception of the nature and purpose of God. This theory may take the form either of deriving the " fallen " condition of nature from the sin of man (as for example in the Jewish Apocalyptists and, possibly, in Paul) or of deriving both the " fallen " condition of nature and the " fallen " condition of man from some more ultimate and primordial Fall preceding both. The latter is the one which any modern rendering of the theory must, in view of the fact of man's relatively late appearance in the evolutionary process, adopt. Thus we have Dr. N. P. Williams recently advocating what he calls a " precosmic vitiation of the whole Life Force at the very beginning of cosmic evolution ", partly on the ground that thus, and only thus, can the " red in tooth and claw " aspect of nature be explained.[1]

The main objection to this theory is that it is speculative in the bad sense of that term ; that is to say, it posits a reality and an event so completely unrelated to anything of which we have experience that it is almost impossible to give them any precise meaning. It substitutes for mystery a darker mystery, and seeks to explain *ignotum per ignotius*. Moreover, since Dr. Williams expressly denies any moral quality to what he rather misleadingly terms the " ruthless *ego*tism " of animate nature, it is a little difficult to see why it is necessary to conceive as lying behind it a mysterious moral lapse in some hypothetical Life-Force. It would be simpler and more intelligible to attribute these things to a mysterious necessity in the divine process of creation which

[1] *The Ideas of the Fall and Original Sin*, Lecture VIII, *passim*.

we cannot grasp, but which, by a judgement of faith, we believe will be ultimately justified in the consummated purpose of God.   In other words, if we are going outside what is empirically observable in our endeavour to make sense of " the cobra, the tarantula, and the bacillus of diphtheria ", it is enough to move *forward* to the eschatological hope, which has its roots, as we have seen, in the immediacies of Christian experience, and not in the least necessary to move *backward* to a speculative lapse in some speculative world-soul, which is hardly related to immediate experience at all.

This indicates the third line of thought, which in our judgement is the right one.   It is to accept these inscrutabilities of the world as part of the infinite and utterly trustworthy divine purpose, which, while being wrought out in and through the travailings and confusions of nature, nevertheless transcends these in a way which makes impossible for us anything but the dimmest comprehension of what is being done.   It is, of course, not inherently impossible that some unimaginable corruption has entered into the order of nature, but in default of any conclusive evidence for that, it seems better to be content to be agnostic, committing everything unto Him who assuredly doeth all things well, and with whom in the end are the kingdom and the power. So regarded, the inscrutabilities of the natural order may, as was earlier suggested, play a not unimportant part in preserving in the soul of the reconciled man a due sense of the mystery and the transcendence of God.   He might even bow his head in awed thankfulness for the earthquake, the blazing comets, the mountainous seas, the teeming fecundity of life, the " tyger, tyger, burning bright ", for that thus again and again he has been compelled with the Psalmist, beholding what desolation He hath made in the earth, to be still and know that God is God.   Such a mood, however, would be incomprehensible to the unreconciled man who knows nothing of the assurances of God in his inner life through Christ.[1]

There still remains the question whether, and in what sense, the natural order as a whole, and apart from the problems which its empirically observable content raises for faith, may be conceived to have a permanent place in the realised kingdom of God. This question, however, inevitably arises again in relation to our interpretation of human history, and such answer to it as it is possible to give can, therefore, be conveniently set forth in that connection.

(2) Providence in history.

The word history is, in popular usage, somewhat ambiguous and ill-defined. We propose to mean by it in this

---

[1] Blake's " Tyger, tyger, burning bright " seems to express a much more proper response than an attempt to explain the " tyger " in terms of a pre-cosmic fall. Cf. Barth (*Commentary on the Epistle to the Romans*, Eng. Trans., p. 46) : " What are all those enigmatic creatures of God— a zoological gardens, for example—but so many problems to which we have no answer ? "

It is said that in the course of an argument with Tolstoy a sceptic said : " How can I believe in God in face of a cholera microbe ? " To which Tolstoy replied : " Don't be flippant." The sceptic is probably still wondering what he meant.

The panpsychist or pluralist hypothesis, which was suggested in Chap. X as at least one possible way of so conceiving the order of nature that room is left for God's living activity within it, might also be invoked here as providing some alleviation of the problem of the travail of nature. It is so used, for example, by Ward in his *Realm of Ends*. According to this theory the aspects of nature described by Mr. More in the passage quoted are due to the fact that nature is a system of monads each of which has a measure of spontaneity and is under necessity " to work out its own salvation " both through competition and through co-operation with other monads. This theory, interesting and illuminating as it is, hardly falls to be included among alternative solutions offered by specific Christian thought and experience. It is purely philosophical in origin and intention, even though it may be compelled, as with Ward, to introduce at the end the thought of God and His providence in order to provide some guarantee that such a collection of competitive entities should be a cosmos and not a chaos. The Christian, however, begins where the philosopher ends, namely, with faith in God, and though he need not be averse to getting light from a pluralist, or any other philosophical, treatment of the problem, he will probably feel that, when all is said, most of the inscrutability of nature still remains, and must be committed to Him whom he has believed and known in Christ.

connection what we mean when we speak of history as a science, namely the study of the evolution of human affairs considered as manifesting connections and significances which transcend the life-span and the conscious purposes of individuals. History as a science is sometimes said to be distinguished from the natural sciences by the fact that it concerns itself with the individual, the *sui generis*, the unrepeatable, whereas the latter are interested in general laws, which so far as possible leave these out of account. Thus, in Windelband's terminology, history is idiographic and natural science nomothetic. Yet Titius is surely right when he says that the distinction, true and important as it is, needs somewhat closer definition. History as a science is not interested primarily in recovering the past of an individual as such, merely for the sake of grasping his idiosyncrasy and the significance which he had for himself and for his intimates. That is the task of biography, if any care to undertake it. History is interested in the individual only as he has significance in a context of events wider than the individual. There is, therefore, as Titius says, in a sense a process of generalisation, whereby the individual is lifted out of his isolation, not in order to dissolve him into a scheme of abstract concepts, but rather in order to set him in the dynamic framework of a larger whole, whether the larger whole be that of an institution, a nation, or humanity in general.[1]

To discuss the relation of providence to history in this sense is thus in effect to propose and apply a Christian philosophy of history. All historical research, which goes beyond the mere accumulation of facts just because they are facts, presupposes a philosophy of history, whether consciously or unconsciously held, for only by the aid of such a philosophy can the historian in the last resort select those facts which he considers to be significant, and interpret

[1] *Op. cit.*, p. 705.

them into the " dynamic framework of a larger whole ".[1]
The difference between a Christian interpretation of history
and others lies in the principles with which it sets out, and
the extent to which it is prepared to make its adhesion to
those principles depend upon its success in construing the
facts satisfactorily in the light of them. The principles with
which it sets out are those implicit in the individual's own
experience of reconciliation to God through Jesus Christ,
and though these may be modified and re-expressed in the
light of what appears to be the historical facts, they must in
their main content be held to, even though these facts
should as judged by them remain an enigma. Here again
appears the difference between the religious and the more
theoretical approach. To the latter the refusal of the facts
to fit its principles of interpretation is, so far, merely an
indication that those principles are wrong and must be
discarded ; to the former, on the other hand, such a refusal
may come rather as a call to faith, and as an indication that
it is not given to us to know the mind of God save in so far
as it meets us in our own immediate personal situation. In
other words, the affirmation of the working of God's providence in history must ever remain at bottom a judgement
of faith ; yet just because faith does, as we have seen, have
a super-individual reference, it is compelled by its own inner
necessities to look out across the wider scene of human
history, and at least attempt to interpret it in terms of what
is given in the intimacies of its own life. In the nature of
the case such an interpretation can hardly be more than an
observation of broad tendencies, seen as in a glass darkly.[2]

[1] Cf. Whitehead, *Adventures of Ideas*, p. 4 : " The historian in his
description of the past depends on his own judgement as to what constitutes
the importance of human life. Even when he has rigorously confined
himself to one selected aspect, political or cultural, he still depends on
some decision as to what constitutes the culmination of that phase of
human experience and as to what constitutes its degradation."

[2] Rom. ix–xi gives an interesting example of the Christian mind moved
by the spirit of love to consider problems of history. The Apostle's

We may first note that the Christian experience of reconciliation through Christ points at once to one place at least in history where God's providential ordering of events might be expected to be more than usually discernible. We asserted earlier[1] that if there is to be a succouring and reconciling revelation of God which shall meet the facts of man's sinful situation, it could not be other than through a historic personality ; and, indeed, Christian thought has, as a rule, insisted on the indissoluble connection between the experience of reconciliation and the historic figure of Jesus Christ. To affirm that God acted uniquely to save mankind in the man Christ Jesus is to affirm that the historic conditions, without relation to which He could not be a man at all, were uniquely grasped within the providence of God and ordered to that end. Doubtless there is a sense in which each human life lies not only within the causal processes of the time-series, but also within the overshadowing providence of God, yet in so far as we are prepared to attribute to Jesus an unique relationship to God's saving purpose towards the race, we shall not without reason expect to be able to discern a special appropriateness in the time, place, and circumstance of His appearing.

Much has been written by various writers on this matter, which it is not necessary to review here.[2] That the Jewish, Greek, and Roman civilisations at that time had reached a peculiarly critical stage in their evolution and mutual interplay, and that Jesus came, so far as can be judged, at the point where the unique content of His personality and message had a singularly high chance of making the

passionate concern for the fate of his own people impels him to try to set the actual facts in some relation to the divine providence ; yet he does not get very far in his interpretations, and is soon forced back on a very agnostic, yet none the less confident, affirmation of faith.

[1] See above, p. 197.

[2] For a short, recent statement see Wood, *Christianity and the Nature of History*, Lecture III.

tive and self-destructive, breaking up even that minimum of social order and co-operation which it requires even to achieve its own purposes. This so far is confirmatory of the Christian faith. Yet it really carries but a little way towards the specifically Christian thought of God. For the judgement which overtakes unrighteousness might be interpreted, in a humanistic way, as the working out of principles which are inherent somehow in the biological and psychological structure of humanity, but which point to no transcendent and overshadowing personal purpose. Moreover, if our standards of righteousness are those of Jesus Christ, it is by no means evident that unrighteousness brings disaster; the facts would seem to show rather that it is only unrighteousness running to a certain imprudent excess which works obvious destruction. The worldly mind is in many ways excellently adapted to this world in public as in private affairs, especially if it chances to have favourable opportunities and knows how to seize them. It is true that the concessions which unrighteousness must make in order to achieve its own ambitions—the honour, for example, which is requisite even amongst thieves—points in the direction of the Christian ethic, but that there is operative in the world a divine purpose which visits all unchristian policies with judgement is no more evident in the larger sphere of history than in the narrower limits of individual lives. Again, there is a certain impersonal wholesaleness in the working out of such judgement upon evil as history does evidence, which, considered in and for itself, hardly accords with the Christian conception of God as a holy love profoundly concerned with the individual soul. When ruin and disaster follow unrighteousness, they are wrought out in the lives of countless men, women, and children, who find themselves helplessly caught in a flood of consequences apparently as pitiless and undiscriminating as the very unrighteousness from which they spring.

U

The position, then, seems to be that beyond question there looms through history, as the general shape of a mountain might loom through the mist, certain broad contours of judgement which in some degree point in the direction of the Christian conception of the righteousness of God. Beyond that the facts, strictly taken, hardly entitle us to go. The Christian may, however, be led by this somewhat equivocal appearance which history presents, to a deeper understanding of the significance of this present life and of the ways of God with men. Thus it is necessary that there should be some sort of observable limit set to unrighteousness in order to sustain in men's minds the fundamental conviction, without which serious living is impossible, that in their ethical life they are dealing with an objective order, and not merely with the " devices and desires of their own hearts ". On the other hand, that the limits should be so broadly set that they allow a certain measure of success to a prudent worldliness, and provide no exact and observable equivalence between unrighteousness and judgement, might be interpreted as evidence of a wisdom which has designed this world for the fashioning of personalities who must learn to love righteousness for its own sake and not for its prestige or its immediate consequences ; as evidence also of a patience and a forgiveness which are themselves that highest righteousness which men in their own lives must seek to share. And in the apparently impersonal and wholesale working out of the judgements of history the Christian will be impelled to see, as has already been indicated in the previous chapters, on the one hand, a solemn manifestation of a divine righteousness, revealed in the Cross, which, being what it is, has no option but to set men in a personal order wherein the innocent suffer with and for the guilty ; and on the other hand, an indication that not in history can the final meaning and consummation of God's purpose with men and women be found, but in something which transcends history altogether. These, however, are religious insights and interpretations springing from the Christian's personal and growing experience of God through Jesus Christ.

Second, the idea of progress.

Bury has familiarised English readers with the fact that the idea of progress, which is still so central and formative in the thought and action of Western peoples, is a comparatively recent addition, dating from the Renaissance. He has also insisted, along with other writers, on the important and indispensable part which Christianity played in making the emergence of the idea possible.[1]

The idea of progress, whatever else may be incorporated into it, includes two thoughts, which mutually involve one another : First, that this world has a certain intrinsic significance which is harmonious with the purposes of men, and in relation to which, therefore, the latter have a meaning and a worthwhileness which they would otherwise lack. Second, that this intrinsic significance is teleological ; there is in things generally a movement, of which man's activity is a part, towards an end-state of realised well-being which will be the ample justification of all that has gone before. The affinity of these ideas with the Christian outlook hardly needs pointing out. Thus we have already said that Christianity, in so far as it remains true to its fundamental conviction of the personal quality of God's relation to man, must insist that this world, the time-process, has a certain intrinsic significance as the sphere in which God's will meets man and asks his co-operation ; even though, somewhat paradoxically, this significance, though intrinsic to the world, is declared to transcend it. Furthermore, and bound up with this, we have seen how the eschatological hope, the belief in a " telos " of history, has always been organically related to the Christian experience of reconciliation. It is

[1] *The Idea of Progress*, Introduction.

generally recognised that it was these Christian ideas which broke through the pessimism of the antique world, which saw no future for the world save a futile, cyclical repetition of all that had gone before ; and though in mediæval times the form in which these ideas found expression in many ways postponed and suspended the rise of the idea of progress, none the less it was the inherent vitality and significance of them in Christian experience which made such a rise possible at all. The doctrine of progress in its purely rationalistic statement is a secularisation, on the one hand, of the idea of God at work in the world, and on the other hand, of the eschatological hope. For the providence of God is substituted the working of an inherent and necessary law of progress (later identified with the so-called law of evolution) and for the " telos " which transcends this world, and depends on other than terrestrial forces for its inception is substituted a more or less perfect end-state, or utopia, within this world itself.

There is plainly, therefore, a relation of some sort between Christian faith and the idea of progress, which it is necessary to think out as clearly as possible. Obviously the Christian faith cannot tolerate the secularised idea of progress which makes it the automatic and necessary working-out of merely immanent process towards a purely this-worldly consummation ; nor, on the other hand, can it tolerate that false form of eschatological hope which in effect, if not in intention, evacuates man's work in this world of any intrinsic significance whatsoever.

Let us consider the two aspects of the secularised idea of progress indicated above.

First, the belief that there is an inherent, necessary law of progress in human affairs.

The prime question here is one of fact. The secularist view has no grounds for its faith except as the facts can be shown to support it, and the Christian faith in providence, though its roots are in something other than the mere observation of facts, is, as we have seen, properly eager to see what the latter may have to reveal concerning the way of God's working in the world.

It is hardly open to question that there has been in human history a movement, or movements, bringing about the gradual realisation of ends generally recognised as desirable, each new stage in the process resting on, and in some cases taking up into itself, what has gone before, i.e. movements not improperly called progress. Wherever there is an end sought, then it is legitimate to speak of progress towards it, without necessarily making any judgement whether the end is ethically good or bad. The most obvious example of progress in this sense is the gradual accumulation of knowledge and the extension of man's power to make his world subserve his own purposes. Again, though in a less obvious and unqualified way, and in some sections of mankind far more than in others, there has been progress in the cultural and social life of mankind, certain generally recognised " evils " of life, such as slavery, infanticide, superstition, short expectancy of life, illiteracy, unrelieved sickness and pain, having been put under more or less effective check, certain generally recognised " goods " of life, such as education, leisure, just legal process, opportunity to enjoy and even to participate creatively in culture through books, radio, museums, etc., being now, if by no means guaranteed to all, at least more assured to a larger proportion of people than they once were. If we concentrate our minds on these aspects of history, the impression is difficult to resist that there is something almost automatic and necessary in progress, provided only we assume that nature will continue to produce men with much the same basic impulses and capacities, and to furnish them with an environment not radically unsuited to their powers. So long as men have instincts of curiosity and creativeness and sympathy, and increasingly find that a mutual protection against ills and a mutual guarantee of pleasures and delights are more effective than isolated action, there seems to be no reason why progress of the sort indicated should not go on, and extend ever more widely over the whole of mankind ; but rather every reason why it should. The continuous pressure of instincts within and circumstance without seems guaranteed to keep man moving, and if he retains any capacity to learn by experience, even though it be only very slowly and after much suffering, the movement, it seems not unreasonable to think, will in the long run be in the direction of an increasing accumulation of " goods ", and an increasing opportunity for most to satisfy some at least of their major desires.[1]

Yet, even if we grant that there is in the interplay of man's innate desires and his environment something calculated to push him forward along these lines, it is clear that that covers but a small section of the facts and therefore is much too narrow a basis on which to build the doctrine of a universal, necessary, inherent principle of progress at work over the whole area of human existence. Four things at least are overlooked :

(*a*) It is overlooked that there are other powerful instincts and urges in human nature besides those which make for the accumulation and extension of generally agreed " goods " and enjoyments. Man's unregenerate nature is always liable to break out in corrupt and senseless courses, seeking immediate at the price of future satisfactions, wittingly or unwittingly using the means which increased knowledge has put into his hands for selfish and destructive ends. History,

[1] This appears to have been the position of some of the Encyclopædists of the eighteenth century, e.g. D'Holbach, quoted by Bury (*op. cit.*, p. 171) as saying : " All the successive inventions of the human mind to change or perfect man's mode of existence and render it happier were only the necessary consequence of his essence and that of the existences which act upon him."

and not least recent history, affords ample evidence of this, and though it may be said by the optimistic believer in progress that mankind will gradually learn from bitter experience not to do this, that is clearly going beyond what the facts of the past warrant. There seems to be no final reason, so far as the facts show, why what we know as civilisation should not pass into a period of disintegration, which relatively to what most men think desirable, and in the light of what has gone before, would have to be called decadence rather than progress.

(b) It is overlooked that inasmuch as changes in man's life are the outcome of the interplay of his instincts and his environment, the possibility is always open that from the latter may come destructive forces and impacts which shall mock his dreams of a more satisfactory life. That there is what Whitehead calls a " senseless side of history ", what the Greeks called ἀνάγκη (compulsion) or βία (violence), the facts show only too clearly. Geographical, climatic, and other changes may help or hinder man's endeavours, and there is no indication from past history which they will do in the future. The possibility always remains open that unforeseen and uncontrollable disturbances may grossly impoverish, or even totally wreck, the life of large sections of mankind. Moreover, man's own tamperings with nature often produce destructive results which he did not foresee. Thus the frightful droughts and dust-storms of the Middle West of America are due to man's denuding of the area of its grass, and the hideous and entirely unforeseen results in many directions of the invention of machinery and the beginning of the industrial age are well known. It is at least possible that a scientist tampering with the atom may at some future date blow everybody to bits. If it is said that such dismal things will not happen, then that is faith and again to go far beyond what the facts warrant.

(c) It is overlooked that the process of satisfying present

desires and solving present problems continually creates new desires and new problems ; the latter, indeed, appear to accumulate by a swift geometrical progression, whereas the means for solving them make only a slow and uncertain arithmetical advance. The feast of good things which progress is supposed to be spreading before us thus takes on a more than superficial likeness to the torments of Tantalus. " Man never is, but always to be blessed." No one, for example, can live in a great modern city like New York without being impressed by the enormous technical progress which its sky-scrapers, subways, automobiles, telephones, etc., represent, and depressed by the crowds of restless, dissatisfied, worried, unhealthy, overworked, de-socialised, individuals who throng its streets, factories, and offices—without wondering where, on balance, this thing called Progress can have its dwelling-place. It is only necessary to dig a little beneath the surface to come across antagonisms and conflicts within the industrial, political, social, economic system, which an earlier and simpler age did not know, and which mere technical efficiency, though it has done much to create them, can do little to solve. This radical dissatisfaction which is at the heart of humanity has been the familiar theme of observers all down the ages, and though it may make for restless, ongoing *change*, it can not be said to indicate an inherent law of progress, even if progress be judged, as it usually is in secularist philosophies, by eudæmonistic standards.

(*d*) Most important of all, the moral elements in human experience are overlooked. Much might be said for the view that the mere interplay of man's instincts and his environment never could have resulted by itself in the accumulation and distribution of " goods " and satisfactions above referred to ; that, had it not been for the continuous entry of the moral-religious awareness of absolute values, apprehended and responded to as deriving from a source other than the process itself, the latter could never have got started, nor, once started, its products preserved.[1] But be that as it may, the secularist faith in progress cannot avoid facing this dilemma : Either man and all he does are, as D'Holbach said, a " necessary consequence ", a mere " effect of what universal nature has made him ", or he is a genuine moral agent capable, in the midst of all the determining influences which play upon him, of choosing his own path in some sense and in some degree. In neither case is there any basis for belief in an inherent and necessary progress. For if man is a purely determined phase of the historical process then, as already indicated, there is no evidence that things are moving steadily forward in the direction of what man, even on a purely eudæmonistic basis, would desire. To believe that the process is making for the happiness of one of its phases becomes a pure, unsupported act of faith. On the other hand, if man is in some sense a moral agent, then there can be no guarantee of progress in the process itself, for there is now in the midst of it the contingency of free choice ; a realm of necessity and a realm of ends are a contradiction in terms. The only possible guarantee of progress on this basis would be an overruling providence which can by an infinite mercy, wisdom, and judgement take note of the choices of men and adjust itself to them to achieve its own purposes.[2]

How then are the facts to be interpreted from the angle of the Christian belief in providence ? Is the Christian,

---

[1] See quotation from Oman, p. 47, above.

[2] The rationalist thinkers of the seventeenth and eighteenth centuries, as Bury indicates, opposed the idea of providence to the idea of progress. This was because it was supposed that to believe in providence was to believe in the possibility of capricious and incalculable interferences from above. Apparently man was regarded as a more reliable and calculable factor than God, a curious inversion of the religious position, and as it concerns man pathetically and obviously wide of all that the facts would suggest. As Wood says in the book already referred to, the true opposite of providence is not progress, but chance or fate or natural necessity.

equipped as he believes himself to be with a truer knowledge of ultimate reality, in any better position to discern an ongoing purpose in history ?   That there should be such dubious and equivocal evidence of progress by eudæmonistic standards will hardly trouble him ; but is there any better evidence by his own standards of what constitutes human well-being ? Plainly not ; rather, if anything, the reverse. Though Christian ideals have in a measure permeated and ameliorated human life in some parts of the world, it would be difficult to maintain that, judged in the light of Christ, the reign of sin, both in individuals and in society, is markedly less extensive than it has been in previous ages. The Christian Church has spread over the world, but there has also spread, particularly in recent years, as Brunner says, a mass atheism and secularism which is without parallel.[1] For the Christian also, therefore, history, like nature, wears an inscrutable face. We have insisted, however, that the Christian does not start from the observation of history at all, but from what is given in his own individual experience of the love of God. The question, therefore, becomes for him how far the latter sheds any light on what God may be doing in and through this daunting mixture of order and confusion, progression and retrogression, achievements and disasters, glories and shames, designs and accidents, which is the human story.

Starting from the revelation of God's austere and saving purpose which has come through the experience of personal redemption, the Christian is bound to read back that saving purpose into the whole order of creation itself. There can be for him no final cleavage between the order of creation and the order of redemption, for the same divine purpose is at work throughout. The divine purpose which is now apprehended as at work within the world through Christ " soul-saving", must have originally made the world so that

---

[1] *Das Gebot und die Ordnungen*, p. 265.

in its essential constitution it is suitable to " soul-making".
This at once sheds light on the strands of creative progress
in science, art, social organisation, etc., which can be
discerned running through the chaos and confusion of
history. A world in which there was no opening up of fresh
tasks, new possibilities of achievement on the basis of what
has already been done, no permanency of acquisition, no
heritage of the past of any sort, a world where every castle
was of sand, to be washed away within a few hours by the
tide, would be no fit place for personality to grow in. The
very idea of rational will, without which personality has no
meaning, necessitates a world that can be altered pro-
gressively in the direction of foreseen ends. Nor could anything in the nature of social co-operation between wills,
as distinct from the mere gregariousness of a herd or swarm,
arise except on the same basis. This is the more clear when
there is added, as there must be in a Christian interpretation,
the thought that the world is a place where the Eternal
will meets and challenges the finite will of man and invites
it to enter into fellowship with itself. It is impossible to see
how that continuous process of activity and change, without
which the finite will could have no awareness of itself,
could not, in fact, be a will in any intelligible sense, could
ever mediate the Eternal unless it revealed elements of
permanence, unless, in other words, there were in it something which could be identified as progress. For the concept
of progress is the concept of permanence in change in the
sphere of will.

Yet, if the Christian can thus interpret the possibility
of progress as part of a created order designed to fashion
personality, by the same token he can interpret the confused
evidence of it which history actually affords. For, in
the first place, if at the heart of the matter there is the will
of man as related to the will of God, then that means that
at the heart of the matter there operates the disturbing

factor of sin. The Christian is not called upon to trace out in detail how this factor has in the past churned up what might have conceivably been a broad and lovely stream of progress into an erratic and incalculable torrent, swirling, back-eddying, overflowing, sometimes in overwhelming floods, sometimes into stagnant and weed-infested pools. Indeed, it is impossible for him to do so. But he can observe his own heart, and his own age, and there the evidence is unmistakable that though man's achievements go on, yet every fresh achievement becomes instantly a new instrument and opportunity for sin to use. Even the ministries of medicine can be used to ward off the consequences of wrong living and give new latitude to the evil will.

On the other hand, though the world in its essential constitution must contain the possibility of progress if it is to be a meeting place of man's will with the eternal, yet also it must in its essential constitution be such as to preclude the possibility of any completely and finally satisfactory achievement whether by the individual or by the race. A historical process which was a mere ploughing of the sands could not mediate the Eternal as *will* ; a historical process on the other hand, which was *not* in some measure a ploughing of the sands, but could come to an end-point of complete fulfilment in itself, could not mediate the divine will as *Eternal*. Hence into the historic process there enters of necessity the element of transiency ; nothing abides, nothing can ever be rested in, nothing satisfies without immediately beginning to engender dissatisfaction, nothing escapes " time's corroding tooth ". Most sensitive minds, to be sure, are saddened and challenged at one point or another by this tragic quality of impermanence and decay, which attaches to all human achievement ; but to the Christian, though he would be hardly human, and indeed hardly Christian, if he did not feel its burden, it is swiftly taken up into the eschatological faith, and is seen as part of the wisdom of a divine purpose which is fashioning men in time for that which time cannot contain. He knows that he has here no continuing city, but seeks one to come whose builder and maker is God. Yet he is prepared for the latter only as he faithfully serves God's will here in all the uses and tasks of this world. It is precisely the paradoxical meaning of this world in the providence of God that he is called upon to seek to realise with all his powers a kingdom which in this world is not fully realisable at all. The Christian is the most dissatisfied of men, yet also the most at peace.

Thus there enters into history, even for the Christian, not only the disturbing factor of sin, but also an element of profound and necessary inscrutability. He cannot say in detail what the Eternal is doing in and through the radical transiency and flux of time, for if he could, it would not be the Eternal. But he can say, in general, that the divine purpose, whatever it is, is certainly one of love and that it has every individual in its grasp ; also that he is under obligation to serve that purpose as it presents itself to him in and through his historical situation, committing everything else unto Him. This involves that the Christian believer will of necessity bring to the observation of human affairs a mind which to the unregenerate and uncritical enthusiasms of men will often seem sceptical, and even aloof. The great ones of history—great, that is, according to the intra-historical standards of men, the Cæsars, Napoleons, Mussolinis, Hitlers—he will know may count for nothing, and less than nothing, in relation to the trans-historical purposes of the eternal ; on the other hand, the insignificant ones who tread the way of self-forgetfulness and love must count for much. This thought has always run through Christian piety, though, unhappily, it has not very consistently determined Christian conduct. " The first shall be last and the last first ". " He hath pulled down the mighty from their seats and exalted them of low degree." It is an essential element of eschatological faith. It involves, further, that, for the Christian, circumstances will often arise wherein he must act in defiance of every consideration of possible or probable historical consequence, believing that his obedience to God is related to an eternal end, even though apparently it cannot be justified in terms of historical ends. This, we suggested earlier, is illustrated in Christ's going to the Cross. The "here stand I, I can do no other, no matter what estimations of historical consequence you may set before me," is likely at any moment to be forced to the lips of every one who is in living touch with God.[1]

It might be thought that at this point the question could well be left, it being neither possible nor necessary from the Christian point of view to say more. That in the main is so ; yet the more reflective mind can hardly avoid asking one further question. Granted that this world has been created so as to serve as a "vale of soul-making" and that we must read the meaning of the historical process in the light of that purpose—are we to suppose that that exhausts the meaning of the world for God ? Is the created order merely to fashion personalities for the divine kingdom, so that when that end is achieved it will pass into nothingness, having no further utility, or has it a significance, which, while not apart from the destiny of individuals, is not to be exhaustively stated in terms of the destiny of individuals ? This leads us to say a word on the second aspect of the popular secularised idea of progress, namely, the belief that the processes of history are inevitably tending towards a more or less perfect end-state to be realised within, and therefore to include, this world itself.[2]

---

[1] Cf. Heim, Glaube und Denken (2 Aufl.), p. 329 : "*Eine Tat kann ewige Frucht tragen, die irdisch gesehen eine sinnlose Kraftvergeudung ist, ein einsames Sterben auf verlorenem Posten, von dem nie ein Mensch etwas erfährt und das nie in die Tafeln der Geschichte eingetragen wird.*"

[2] Cf. Wells' picture of a world physically transformed by man in *The Shape of Things to Come*, referred to by Horton in *Realistic Theology*, p. 61.

Much that has already been said will have shown the *naïveté* and inadequacy of this belief, from the point of view both of Christian faith, and of the evidence afforded by the facts. Apart from the fact that there is such ambiguous and equivocal witness to the reality of any ongoing progressive movement in history, the idea of such a utopian end-state, even if it could be achieved, falls foul on the one hand of the Christian valuation of those individuals who had lived and died prior to its arrival and who, presumably, would have no part in it ; and, on the other hand, of the law of entropy which, the scientists tell us, render it highly probable that at long last the world, however improved it may be meanwhile, will not be habitable at all. Yet it may be that such a utopian hope preserves in its own inadequate way a truth which was not absent from the older eschatologies and which we cannot altogether set on one side, the truth, namely, that the natural order does have some sort of permanent place in the purpose of God and is not merely a framework and stage for the fashioning of men.[1]

Two reasons at least suggest themselves for thinking that the natural order has some such intrinsic significance. First, it is very difficult to believe, though there is nothing logically impossible in the idea, that the whole order of animate and inanimate nature, in its infinite richness and complexity and beauty, has no other significance than to provide a temporary setting for the training of human personality, and does not rather express some necessity of the divine nature which, while never running counter to the latter, and always serving it, none the less goes far beyond it. This thought becomes quite irresistible when the eyes are lifted to the infinite extent and majesty of the heavens. Second, we must take note of the kind of experience which finds

---

[1] The belief in a mundane state of perfection to which Progress is inevitably moving is the secularised form of the millenarian hope, and doubtless was in some degree historically derived from it.

highest expression in art, especially art when it is informed
by the spirit of religion. Man's creative manipulation of his
physical environment into a vehicle of order and beauty is
felt at its highest to be far more than a mere disciplinary
exercise of powers, which ultimately are to be used in a
totally other world for totally other ends, as a man might
develop his muscles on a rowing-machine which never
carries him an inch beyond where he now is. Indeed the
entry of such a thought would tend to kill the artistic
impulse altogether. The artist may be well aware that his
artistic product, like everything else, is subject to the decay
of time, yet he is aware—and because of such awareness
what he does is infinitely more significant—of somehow
sharing in the creativeness of God. The making of matter
a vehicle and expression of spirit is thus felt to be an essential
element in the divine purpose itself, and it is only as the
artistic task is so interpreted that it becomes other than a
merely sportive embroidery upon life, or has any power to
train the soul for higher things. It can hardly be questioned
that some awareness of this has entered into the popular
hope of an end-state towards which this world is moving,
mainly through the creative efforts of man. Even the
millenarian fancies of some of the older eschatologies—as
for example the oft-quoted picture in the Apocalypse of
Baruch of a messianic age wherein " on each vine there
shall be a thousand branches, and each branch shall produce
a thousand clusters, and each cluster shall produce a
thousand grapes "—crudely materialistic and eudæmonistic
as they tended to be, might be supposed to have been not
totally devoid of a sense of the divine creativeness which
can fashion even this brute world into an order and loveliness
not known before.

Christian theology on the whole has tended to insist that
the world is not merely instrumental to the fashioning of
personalities, after which it will pass into nothingness, but

will itself be somehow taken up in a transfigured form into the realised purpose of God.[1] It will be in the fullest sense a new world, but the point is that there will be a *world* in the Kingdom of God ; the latter will not be merely saints subsisting in some sort of disembodied relationship with one another. Such a thought, difficult as it is, does at least protect from the parochialism which sees all the " furniture of earth and choir of heaven " merely as a setting for man, and from the narrow moralism which would deprive the creativeness of man in art of any intrinsic significance. On the other hand, the difficulty is to know just what is meant by the word *new*, when we speak of a new world. The Christian faith must affirm that the new world is exempt not only from sin and death, but also from the essential limitations of the time-form as such. Such a new world is by definition so profoundly discontinuous with the world we now know that it might seem that it would involve after all the annihilation of the latter, even though another of an utterly inconceivable sort be substituted for it. It is in part this sense of the radical discontinuity which is necessarily involved in the very idea of the realised kingdom of the eternal God which makes the eschatological hope rest in a transcendent act of God. Yet, as against this, the thought that this world is somehow taken up into the kingdom, the old being thus somehow continuous with and consummated in the new, has its value, even from the narrower point of view of understanding it as a training place for personality.

Any rational solution of these contrarieties must, it seems, lie ever beyond us, if only for the reason that they arise from the bringing together of two disparate dimensions— time and eternity, the finite and the infinite—and the

---

[1] For a brief review of Christian doctrine in this regard, see Althaus, *op cit.*, p. 330 f. It has been the incursion of mysticism of a neo-platonic type which has tended to deflect Christian theology from this line of thought.

x

attempt to grasp them both in categories appropriate to one of them only. All we can do is, as was said in the chapter on eschatology, to rest in, and commit ourselves to, the continuity of the will of God, that will which, whatever else it may comprise, will always, we are assured, be that which has been shown unto us in the face of Jesus Christ, namely, a saving love which we must utterly trust and utterly obey as it meets us where we now are in this world. For the rest we may be confident that if anything is of real value in this present world it will never pass into nothingness, and that if anything passes into nothingness it will not be of real value, and need cause no regrets.

INDEX

I. NAMES

II. SUBJECTS

Printed in Great Britain by
Unwin Brothers Limited, London and Woking